MAP OF PENNSYLVANIA, SHOWING THE AREAS SURVEYED IN 1874, 1875 & 1876.
THE LETTERS INDICATE THE REPORTS OF PROGRESS PUBLISHED.

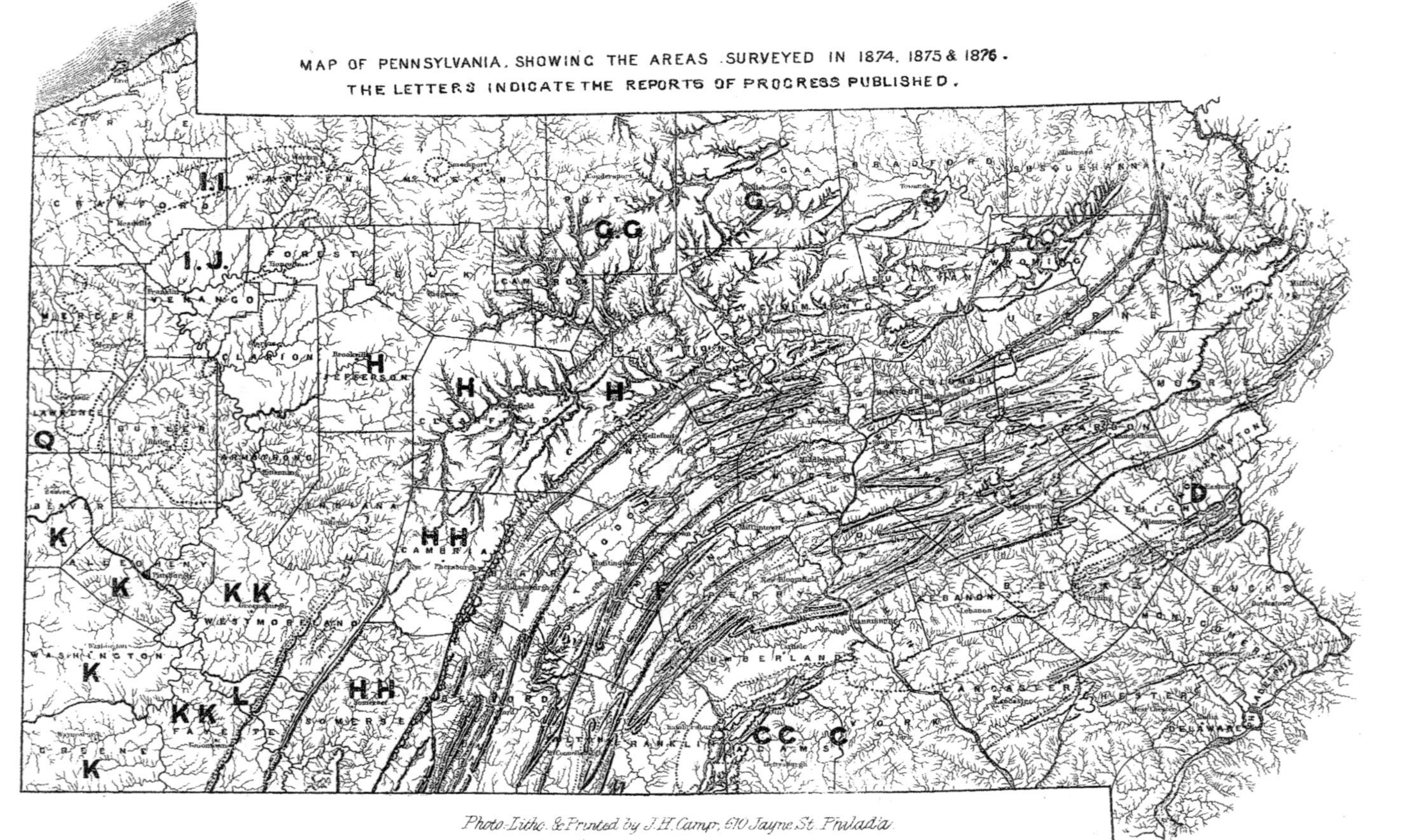

Photo-Litho. & Printed by J.H. Camp, 610 Jayne St. Philad'a.

SECOND GEOLOGICAL SURVEY OF PENNSYLVANIA:
1875.

SPECIAL REPORT

ON THE

COKE MANUFACTURE

OF THE

YOUGHIOGHENY RIVER VALLEY

IN

FAYETTE AND WESTMORELAND COUNTIES.

WITH

GEOLOGICAL NOTES

OF THE

COAL AND IRON ORE BEDS.

From Surveys by CHARLES A. YOUNG.

BY FRANKLIN PLATT.

TO WHICH ARE APPENDED

I. A Report on methods of Coking.
By John Fulton, M. E.

II. A Report on the use of Natural Gas in the Iron Manufacture.
By John B. Pearse and Franklin Platt.

HARRISBURG:
PUBLISHED BY THE BOARD OF COMMISSIONERS
FOR THE SECOND GEOLOGICAL SURVEY.
1876.

Printed by
B. F. MEYERS, *State Printer,*
HARRISBURG, PA.

BOARD OF COMMISSIONERS.

SECRETARY OF THE BOARD

STATE GEOLOGIST

ASSISTANT GEOLOGISTS.

PERSIFOR FRAZER, JR.—Geologist in charge of the Survey of York, Adams, Franklin and Cumberland.

A. E. LEHMAN—Topographical Assistant.

FREDERICK PRIME, JR.—Geologist in charge of the Survey of Lehigh, Northampton, Berks and Lebanon.

A. P. BERLIN—Topographical Assistant.

JOHN H. DEWEES—Geologist in charge of the Survey of the Fossil Ore belts of the Juniata country.

FRANKLIN PLATT—Geologist in charge of the Survey of Clearfield, Jefferson, Cambria, Somerset, Armstrong, Blair, &c., &c.

W. G. PLATT—Geological Assistant in Cambria, Somerset, and Indiana.

R. H. SANDERS—Topographical Assistant in Blair, and Somerset.

J. J. STEVENSON—Geologist in charge of the Survey of Greene, Washington, Fayette and Westmoreland.

I. C. WHITE—In charge of the Survey of Beaver, Lawrence, Mercer, &c.

J. F. CARLL—Geologist in charge of the Survey of the Oil Regions.

H. M. CHANCE—Geological Assistant for the Survey of the Water Gaps, and in Butler, Beaver, Mercer, &c., &c.

C. A. ASHBURNER—Geological Assistant in Mifflin and Blair, and in charge of the Survey of M'Kean, Elk, Forest, &c.

C. E. BILLIN—Topographical Assistant in Mifflin and Blair, and in charge of the Survey of the Huntingdon Valley and Seven Mountains.

ANDREW SHERWOOD—Geologist in charge of the Survey of Bradford, Tioga, Potter, Lycoming, &c.

F. A. GENTH—Chemist and Mineralogist at Philadelphia.

A. S. M'CREATH—Chemist, in charge of the Laboratory of the Survey, 223 Market street, Harrisburg.

C. E. HALL, Fossil Zoölogist, in charge of the Collections for the Museum.

LEO LESQUEREUX—Fossil Botanist, Columbus, Ohio.

E. B. HARDEN—In charge of Illustrations for the Reports, 1008 Clinton street, Philadelphia.

CHARLES ALLEN—In charge of the Collection of Records of Railroad and other Levels, Harrisburg.

F. W. FORMAN—Clerk in charge of the Distribution of Reports from the rooms of the Board, 223 Market street, Harrisburg.

PHILADELPHIA, *December* 31, 1875.

To PROFESSOR J. P. LESLEY,

State Geologist:

SIR:—I have the honor to submit the following report upon the Coke Manufacture at Connellsville, Fayette county, Pa., and other points along the Youghiogheny River Valley.

In accordance with your instructions I directed Mr. Charles A. Young to examine the mineral deposits which furnish materials for the groups of Coke Ovens and Iron Furnaces, as well as to gather statistics for an Economic Report. But as the general geology of the region is described in the Final Report of the First Geological Survey of Pennsylvania, published in 1858, and as the Second and more elaborate survey of Fayette and Westmoreland counties is to be made by Prof. Stevenson in 1876, I have briefly re-stated the principal facts so that the general structure of the country may be easily understood.

Mr. Young pursued his survey in the Valley from May 20th to September 15th, 1875, and the facts and tables presented in this report are substantially in the form in which they were returned by him.

Much assistance was rendered by persons residing in the Valley, or interested in its prosperity. I am especially indebted for information and good offices freely tendered by Mr. E. C. Pechin, C. E., of Dunbar Furnace; Mr. Frick, of Broad Ford; Mr. Davidson, of Connellsville; Mr. Frank D. Howell, of Philadelphia; and Mr. Oliphant, of Uniontown. But kindness to Mr. Young and myself, and interest in the special survey of this important business of South Western Pennsylvania, were uniformly and universally manifested throughout the district.

I remain with much respect,

Your obedient servant,

FRANKLIN PLATT,

Assistant Geologist.

TABLE OF CONTENTS.

OF THE SEVERAL CHAPTERS.

SPECIAL REPORT ON COKE.—BY FRANKLIN PLATT.

Page

1. The Coal Measures of the Youghiogheny, - 1
2. The Geological column at Connellsville, - 13
3. The Coal Measures of the Connellsville Basin in West Virginia, - - - - - - - - 33
4. The Connellsville Coke Trade and description of the Coke works, - - - . - - - 40
5. On Coking the Connellsville coal, - - - 61
6. The Youghiogheny Gas Coal Trade, - - 88
7. On the Iron Ores, Fire Clays, and Salt Wells and Cement quarries, - - - - - - - 98

Appendices.

A. On the methods of coking coal for Furnace use; its efficiency and economy as compared with the anthracite coal in the Metallurgy of iron. By John Fulton, G. M. E., Cambria Iron Co., - - - - - - - - - 117

B. Analyses of Gas issuing from Oil wells. By Samuel P. Sadtler, As't. Prof. Chem. in the University of Pennsylvania, - - - - - - - - - 146

C. On the durability of the natural gas supply. By Franklin Platt, - - - - - - - - - 161

D. On the use of Natural Gas in Iron working. By John B. Pearse, - - - - - - - - - 173

E. On the record of the Boyd's Hill well at Pittsburg, as compared with that of the gas well at Leechburg and other geological data of the region. By J. P. Lesley, - 215

SECOND GEOLOGICAL SURVEY OF PENNSYLVANIA.

1875.

SPECIAL REPORT ON COKE.

BY FRANKLIN PLATT.

CHAPTER I.

The Coal Measures of the Youghiogheny.

It is proper to preface a report upon the Coke Manufacture of the Youghiogheny River Valley, in Westmoreland and Fayette counties in south-western Pennsylvania, with a geological description of the Bituminous Coal Beds, and especially of the large Pittsburg coal bed from which, practically, *all* the material of that manufacture is obtained: its altitude on the hill sides; the depths to which it sometimes sinks beneath the river; its eastern outcrop, facing Chestnut ridge; its covering rocks; and the measures which underlie it at various depths.

This bed, named by Messrs. M'Kinley, Jackson and other assistants of Prof. Rogers in 1836–1840 the "Pittsburg Bed," was traced by them from Pittsburg to Connellsville; and by Dr. Jackson, from Connellsville southwards to the Virginia line, and back by the Monongahela to Pittsburg; and northwards by New Alexandria, Blairsville and Saltsburg, through northern Westmoreland, to Pittsburg. Its geological position as the bottom bed of the Upper (Monongahela) Coal Measures, its outspread throughout Westmoreland and Fayette counties, the basins in which it lies, and the gentle anticlinal rolls which separate these basins—were all perfectly well known before the end of the First Geological Survey in 1842, and are minutely described in the second volume of the Final Report of 1858.*

* Book IX, Subdivision III, *Chap. 23*, (pages 599 to 602,) Third basin, Blairsville, Saltsburg, Chestnut Ridge; *Chap. 24*, (603-616,) Lower Coal Measures along Chestnut ridge, south to Connellsville and Maryland; *Chap. 25*, (616-628,) Pittsburg Bed facing Chestnut Ridge; *Chap. 26*, Pittsburg bed in the

Along the Youghiogheny the connection of the Pittsburg area of the bed with the Connellsville area is broken; the bed rising into the air and descending again; the intermediate portion being swept away. The map accompanying this report (Plate 1) therefore shows no coke ovens and no coal mines in this intermediate area. People in the Connellsville region have imagined that the bed at Connellsville is a different bed from the bed at Pittsburg. But its identity, as has just been said, was demonstrated many years ago, by tracing its outcrop in a semicircle by the south, from Connellsville to Pittsburg; and the identity is shown upon the long sections of the Final Report of 1858; and by numerous local sections in the text of that report. It is again exhibited by the section along the Youghiogheny river prepared, from measurements of outcrop heights along the river, by Mr. Young, and published with this report (Plate 2,) adding indeed no new force to the old evidence, but making more evident the exact shape of the swells which carry the bed into the air, or plunge it under water level. The repugnance manifested towards an identification of the bed at Connellsville with the bed at Pittsburg has arisen out of the fact, that at Pittsburg it is not in its best condition, whereas at Connellsville it is at its largest size and of the finest quality. Its various aspects in south-western Pennsylvania will be fully discussed and described in the Report of Progress of 1876, from a thorough re-survey of the entire field which it occupies west of the Monongahela and south of the Kiskiminetas. Its changes along the left or west bank of the Monongahela are shown in Prof. J. J. Stevenson's Report of Progress, 1875, on Washington and Greene counties.

This Coke Report of 1875 is especially confined, by order of the Board of Commissioners, to the local districts of Westmoreland and Fayette counties, where the Coke establishments are found, a list of which, 45 in number, will be given further on. But a Report on the Coke Manufacture, by Mr. John Ful-

---

fourth basin at Greenburg, &c.; *Chap. 27*, (630-635,) around Pittsburg; *Chap. 28*, (636-650,) south of Greensburg. A multitude of local sections from Dr. Jackson's notes illustrate these chapters; and these will be used in our Report of Progress of the Second Geological Survey in Westmoreland and Fayette, in 1876.

ton, published, by permission, at the end of the volume, will compel some notice of the Coke district of the Upper Conemaugh, in Cambria county, and the lower Coal beds there mined for coking purposes.

The Coke Region now in question embraces:—1. The Valley of the Youghiogheny from its mouth at M'Keesport, to the Gap through Chestnut Ridge, at Connellsville, 44 miles*; 2. The Valley of Dunbar Creek, at the base of Chestnut Ridge from Connellsville south to Uniontown, 10 miles;—3. The Valley of Mount's Creek, at the base of Chestnut Ridge, from Connellsville† north to Mount Pleasant, 9 miles; and 4. The line of the South West Pennsylvania, Railroad from Connellsville north towards Greensburg, 12 miles.

This Coke Region is served by four railways: — 1. The Pittsburg, Washington and Baltimore (Pittsburg and Connellsville) main line, running along the right or north bank of the Youghiogheny River; Connellsville being 57½ miles from Pittsburg, and 287 miles from Baltimore‡; — 2. The Uniontown Branch, 10 miles long;—3. The Mount Pleasant Branch, 9 miles long;—4. The South West Pennsylvania Railroad, (a branch of the Pennsylvania Railroad,) 24 miles long, from Greensburg to Connellsville.§

Surveys have recently been made looking to the extension of the Slackwater navigation of the Monongahela river, up the Youghiogheny river, to Connellsville.¶

The streams which afford convenient road-beds for the above named railways are affluents of the Ohio; the Youghiogheny

* 43 to Connellsville; 44 to White Rock junction of the Pittsburgh and Connellsville Railroad, with the Uniontown Branch Railroad.

† Properly from Broad Ford junction (2 miles below Connellsville) along the Mount Pleasant Branch Railroad.

‡ After going east from Connellsville, through the two gaps of Chestnut Ridge and Laurel Hill, and over the summit of the Allegheny Mountain, and descending to the Potomac waters at Bridgeport, 78½ miles, the coke for Middle Pennsylvania switches off north on to the Bedford, Broad Top and Huntingdon Railroad, and descends to Harrisburg by the Pennsylvania (Central) Railroad, reaching Philadelphia in 357 miles from Connellsville.

§ By this route the coke from Connellsville reaches Pittsburg in 56 miles, and Philadelphia in 346½ miles.

¶ For levels see Report on the Levels of Pennsylvania, 1875, by Charles Allen, Assistant in Charge of Collection of Levels for the Second Geological Survey.

being a branch of the Monongahela; and the Monongahela together with the Allegheny forming the Ohio, at Pittsburg.*

The map will show, better than any description, how the general drainage of the district under review is towards the west; how the Little and Big Sewickley creeks and Jacob's creek cross southern Westmoreland from Chestnut Ridge to the Youghiogheny river; and how the Redstone, Dunlap's, Brown's and George's creeks traverse Fayette from Chestnut Ridge to the Monongahela river.

This general drainage westward has been produced, geologically, by the great anticlinal of Chestnut Ridge, which throws: 1. The Upper Coal Measures;—2. The Pittsburgh bed;—3. The Barren Measures under it;—4. The Lower Coal Measures next lower, and —5. The Conglomerate (No. XII) into the air; while it upheaves, in a long straight north-east line, the Sub-Carboniferous rocks (XI, X,) in the shape of a mountain ridge with broad flattish top, to the height of about 1,300 feet above the river bed at Connellsville, and about 2,200 feet above the ocean level.†

On this rounded mountain crest, overlooking Connellsville, may be seen still lying in place massive square fragments of the conglomerate No. XII, the bottom rock of the Lower‡ Coal Measures; while the outcropping edge of the Pittsburg or Connellsville coal, the bottom bed of the Upper Coal Measures, dotted with coal drifts, may be noticed far down below, ranging along the east face of a line of low hills, fronting the west foot of the mountain; the valley of Dunbar creek flowing north, and of Mount's creek flowing south, into the Youghiogheny at Connellsville, intervening between this outcrop and the mountain.

In other words: the bottom rock of the Lower Coal Measures occupies the top of the mountain, while the Upper Coal Measures occupy the rolling low country of Fayette and Westmore-

* The Coke of the Youghiogheny Region descends the Ohio, by boat and by rail, and is distributed through the Western States as far as St. Louis and New Orleans. Statistics will be given in the following chapters.

† The Elk Rock is by barometer 1,450′ above Connellsville; but this is doubtless too high. Cow Rock 650; Dunbar Furnace, 165.—J. P. L., 1865.

‡ Meaning thereby the Lower *Productive* Coal Measures.

road
Ground-plan.
The Elk Rock.
From Connellsville
S-50°E
1865

land, spreading westward from its foot, the geography and geology being exactly reversed.

From the summit of one of these huge remnants of No. XII called the Elk Rock,* the geologist looks westward down upon undulating bituminous coal country of, western Pennsylvania, through which the Youghiogheny and Monongahela rivers meander with their hundred tributary streams and streamlets, exposing in thousands of hillsides, each from two hundred to four hundred feet high, the outcrops of the three beds of the Upper Coal Measures — the Pittsburg, the Redstone (50 feet above it,) and the Sewickley, 50 feet above this again.

Two beds, still higher in the series, the Waynesburg and the Washington have been eroded from a good deal of the country, but the geologist can see with his mind's eye, their outcrops lining the far distant and more elevated hills beyond the Monongahela river.†

The country is *geographically* undulating; for only along the water sheds between the principal streams is there any level surface, and scarcely there. The whole country is a labyrinth of shallow vales and valleys with rather steep hillsides, marked by the outcrops of coal, limestone, shale and sandstone beds, in nearly horizontal attitudes, the dips being measured, not by degrees, but by feet in the mile, as Mr. Young's section shows.

And *geologically* the country is undulating; for the Coal Measures, although lying so nearly horizontal, do really rise and fall, in exceedingly flat broad waves (parallel with the

---

*Fig. 1, is from a sketch of the north side of the rock, made in 1865. Fig. 2, shows the decayed east end, with a ground plan of the whole. The ascent to this point of view from Connellsville is easy, and the distance about three miles. It will undoubtedly become a place of resort for the lovers of fine scenery. The Elk Rock is one of two large fragments, with several smaller detached pulpit rocks close by, one of which is seen to the left of the sketch at the North end of the Elk Rock. The "Conglomerate" is here a soft yellowish friable sandstone, from 40 to 60 feet thick, showing no lines of bedding, and few cleavage planes. It weathers easily and in rounded contours, is hollowed into bear caves, and exhibits curious reticulations of sandy iron ore. Further down the mountain towards Connellsville, and near the edge of the gorge of the Youghiogheny, a flat rock, over which the road passes, is covered with Indian sculpture, and is called the Cow Rock.

† In Prof. J. J. Stevenson's Report on Greene and Washington counties, (1875,) are described more than twelve *persistent* coal beds of the Upper or Monongahela series; adding thus, several to those already known and described in the Final Report of 1858.

mountain) so as to divide the region into regular basins, carrying the outcrop of the Pittsburg sometimes to the hill tops, and sometimes bringing it down near to the river bed; even putting it under river level from Sedgwick station as far as Jacob's creek. In this interval of 13 miles, as measured by the sinuosities of the railroad, or of 8 miles as measured straight across, this coal bed can only be reached by shafts. Everywhere else between Connellsville and Pittsburg gangways enter the bed at various heights on the hill slopes.

Approaching the mountain, a sudden and rapid steepening of the dip to 20° * brings the Bituminous Coal Field to an end eastward; throws the Pittsburg bed into the air along a straight outcrop of seventy miles;† hollows a series of little valleys in the Barren Measures all along the foot of the mountain; brings up the Lower Coal Measures on the flank of the mountain;‡ and throws out the Conglomerate near the mountain top in a line of little terrace knobs.

The dip then suddenly flattens again and lays the Conglomerate flat upon the broad summit of Chestnut Ridge, in patches, as above described.§

The mountain itself (Chestnut Ridge) consists of a grand arch of the Catskill Formation (IX and X;) and the Youghiogheny river, which cuts through it to its base, (1,300 feet,) exposes these formations in cliffs and precipitous slopes on both sides of the gorge.¶

---

*The dip measured at one place near Connellsville, was 19°; but further north it is 30°.

†That is from ten miles north of Blairsville, to the Virginia line, and far south of that.

‡Sometimes with a low, sharp intervening little ridge of Mahoning Sandstone.

§ When the dip is reversed, descending eastward into Ligonier Valley, the Conglomerate first comes in, making another row of little terrace knobs; then the Lower Coal Measures and the Barren Measures; but the Pittsburg bed is not preserved along the centre line of the Ligonier Valley except in one little sharp high hill far to the north. A larger area of it is left in Somerset county at Salisbury; and a still larger one in the Cumberland Coal Basin in Maryland. One very small piece remaining on the highest summit of Broad Top mountain in Huntingdon county, attests the undeniable fact that this wonderful Coal Bed once spread throughout Central Pennsylvania.

¶ Wood Cut, Fig. 3, gives a section at Connellsville (looking N. 40° E. to show the structure. See also Figs. 472 and 474, of Jackson, in Rogers' F. R. 1858.

The Elk Rock (Piedmont Sandstone) on Chestnut Ridge over Connellsville

The outcrop of the Pittsburg bed may be said to run at an average distance of about two miles from the crest of the mountain, and always on the slope of a hill facing the mountain.

The Connellsville Basin is shallow; for a shaft sunk at a point one mile north of Connellsville, where the centre line of the basin crosses the river, struck the Pittsburg bed at a depth of only 120 feet beneath the river.*

When the bed emerges further down the river it rolls slightly, but keeps above water level, low on the hill side, for about a mile, and then rises rapidly to the hill tops, and leaves them at Dawson's Station.†

The Pittsburg bed does not descend again westward into the hill tops until we reach the mouth of Jacob's Creek, where it is first met with at an elevation of 300 feet. It then sinks rapidly, down stream, and goes under the water about a mile below the mouth of Jacob's Creek.

Hence to White Heath (one mile below West Newton) the Pittsburg bed lies under water level, in a synclinal trough as shallow as that of Connellsville, the dips being exceedingly gentle.‡ At West Newton a shaft strikes it at a depth of 60 feet.

Emerging again at White Heath, and gently rolling up and down the hill slopes, over a flat anticlinal, which crosses the Youghiogheny a short distance below the mouth of the Big Sewickley creek, the Pittsburg coal bed descends into its next basin, and reaches its lowest elevation on the hill sides at Suter's Station.

Thence it rises slowly to Armstrong station, and again descends gently to Guffey's station.

Thence it rises to 200 feet above the river at Alpsville, and sinks to 100 at Elrod's station.

Thence it rises to 200 feet at M'Keesport, and so continues

* The basin is described in the Final Report of 1858, P. 611, Vol. 2, as subdivided by a roll or anticlinal along its centre line, not only here at Connellsville, but further north on Mount's Creek.

† The hills immediately on the river at the Station are not high enough for it; but those a mile back from the river to the north are. The coal is there mined for local use; and a beautiful bench or terrace made by this bed is plainly traced on the landscape.

‡ As seen at the Waverly Colliery, a little more than a mile below Jacob's Creek.

slightly rising all the way down the Monongahela river to Pittsburg, where it is 320 feet above water level.

The following table of levels along the Pittsburg and Connelsville railroad was made by Mr. Charles Allen, from an inspection of the profile of that road in the office of the company at Connellsville, and *corrected for mean tide at Baltimore*, in accordance with instructions from Mr. W. H. Taylor, R. E.:*

PITTSBURG..........	(0.0)	751′	Laurel Run..........	(50.0)	856′
Birmingham bridge..		751′	Dawson..............	(51.9)	864′
Soho................		769′	Sedgewick..........	(52.9)	868′
Copper works........		763′	Broad Ford..........	(55.0)	872′
Laughlin............		770′	CONNELLSVILLE......	(57.4)	894′
Frankstown..........		783′	White Rock..........	(58.6)	921′
Hazelwood..........	(3.6)	789′	Sand works..........		921′
Grove................		784′	*Indian Creek*.........	(64.0)	982′
Brown's..............		757′	Ohiopile, F..........	(74.9)	1,237′
Salt works...........		766′	Egypt station.........		1,302′
City farm............		761′	Drakestown R........		1,319′
Braddock's..........	(9.3)	769′	*Confluence*...........	(84.4)	1,346′
Port Perry Junction..		765′	Brook Tunnel........		1,558′
Saltzburg............	(11.8)	765′	Shoofly Tunnel.......		1,614′
Riverton.............		765′	Pinkerton Pt.........		1,649′
McKeesport..........	(14.3)	765′	Castleman............	(98.4)	1,757′
Long Run	(16.6)	765′	*Mineral Pt*...........	(101.6)	1,825′
Ellrod...............	(17.6)	768′	Pinegrove...........		1,874′
Osceola..............	(20.0)	768′	Garrett..............	(108.0)	1,947′
Alpsville............	(21.0)	768′	Myerdale.............	(112.0)	2,063′
Coultersville.........	(22.0)	768′	Sandpatch Tunnel....	(116.0)	2,226′
Robbinsville..........	(23.4)	768′	SUMMIT ALLEGHENY MTN....		2,286′
Armstrong's..........	(26.1)	779′	Philson's Mills........	(123.0)	1,861′
West Newton.........	(32.6)	782′	Glencoe.........		1,633′
Snyder's.............		788′	Southampton.........	(127.9)	1,664′
Port Royal...........	(36.9)	792′	Fairhope.............	(130.0)	1,384′
Jacob's Creek.........	(40.3)	794′	*Bridgeport*...........	(135.9)	938′
Barring's............		804′	Cook's Mills..........	(140.0)	784′
Layton's.............	(44.5)	818′	Ellerslie.............		730′
Oakdale..............		852′	CUMBERLAND........	(149.7)	——

It appears from the above table (taking the railway grade as approximately parallel with the river water level) that the Youghiogheny river cuts its bed down 255′ in 11 miles, from the axis of Ligonier Valley synclinal at Ohiopile falls, to the axis of the Chestnut Ridge anticlinal at Indian creek, or - - - - - 23′ per mile.

* The profile itself has an empirical datum of 200′ below low water at Pittsburg, or 514′ above mean tide at Baltimore. Distances, in miles, taken from Anderson's railroad map, are given in parenthesis.

From the axis of the anticlinal (Indian creek) it cuts down to the axis of the Connellsville basin (Broad Ford) 110′ in 9 miles, or - -	12′ per mile.
From Broad Ford to the mouth of Jacob's creek, a distance of 14.7 miles, it falls only 78′, or -	$5\frac{1}{3}$′ p. mile.
From Jacob's creek to Pittsburg, a distance of about 40 miles, it falls only 43′ feet, or about	1′ per mile.

But when the above intervals are measured, not by the windings of the river, but in straight lines, the result obtained is quite different; for by the *bee-line distance* from

Ohiopile to *Indian Creek*,	$7\frac{1}{2}$ miles, it is	34′ per mile.
Indian Creek to *Broad Ford*,	$6\frac{1}{2}$ miles, "	17′ per mile.
Broad Ford to *Jacob's Creek*,	10 miles, "	7.8′ per mile.
Jacob's Creek to *Pittsburg*,	25 miles, "	1.7′ per mile.

Even this does not corrctly express the slope of the general erosion of the country westward; for if we measure the above intervals *at right angles to the strike* we get the following distances and percentages of fall:—

Ohiopile to *Indian Creek*, about 5 miles,	=	51′ per mile.
Indian Creek to *Broad Ford*, about $6\frac{1}{2}$ miles,	=	17′ per mile.
Broad Ford to *Jacob's Creek*, about $9\frac{1}{2}$ miles,	=	8′ per mile.
Jacob's Creek to *Pittsburg*, about 23 miles,	=	1.85′ p. m.

The law of surface topography thus comes out more and more clearly: *the steeper the dip the sharper the erosion.* And that it holds out, eastward, on the headwaters of the Youghiogheny (Castleman's River) to the Summit of the Allegheny Mountain is also shown by the table; for, measuring at right angles to the slope from point to point in that direction, the bed of the river is seen to rise

From Ohiopile to Confluence,	109′ in 7 m.	=	15.4′ p. m.
From Confluence to Meyersdale,	717′ in 15 m.	=	48′ p. m.
From Meyersdale to Sandpatch,	163′ in 4 m.	=	41′ p. m.

As to the extent of the erosion, it is evident that the Pittsburg (Connellsville) Coal bed and Upper Coal Measures once lay upon the top of Chestnut Ridge; for fragments are left still existing, beyond, at Ligonier and Salisbury. No reason has been given for doubting that the still higher Upper Barren Measures also once passed over the mountain. Nearly three thousand feet, therefore, must be added to get its original height. When the erosion began the crest of the ridge must have stood at between 4,500 and 5,000 feet above tide level,* and the average of the general slope must have been then about 1,840† feet in 40 miles, or 46′ feet per mile.

But this gives a very false idea of the original face of the country. To rightly see it, we must not average the 1,840′ over for the whole forty miles, from the summit of Chestnut Ridge to Pittsburg, but take it in detail. The fall of the very first five miles, from the top of the mountain to the bottom of the Connellsville basin was 60′+1,300′+740′=2,100 feet; or 420′ per mile; and it was down this tremendous slope that the erosion began to plough out those numerous sharp ravines, which still continue to drain the mountain along its whole length; undercutting the sand rocks and revealing the edges of the coal beds, limestones and iron ores. We can easily study the process; for it is still going on continually before our eyes, at all seasons of the year, but especially in the spring time, when the melting snow and heavy rains wash down the clay and sand and fragments of rock which the winter's frost has loosened and softened, ready to topple over and slide down at the melting of the ice.

No one can rightly understand the geology of the Connellsville and Youghiogheny River Coke District who does not get a clear idea of the nature and extent of the erosion which the country has suffered in the lapse of all the geological ages since the close of the coal era and the uplift of the continent.

* A very interesting inquiry arises here. Did the Continent at that time stand out of sea level at about the same general height then as now? We know that the ocean flowed up through Bucks, Lancaster, York and Adams counties immediately after the rise of the coal fields, and that the bed of that New Red estuary was afterwards lifted many hundred feet. But this lifting seems to have been confined to the south-east counties of the State; for Pittsburg is only 750 feet above sea level now, and there are no New Red deposits around it; and the New Red rocks are all tilted towards the north and west. Western Pennsylvania, then, may have been *higher* above sea level, but could hardly have been *lower* than now, that is, considering the *formations*. But the *surface* of Western Pennsylvania was evidently at one time several thousands of feet higher than it is now, and has been degraded by the ceaseless activity of its streams, small and large.

† Adding together the difference of level between Pittsburg and Connellsville, 143′, the height of Chestnut Ridge, 1,300′, and the thickness of coal measures from XII up to the shales in the Ohio at Pittsburg, 400′; say, 1,840 feet.

When we speak then of the Connellsville basin and of the Pittsburg coal bed as being limited by certain geographical lines and confined to certain areas, it must be distinctly understood, that *it was not so limited formerly*, but was originally with the Barren Measures below it and the Upper Coal Measures above it, spread out in an unbroken continuous sheet, from Middle Pennsylvania to Middle Ohio, and far into Virginia; and it can in fact be recognized at such widely distant localities by its qualities and by its companion rocks.

The description of the general appearance, risings and fallings, of the Pittsburg bed along the Youghiogheny river given above will serve equally well to describe its attitude along Jacob's creek, which, rising in Chestnut ridge, flows westward, with innumerable sharp windings, to fall into the Youghiogheny 17 miles below Connellsville and 40 above Pittsburg. For ten miles it flows in the Connellsville basin with the Pittsburg bed mostly below water level. Then for eight miles it flows between hills not high enough to take in the Pittsburg bed.

The Big Sewickley also heads in the Connellsville basin and enters the Youghiogheny below West Newton, ten miles below Jacob's creek. For six miles at its head near Pleasant Unity, the Pittsburg coal is under its bed, but emerges and goes into the air, coming down again and lying in the hill sides for six miles* above the mouth of the creek. From the ten miles of intermediate country the bed has been eroded, and the creek flows through the Barren Measures.

Redstone creek (south of the Youghiogheny) heads likewise in Chestnut Ridge; cuts the Connellsville basin (holding the Pittsburg bed around Uniontown) for three miles; then flows five miles through Barren Measures; then six miles between hills carrying the Pittsburg coal bed, and enters the Monongahela at New Albany.

Dunlop's creek, Middle run, Brown's run, and George's creek, still further south, flow wholly in the Upper Coal Measures. †

* These measurements are not following the stream, but in a straight line.

† The details of this general statement are given in the Report of 1858, and will be enlarged in the Report of 1876. Many of the names of places referred to in the Report of 1858, printed from Jackson's manuscript of 1840, are obso-

The Pittsburg coal bed will be described in its details in the next chapters, and in immediate connection with the collieries and coke-works. It is enough to say here that, while it varies slightly in thickness*, it is always a fine minable bed, from eight to eleven feet thick, with a good roof, an even floor, and a small bearing-in slate-parting at about one and a half feet from the floor. Along the Youghiogheny it yields an admirable coking coal, containing about 30 per cent of volatile matter. As the percentage increases to 40 in the region of Pittsburg, the coal is preferred for the gas coal market.

Above it rest about 250 feet of Upper Productive Coal Measures, (*Monongahela System.*)

Under it lie about 450 feet of Barren Measures. Under these lie 250 feet of Lower Productive Coal Measures, (*Allegheny System,*) containing at least two workable coal beds.

Then comes the Conglomerate, say fifty feet thick.

Then the red shales of XI, with iron ore, limestone and a little coal, not one hundred feet thick, all told.

Under these lie the grey sandstones of X, the red sandstones of IX (Catskill,) the grey shales of VIII (Chemung oil rocks,) &c., &c., only to be reached by oil-well borings or deep shafts.

---

lete, being names of property owners, re-placed by later purchasers. But most of the description in the Final Report of 1858 is as intelligible now as it ever was. The facts, however, were meagre compared with those forthcoming, after thirty years of business life has multiplied villages and dépôts, created industries, and established mines, collieries and coke-works. In this Report only such as relate to the Youghiogheny valley are now published. Those on the Big Sewickley are connected with the development of the Kiskiminetas or Conamaugh river, and the Pennsylvania railroad.

*Its thickness increases towards Connellsville, and diminishes towards Pittsburg.

CHAPTER II.

The Geological Column at Connellsville.

Dr. R. M. S. Jackson reported to Mr. Rogers the following section of about 250 feet of the Upper (Monongahela) Coal Measures, immediately overlying the Pittsburg coal bed.* All the rocks higher in the series have been swept away, in the lapse of ages, from the hills in this neighborhood. Nor is it necessary, for the purposes of this report, to describe them as they appear further south and along the Monongahela river. This will be done in the Report of Progress for 1876 in Fayette and Westmoreland counties. A full description of the Upper Coal Measures is given in Professor J. J. Stevenson's Report of Progress for 1875 in Washington and Greene counties.

Section below Connellsville.

Slate and sandstone		? 30′ 0
Limestone		?
Sand and slate		20′ 0
Limestone and slate, alternate		48′ 0
Micaceous sandstone, thick and thin†		36′
Coal (Sewickley bed?)		0′ 3″
Limestone and black slate, ‡	*Great limestone,*	22′ 0
Limestone, yellow, nearly solid,	*Great limestone,*	7′ 0
Coal (Redstone bed?)	*Great limestone,*	1′ 3
Limestone with slate.	*Great limestone,*	24′ 0
Slate and micac. sandstone §		60′ 0
Pittsburg coal bed		9′ 0
Above the Youghiogheny river		24′ 0
Total		281′ 6″

In this section, the Redstone and Sewickley beds amount to nothing; but on the Redstone creek the Redstone coal be-

* See Final Report, 1858, Vol. II, pages 621, 622, fig. 500.

† Upper part flaggy.

‡ Upper part black limestone with black slate, and three inches of coal, and five inches of black slate.

§ With some black shale.

comes three and a half feet thick, and on Sewickley creek the Sewickley coal becomes five feet thick.

The chief feature of the country is the limestone deposit connected with these coals, overlying the Pittsburg bed and outcropping in all the hill sides of the Connellsville basin. A very good description of this remarkable deposit, as it appears along the Monongahela river from Pittsburg to the Virginia line, is given on page 635 of the Final Report of 1858, substantially as follows:

The Great Limestone is non-fossiliferous; variable in thickness and composition; made up of numerous beds, in contact, or separated by thin layers of shale, and sometimes by deposits of shale from one to eight feet thick; separated occasionally by calcareous sandstones, instead of shale, insensibly passing into limestone.—Color, generally blue and blueish.—Hard; breaking with a semi-conchoidal fracture.

Some of its layers are of a light yellow color, containing transparent specks of crystallized carbonate of lime, and take a polish as a beautiful marble. Other slaty layers of a black color, very hard, and giving out under the hammer a fœtid bituminous odor, lie in contact with and pass insensibly into black shale, in which case the black slate itself effervesces with acid, splitting smoothly. Most of the interbedded deep blue and yellow shales are soft, mouldering to clay on exposure, and contain limestone nodules. Some of the soft shales are black like a coal crop; and two of these form locally the Redstone and Sewickley coal beds.*

In Allegheny county and north-west Westmoreland county, the lower layers of the *Great Limestone* cap the isolated knobs with what looks like an artificial pavement.

Up the Monongahela, the sub-divisions of the *Great Limestone* surround all the vales and ravines with regular terraces.

Mr. E. C Pechin, of Dunbar, read a valuable paper before the meeting of the American Institute of Mining Engineers, at New Haven, in February, 1875,† in which the following description of these limestones is given:

Nothing definite is known about the upper layers of the

---

* Prof. Stevenson limits the "Great Limestone" by these beds.

† Transactions American Institute of Mining Engineers, vol. III, page 399.

great limestone mass, except that one of them, overlying the Pittsburg bed by about 300 feet, is a very valuable ledge of cement stone, from which the Phœnix Hydraulic cement is manufactured on a large scale.*

Two ledges of limestone, separated by eight or ten feet of shale, and having together twenty-five or thirty feet of outcrop immediately overlie the Sewickley (Uniontown?) coal bed, here four to four and a half feet thick, good and clean, and mined for the farmers' use.

Another layer of limestone, ten feet thick, underlies the above coal bed thirty-five or forty feet; and overlies the Redstone coal bed about forty feet.†

The Redstone coal bed is therefore about ninety feet *below* the Sewickley (Uniontown?) bed, and thirty-five feet *above* the Pittsburg (Connellsville) bed; no mention being made of any limestone in this last interval.

"There is practically no difference between these various ledges of limestone, and the analyses given below will serve for all. These ledges supply the local furnaces, and ship large quantities for the Pittsburg furnaces and city limekilns:—

Carbonate of lime	86.589
Carbonate of magnesia	3.715
Carbonate of protoxide of iron	1.685
Alumina	4.576
Silica	0.760
Organic matter	0.213
Water	0.003
Ignited insoluble residue	2.836

which last consists of silica, 2.445; alumina, 0.283; sesquioxide of iron, 0.062; lime, 0.038; magnesia, 0.006."

* It is evident that Mr. Pechin does not confine the term *Great Limestone* to the calcareous strata overlying the Pittsburg Coal Bed within the first 100 or 150 feet, but that he includes all the lime rocks of the Upper (Productive) Coal Measures, in the hills south of Connellsville. The Cement Bed of which he here speaks, does not even enter into the Connellsville section, lying about fifty feet above its highest stratum.

† Mr. Pechin thus places the Sewickley (Uniontown?) Coal Bed 85 to 90 feet above the Redstone Coal Bed. There was great uncertainty felt and expressed in the old survey about the identification of the small coal beds above the Pittsburg Bed, and we must wait until the new report of 1876 shall throw a clearer light upon their relationships.

Pittsburg Coal Bed.

The *Pittsburg Coal Bed* in the Connellsville basin, is thus succinctly described by Mr. Pechin. After stating that it occupies a trough three miles wide and fifty miles long, almost without a fault, he says that it gives from eight to nine feet of workable coal, is soft, easily and cheaply mined, and makes a coke of unusual excellence.

His typical "verified" analysis of the coke may be as conveniently given here as elsewhere:

Analysis of Connellsville Coke, by E. C. Pechin.

Volatile matter	1.296
Carbon, (hydrogen and nitrogen)	89.147
Ash	9.523
Water at 125° C.	0.032
Sulphur	0.084

Ash ignited, as above, 9.523.

Silica	5.413
Alumina	3.262
Sesquioxide of iron	0.479
Lime	0.243
Magnesia	0.007
Phosphoric acid	0.012
Potash and soda	traces.

"A large number of analyses of Connellsville coke have been made, showing less carbon and more sulphur. As regards carbon, I have had a number of analyses made at different times, out of different lots, showing somewhat more carbon than the above.

"This point is worthy of being noted in connection with this coal, viz: that in some localities slate veins (always containing more or less of sulphur) are almost wholly wanting, being confined to a thread of not more than a quarter of an inch in thickness, about two feet from the bottom of the coal, while in other localities not far distant, there are numerous small slate seams. The above analyses were made from very pure coal.

"The cheapness of the fuel is surprising at the present time. The coal is mined, coked and loaded on cars at the ovens for two and three-fourth cents per bushel, or one dollar and thirty-seven cents per net ton."

L.PLATE.I.

SECOND GEOLOGICAL SURVEY OF PA.

——— 1875 ———

YOUGHIOGHENY SECTIONS.

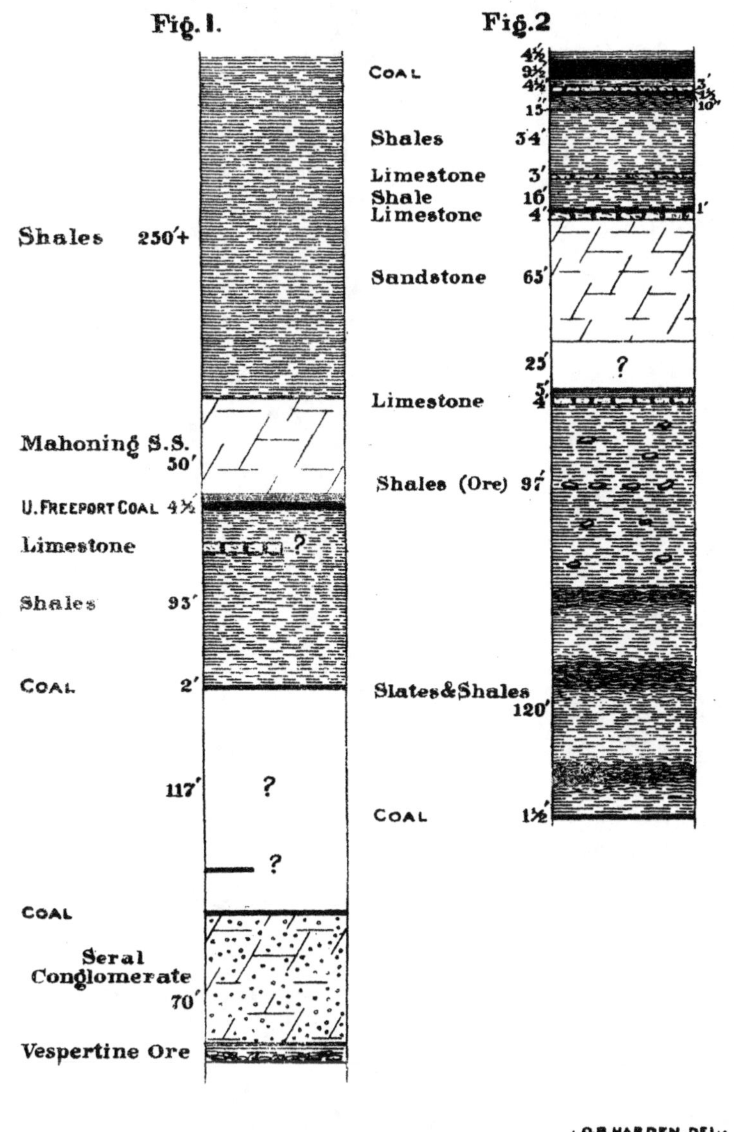

O.B.HARDEN, DEL.

PHOTO-ZINCOGRAPH, by F. A. WENDEROTH & CO., 1328 Chestnut Street, Philada.

Lower Barren Measures.

The Lower Barren Measures beneath the Pittsburg (Con nellsville) coal bed, occupy the valley of Dunbar creek, Young's Mile run and Gist's run, opposite Connellsville. They also rise successively from the bed of the Youghiogheny river, going down stream from the old Lobinger salt works, four miles below Connellsville. This latter section Dr. Jackson gives as follows:—*

	Thickness.	Bottom.
Pittsburg Coal Bed	9′ 0	0
Yellow slate and blue shale	16′ 0	16
Limestone, (Pittsburg)	10′ 0	26
Yellow shale	5′ 0	31
Interval unknown	20′ 0	51
SANDSTONE, (Connellsville) †	25′ 0	76
Interval unknown	15′ 0	91
Olive shale	20′ 0	111
SANDSTONE, (Pittsburg,) micaceous, (Morgantown?)	9′ 0	120
Yellow slate	15′ 0	135
Interval estimated ‡	40′ 0	175
Blue shale	7′ 0	182
Fossil Limestone	0′ 6″	
Blue shale	4′ 0	186
Coal Bed	1′ 3″	
Blue slate	4′ 0	191
SANDSTONE, (bluff)	70′ 0	261
Yellow shale	25′ 0	286
SANDSTONE, (Upper Mahoning)	30′ 0	316
Shale	25′ 0	341
SANDSTONE, (Lower Mahoning) §	40′ 0	381

The characteristic features of the above section are:—

1. The *Pittsburg coal bed*........................base at 0
2. Shales, and *Iron ore* under it.
3. The *Pittsburg limestone;* a well defined horizon, " 26

* Final Report, 1858. Vol. II, page 611.

† Coarse, grey, diagonally bedded. Called also the Ligonier sandstone.

‡ At the Old Franklin iron furnace and forge, and further on down stream, beneath the river bed towards Perryopolis, a village situated on a high hill of Barren Measures, not high enough to take in the Pittsburg coal.

§ The next set come in three-fourths of a mile below East Liberty, at old Strickler's coal bank, and they are estimated to lie 35 to 40 feet under tho preceding yellow slate. The coal bed (Strickler's little bed,) appears again 400 yards lower down the river, and 35 feet above water level, and under it runs the 70 foot sandstone, &c.

4. The CONNELLSVILLE SANDSTONE;* a marked horizon .... base at 76
5. Red variegated shales;† universal.
6. *Limestone, fossiliferous*.......................... " 182
7. *Coal bed*, very small.............................. " 187
8. SANDSTONE, very coarse and large. ‡........... " 261
9. The MAHONING SANDSTONE; very massive §.. " 421

The *Iron ore* beds underlying the Pittsburg (Connellsville) Coal from 8 to 12 feet, and mined for many years six miles south of Uniontown for the use of the Fairchance Iron works, are thus described by Mr. Pechin:

Blue Lump ore bed on top; averaging from 35 to 37 per cent of iron, and only 0.006 of phosphorus. At Dunbar furnace, approaching Connellsville, this dwindles to about one inch of ore imbedded in four inches of a mushy, wet clay. To take its place, economically, a layer of a very peculiar ore, 12 to 15 inches thick, is here found two feet over the clay, and four feet under the coal. This ore resembles baked yellow clay; is richer in alumina, and leaner in silica, than the other carbonates; weathers easily; calcines with great ease, and runs together in great loups; contains of sulphur 1.11 per cent, and of phosphorus 0.44 per cent. The soft clay under it allows it to be cheaply mined, at about $1 50 per ton, at present. The raw ore averages only about 30 per cent iron; but when calcined, smelts with great readiness, and with less fuel and flux. A mixture with equal parts of mountain ores (Red Shale of XI) makes a very soft, fluid and desirable foundry iron; the forge iron is, of course, cold-short, but otherwise good. This bed is now mined in every ore-bank opened between Uniontown and Dunbar, ten miles, and has been found regular far under cover. It has been struck in an artesian well at a depth of 420 feet.

Condemned Flag ore bed lies next below the Blue lump; and under it lies the

---

* The Connellsville sandstone, 65 feet thick, on which the town is built. The high knob opposite the town, and on the south side of the river, is of the same rock.—F. R. 1858, p. 610.

† Reddening the country around Pittsburg.

‡ This is a master rock in Somerset county, if properly identified.

§ Below this appear the top of the Alleghany River Coal Series, with a small coal bed at 427; a workable coal bed at 521, and some of the measures underneath. These turn gently over the anticlinal, and sink again successively beneath the Youghiogheny river towards Pittsburg.

Big Bottom ore bed, over the Pittsburg limestone.

These two beds yield from 28 to 32 per cent ores, with more phosphorus and more silica than the Blue lump ore. When worked together, and especially with charcoal, they make a brand of iron which was well known through the west for its excellence. About Dunbar, however, the Flag and Big Bottom ore beds are practically beds of limestone, with streaks of ore running through the deposit; and in the country north of Connellsville, and down the Youghiogheny, all the three ore beds above described vanish, only two feet of fire clay intervening between the bottom of the Pittsburg coal bed and the top of the Pittsburg limestone. But from Dunbar south-westward, to the Monongahela river and into Virginia, the ores may be mined successfully.*

The Pittsburg Limestone lies 16 feet beneath the Pittsburg coal, around Uniontown, and is from ten to twelve feet thick. Around Pittsburg, on the contrary, it immediately underlies the coal bed and occupies twenty-five feet of outcrop, with six, eight and even ten layers of blue and black limestone, separated by deposits of shale. Usually there is a top layer of limestone just under the coal bed; then most of the shale; and then the remainder of the limestone, composed of layers from 12 to 18 inches thick, close on top of one another, generally of a dark blue color, but sometimes deep black, ferruginous and fœtid. The top layer is sometimes absent or represented by nigger-heads or nodules of limestone in the shale.

The Connellsville Sandstone, (Ligonier sandstone,) is one of the great persistent members of the Coal Measure system, thinning and becoming more shaly towards the Ohio, thickening and becoming a more massive sandrock towards Chestnut ridge. It caps the highest hills in the Ligonier valley, and appears in its place under the Pittsburg coal at Salisbury, in Somerset county. The town of Connellsville is built upon it; and as it rises from the river it forms the bluffs of the ridge west of

* Mr. Pechin affixes to this favorable statement of the ore beds a theoretical condition to be received with caution, namely: "That where the covering is light near the outcrop, the Blue lump and attendant lower ores will be found, and that wherever the cover grows heavy, these will run out and the other vein come in." All that is known of such deposits teaches that the amount of cover has nothing to do with such variations of deposit. J. P. L.

Dunbar creek, and the crest west of Gist's run. Near Pittsburg, the shales over it contain lime-nodules, and the sand layers are separated and soft, but are used for flags and building stone, often showing ripple marks.

A *limestone*, not seen in the Connellsville section, but widely extended through the Monongahela country, underlies the sandstone. It is a square-breaking, hard, heavy, polishable, dark blue, (yellowish outside,) non-fossiliferous layer, three to five feet thick, undermined by a flooring of clay, and its fragments are tumbled down the hill slopes in abundance.

A *limestone* (non-fossiliferous) 12 feet under the last, but only two feet thick, sends its blocks down in the same manner, and for the same reason.

A *limestone* (non-fossiliferous) 35 feet under the last, three feet thick, and supported on a floor of sandy slates and slaty sandstones, does not lose its outcrop thus; but, on the contrary, although frequently seen, is usually covered up by the red, blue and yellow shales and clays which overlie it and intervene between the two upper limestones.* It is a stratum remarkable for weight and hardness; breaks square; smells of clay; is specked with calcite, and contains iron.

Red Shale, averaging 12 feet along the Monongahela waters, makes a bright red mark along all the hill slopes, about 130 feet below the place of the Pittsburg coal bed.

The *Pittsburg sandstone* (Ligonier S. S. ?) is a great deposit of shale above, sand in the middle, and pebble rock at the bottom, 70 feet thick; extremely variable in its composition, however, in different parts of the country. The Pittsburg Court House, Western Penitentiary, and other public edifices have been built from its quarries. It is sometimes so disintegrated at its outcrop as to furnish thousands of tons of coarse sand. The quarries are in its lower layers, and yield a yellowish grey stone, sometimes brownish green or brown; sometimes full of mica, sometimes destitute; much current-bedded; the pebbles in the bottom layers consisting of a fine, hard, drab or bluish clay, containing specks of mica from one inch to 15 inches (!) in

* Coloring the roads of Allegheny and Northern Westmoreland counties. The red shale is only four feet thick, over which lie 18 feet of buff and gray shales, sometimes quite full of lime nodules; and over these ten feet of yellow and purple shales.

diameter, always round, and apparently water-worn; coaly matter in the bed planes, sometimes pure coal; abundance of matted fossil plants; the sand of the disintegrated layers is of white quartz, water-worn, held together by a lime cement, and holding (in the green parts) a minute univalve fossil.

Olive and buff shales, holding lime nodules, with layers of fine flag-stone, and black clay streaks, but no coal beds, occupy the next interval.*

Black Limestone, fossiliferous,† two feet thick, separated by a clay layer from two to four feet thick from an underlying small

Coal Bed of the Barren Measures, varying from six inches to one and a half feet, hard, black, brilliant, and good. This bed lies, at Pittsburg, not many feet above the Monongahela river water level.

Marl, or calcareous blue and red mottled soft shale, the colors irregularly intermixed in spots, blotches and bands, numerous layers of lime-iron nodules occuring in the mass, and some minute fossils.

Sandstones, slaty, argillaceous, graduate downwards into yellow and brown shales, to a

Coal Bed of the Barren Measures, about one foot thick, up the Allegheny river; but it does not appear in the Connellsville section given above.

Mahoning Sandstone.—This great *triple* deposit of sand and gravel, is the base of the Middle Barren Measures; as the Conglomerate XII is the base of the Allegheny River Coal Measures. Along the Allegheny river bluffs it is seen divided thus:—

Upper,	Sandstone	30′ 0
	Conglomerate; quartz; iron nodules	4′ 0
Middle,	Coal bed, (sometimes)	0′ 6″
	Shales	25′ 0
Lower sandstone		35′ 0

* In Rogers' Final Report, the *collated* section on page 631, makes this limestone lie 300 feet below the Pittsburg bed. Jackson's section below Connellsville, makes it only 200 (183) feet more or less below that coal. The interval varies in all parts of the great coal field.

† This is a great store-house of fossils for the palæontologists. The shells are mostly bivalves, *Productus*, *Læptena*, *Terebratula*, *&c.*, but joints of stone lily stems (Encrini) are abundant, some of them half an inch in diameter. A small Orthoceras (cuttle fish shell) is also plentiful. Ammonites are found. Prof. J. J. Stevenson has named a long list of these fossils in his memoir on the West Virginia Coal Measures in the Transactions of the American Philosophical Society. Vol. XV, page 26.

This corresponds very well with its appearance in the bluffs of the Youghiogheny below Connellsville. The Lower Mahoning is seen at the Old Franklin iron works and forge, as a thinly laminated, grey, micaceous sandstone deposit, mixed with dark olive shales, on a gentle east dip. Fragments of coal are found near it, which probably come from the little bed in the middle.

The Mahoning sandstone is the great key-rock of the Bituminous Coal Field in Pennsylvania, Ohio, West Virginia and Kentucky. It was first best studied on the Mahoning river, in Jefferson county,* and hence its name. It is frequently referred to in the Report of Progress of 1874, on Clearfield and Jefferson,† and will be equally prominent in the report of 1875, on Cambria and Somerset. It makes a strong mark in the geology of the Broad Top Coal Field in Huntingdon and Blair, where it is a triple formation, with an intermediate coal bed.

The Mahoning sandstone, however, like the Conglomerate, and like the Mountain sands and Oil sands, still further down, puts on *locally* a thousand varying aspects, being sometimes coarse, pebbly and massive, and again fine grained, thin bedded and shaly. When horizontal, or nearly so, as on the Youghiogheny, it always makes steep slopes, often bluffs, and sometimes towering and continuous cliffs along the valley sides. When dipping more steeply, it always makes the brow of a ridge, like that along Dunbar creek, and that along Mount's creek, near Connellsville.‡

---

* Not the Mahoning river of Ohio.

† See it placed in the Column of Formations, H, page 2.

‡ At the mouth of Washington run, on the Youghiogheny, there is an exposure of—

Mahoning sandstone, coarse and massive	80 feet.
Olive slate	4′ 6″
Coal bed	1′ 3″
Shale, with lime-iron-nodules	4′ 6″
Slate, olive	4′ 0
Sandstone, micaceous	4′ 0
Slate, olive	4′ 0
Sandstone, micaceous	5′ 0
Interval, at Washington run; conjecturally	65′ 0
Shale, blue	4′ 0
Coal bed	4′ 6

and these are the lowest rocks that appear above water level, between Connellsville and Pittsburg.

The Mahoning sandstone forms the rapids of Youghiogheny.

The Mahoning sandstone is largely quarried on Dunbar creek for furnace hearths, and for crushed sand for glass works.*

The total thickness of rocks between the Pittsburg coal bed and Upper Freeport coal bed, is stated by Prof. H. D. Rogers† at 600 feet towards Blairsville, and 700 feet towards the Maryland line. Prof. W. B. Rogers makes this interval, as measured on his Morgantown section in Virginia, 525 feet. Prof. J. J. Stevenson makes the interval between the two coals on the Virginia line, 420 feet.‡ Dr. Jackson's notes down the Youghiogheny, puts the first coal bed under the Mahoning sandstone 427 feet below the Pittsburg bed, and the "four foot bed" 521.§ The generalized section along the Monongahela and Allegheny rivers, around Pittsburg, makes it 470 feet.¶ It is to be hoped that the report of 1876, in Fayette and Westmoreland, will clear up the difficulties which surround the measurement, and give more precision to our knowledge of the persistent members of the Barren Series.

Lower or Allegheny River Series.

MAHONING SANDSTONE.		
Shale, of variable thickness §		6′ to 8′ 0
Upper Freeport coal bed		4′ to 5′ 0
Middle Freeport coal bed		
Limestone and ore		93′ 0
Interval of 60 feet, (Pechin)		
Limestone ore, 2 to 3 feet		
Limestone, 3 to 5 feet		
Interval of 70 feet		
Lower Freeport coal bed		2′ to 4′ 6″
Interval, with small ores and *coals*,		200′ 0 ‖
Ferriferous coal bed	2′ 0	
Interval of 30 feet		
Iron ore, nodular		
Interval, with small *coals*		
Coal bed, (Brookville? Clarion?)		
CONGLOMERATE, No. XII		60″ 0

* E. C. Pechin, Trans. I. A. M. E. III, p. 404.

† § Final Report, 1858, II, p. 500. Jackson's data. ¶ Final Rep. II, 631.

‡ Trans. Am. Phil. Soc., Vol. XV, p. 24.

§ Jackson thought he found this bed of shale in one place on the Loyalhanna, 55 feet thick. See Final Report, 1858, p. 502, Vol. II.

‖ E. C. Pechin. Jackson's measurements varied with every section he made along the mountain. At Dunbar, J. P. Lesley reported 100 feet interval, *including the Conglomerate!* See private report of March 9, 1865, p. 10.

In these coal measures occur the ore beds of the Cambria Iron Company around Johnstown, in Cambria county; the Paint Creek and Elk Lick ore beds of Somerset county; the extensive deposits of brown hematite in Jefferson, Armstrong, Clarion and Venango; and the extension of these through the Hanging Rock iron region of Ohio; and Hartman's ore bed in West Virginia.

But in the Westmoreland and Fayette region no such important ore beds have yet been found. Mr. Pechin, knowing the efforts made to open similar deposits south of Connellsville, says that in the 200 feet of measures beneath the Lower Freeport coal, "occur numerous seams of coal from six inches to two and a half feet in thickness, and, connected with them, *small and unimportant layers of ore.*"

"The Lower Freeport coal gives from four to four and a half feet of workable coal, full of sulphur and slate, but, when cleansed of these impurities, making a strong, excellent coke. It is not now regarded as of any value, but when the day comes that the Connellsville (Pittsburg) coal is exhausted, this coal will play an important part in smelting the vast stores of ore which will still remain."

"Immediately *under* this [Lower Freeport] coal, and for 60 feet *above* it, occur small and unworkable bands of ore. About 70 feet *above* it is found a vein of *limestone ore*, claimed to be two to three feet thick, lying on some three to five feet of *limestone*. An analysis of cropstone gave the following:"*

Sesquioxide of iron		2.211
Protoxide of iron	33.504	78.070
Lime	10.587	
Magnesia	2.495	
Carbonic acid	31.484	
Alumina		1.867
Silica		0.287
Phosphoric acid		0.168
Sulphuric acid		0.160
Combined water		1.883
Hygroscopic water expelled at 100 C		0.292

* In changing the arrangement of Mr. Pechin's analysis, it is not intended to intimate that the carbonic acid is exactly satisfied by the lime, magnesia and protoxide of iron first stated; but merely to place before the reader's eye more prominently the lithological and metallurgical character of the bed; which really contains about 9 per cent of silica; 3 of alumina; $2\frac{1}{2}$ of peroxide of iron; 12 of lime; 3 of magnesia; and $27\frac{1}{2}$ of metallic iron.

Organic matter	2.406
Ignited insoluble residue,	12.100

consisting of silica, 8.667; alumina, 1,203; sesquioxide of iron, 0.476; lime, 1.504; magnesia, .239.

"Some 60 feet above this occurs another vein of limestone ore, which has only been opened on the outcrop, but not analyzed. Above this follows the Mahoning sandstone."

The names Upper, Middle and Lower Freeport coal beds, are adopted from the series on the Allegheny river. But it is a little hazardous to attempt their absolute identification. All we know for certain, is that the three Freeport beds of the country of the Mahoning, Redbank and Moshannon rivers, further north, form the first set of workable beds underlying the Mahoning sandstone.

.The Upper Freeport bed at Connelsville is merely the first *workable* bed under the Mahoning sandstone; and is a *double bed;* its two members getting further and further apart as we go south, until they become separated by 15 or 20 feet of shales towards the Virginia line; thus corresponding to the Upper and Middle Freeport of Jefferson county.

The same uncertain identity attaches to the lower coal beds, and a discussion of it is here out of place.

To the north of Connellsville, the Mahoning sandstone caps the ridge east of Mount's creek, and the lower coal beds outcrop on its east slope, facing Chestnut ridge, and in the valley of White's Mill run. West of Mount's creek the Barren Red shales occupy the base and the Pittsburg bed outcrops along the hillsides. Further north, at the head of Jacob's creek, Jackson found six coal beds in 350 feet of lower Coal Measures, thus:—

Jacob's creek.	Yellow shale, thickness unknown.	
	Coal bed	3' 0
	Yellow slate ... perhaps	20' 0
	SANDSTONE	50' 0
	Coal bed	0' 6"
	Olive shales, thickness unknown.	
Middle Barren Measures.	Interval, nature and thickness unknown.	
	SANDSTONE, coarse	30' 0
	Olive, yellow, sandy slates	30' 0
	SANDSTONE, micaceous	25' 0
	Olive, yellow, black, slates	20' 0
	Coal bed, hard, brittle	1' 2"
	Yellow shales to water level.	
	Interval, nature and thickness unknown.	

	SANDSTONE, MAHONING,* thickness unknown.	
Lower Coal Measures.	SANDSTONE, micaceous, thickness unknown.	
	Yellow shale, thickness unknown.	
	Coal bed, (Upper Freeport)	3′ 0
	Interval, nature and thickness unknown.	
	Coal bed, (Lower Freeport)	3′ 0
	Interval, nature and thickness unknown.	124′ 0
	Sandstone, coarse, over	12′ 0
	Coal bed.	1′ 0
	Blue, yellow shale, micaceous sandstone...	20′ 0

South of Connellsville, the Mahoning sandstone caps the ridge on the east side, and the Connellsville sandstone caps the ridge on the west side of Dunbar creek, which flows in the soft Barren Measures of red, yellow and olive shales with bands of micaceous flaggy sandstone, thin coal seams and limestones.

The Lower Coal Measures crop out on the east side of the ridge facing the mountain. The Upper Freeport coal bed varies from three to four feet in different gangways, and has a four foot roof of yellow clay charged with plants; sometimes dark blue slate. The Freeport limestone hich ought to appear under it is not visible. A two foot coal, rich, soft and crumbling lies 93 feet under it. Another two foot coal bed lies 117 feet under the last; and then follows the Conglomerate No. XII, without pebbles, merely a coarse, dark gray massive sandstone, 60 to 70 feet thick, making the rapids at Rotrock's Eddy two and a fourth miles above Connellsville, and thence rising in cliffs on each side of the gorge to the summit of the mountain. Immediately under the cliffs crop out the ore beds of No. XI.†

Mr. E. C. Pechin gives the latest and most circumstantial account of these ore beds, five in number, and known (beginning at the top) as the Honey-comb; 2, the Kidney; 3, the Flag; 4, the Big Bottom; 5, the Hematite, and he describes them thus:

Ores of XI.

Several small layers of not workable ore underlie the Conglomerate, No. XII, and overlie the uppermost regular stratum:

1. The *Honey-comb ore bed*, five to twelve inches thick; cel-

* This large solid stratum forms the high rocky spurs descending from the mountain, between the head-runs of Jacob's creek. See Final Report, 1858, page 607.

† The above is Jackson's report in Rogers' Final Report of 1858, p. 610.

lular; but almost identical in analysis with the Kidney, but making the better iron of the two.

A small *coal bed* six to ten inches thick, lies one foot under the Honey-comb ore bed, makes the mining of the ore easy, and suffices to roast both the Honey-comb and the Kidney ores at the pit mouth.

Fire clay ten feet thick, underlies the coal; and then comes:

2. The *Kidney ore bed* in two solid and continuous plates; the upper, one to two inches thick, and the lower, three to four (locally eight to ten) inches thick, separated by three feet of gnarled tough slate full of ore balls. The bed is but little wrought.

Interval of twenty feet, unknown rocks, under which lies

3. The *Flag ore bed*, eight to twelve inches thick, in a solid plate; good at the outcrop, but growing siliceous in the hill; "at 30 or 40 yards under cover there is nothing more than a ferruginous sandstone." Once extensively stripped; now abandoned.

Interval of sixteen feet, unknown rocks, under which lies

4. The *Big Bottom ore bed*, averaging 18 inches thick; a dense, hard, protocarbonate; in one, two or three layers, embedded in hard, tough blue clay, the whole, say five feet thick; roof, the same clay, treacherous and costly to keep up; over which lies six feet of fire clay; floor, sandstone.

The ore ground is quite irregular; thickening and thinning, with frequent rolls and faults. Sometimes the ore is found on both sides of a hill and not in the centre, (150 yards in.) "As long as the slate holds, the ore is found; but when the fire clay comes down, it cuts out both ore and slate." *

Interval, seventy to eighty feet, down to the Red shale of XI (Umbral.) In this interval—

5. The *Hematite ore bed* has been found on the mountain, lying about 40 feet above the Red Shale of XI, and has been traced a considerable distance. It was at first supposed to be a surface deposit. But several test-holes 15 to 30 feet deep, proved that it was a regular layer of brown hematite, averaging

* This sounds like the report of the miners, and such generalisations are seldom found to be exactly correct when carefully criticised by the experienced geologist. J. P. L.

thirty inches, and lying in a yellow clay. "It is authoritatively stated (says Mr. Pechin) that at an old charcoal furnace, some miles further up the mountains, a heading had been driven in 150 yards, the ore preserving its continuity throughout, and making an excellent iron. The partial analysis given below, (No. 1, on fine, dirty ore, and No. 2, on lump ore,) show a marked difference from any other ores in this section, containing an exceptionally large amount of phosphorus, and very considerable manganese, which is practically unknown in our other ores." *

The analyses of the Honey-comb, Flag and Big Bottom ores, are thus given:

	Honey-comb.	Flag.	Big Bottom.
Protoxide of iron	45.634	48.291	45.274
Sesquioxide of iron	2.057	trace.	trace.
Protoxide of manganese	0.000	0.000	0.000
Alumina	2.740	0.542	3.445
Lime	0.014	trace.	1.456
Magnesia	1.678	0.973	1.464
Silica	0.424	0.170	0.195
Carbonic acid	29.745	30.583	30.322
Phosphoric acid	0.068	0.143	0.170
Bisulphide of iron	0.754	trace.	trace.
Combined water	0.042	0.021	0.029
Hygroscopic, expelled at 100° C.,	0.074	0.010	0.003
Organic matter	1.324	1.131	0.947
Ignited insoluble residue	15.568	17.548	16.700
consisting of—			
Silica	10.844	13.410	11.046
Alumina	4.240	1.372	4.697
Sesquioxide of iron	trace.	0.107	0.643
Lime	0.034	1.804	0.264
Magnesia	0.439	0.853	0.047
Metallic iron	35.823	37.560	35.664

The ores above described have been traced over one-half of Pennsylvania, being first studied and described by Mr. J. T. Hodge, in his Reports of 1838–'9, around Ralston in Lycoming county, and thence south into Maryland and Virginia.†

* Metallic iron,	No. 1, 24.32.	No. 2, 41.07.
Protosesquiox. mang.,	12.60.	8.77.
Phosphoric acid,	1.27.	1.74.

† From J. P. Lesley's private report of 1865, the following description of the ore, as then worked, is taken:—

At the Bear Wallow drifts, on the brow of the mountain, overhanging the centre of the gorge, 980 feet above the bed of the river below, the bed of blue

Limestones of XI.

Immediately under the Red Shales of XI come the limestones which play so important a role in the subcarboniferous geology of our Southern and Western States, and which are totally absent from Middle and North-eastern Pennsylvania, or only marked by a few nodular concretions.

1. The *Upper Limestone;* a dark-blue fossiliferous stratum, 20 to 30 feet thick, composed of layers separated by shales. The rock is siliceous at the outcrop, and not now used for furnace flux.

2. The *Middle Limestone;* in two plates six feet thick; compact, pea-green; working well in the furnace.

---

carbonate is 10 inches thick. About 5,000 tons, in two years, were obtained from several gangways driven in blue-black shale under the cliffs of Conglomerate. Its two outcrops descend to water level at the paper mill on the river, and to the old furnace on Dunbar creek. On the opposite bank of the creek the outcrop returns up the slope, three miles, to the top of the mountain; and thus it zigzags, going south towards Virginia, up and down, along the sides of Limestone run, Tucker's run, Elk run, and other waters draining the great slope. Add to all this two miles of outcrop on the south brow of the river gorge descending into Ligonier valley, and two on Irishtown run, and we have fifteen miles of continuous outcrop of this bed of ore on the Dunbar furnace property alone. This will give some idea of the importance, as well as of the geology of these ore deposits.

The ore has been stripped extensively around the head waters of Elk run, at elevations of 880 to 1,150 feet above the furnace. Kree's and Watt's incline-planes used to bring down the ore to tramways at their feet. The new tramroad up Irishtown run, one and three-fourth miles long, reaches the outcrop at an elevation of about 600 feet above the furnace. Here, in a stoped face of 20 feet at the top, is seen a layer of ball-ore, some of the masses 12 inches long by 4″ to 5″ thick; and at the bottom the three continuous layers of ore, (sometimes splitting into five,) always measuring about the same total thickness of ore, two and a half feet.

The top layer of the Big Bottom deposit is a hard, heavy clay-iron-stone, 8″ to 10″; on 6″ to 18″ of nearly black fire-clay slate; the middle layer a dark-blue, soft, argillaceous ore, looking like ferruginous fire-clay, on 4″ of soft blue slate; the bottom layer a hard blue carbonate of fine grain, apt to come away (like the top layer) in slabs or flattened nodules of large size, entirely contiguous to one another, on 12″ of slate. Floor, gray flag stone.

Where there are five layers, the soft ore is still the principal layer, 12″ thick, and the other four 6″ or 7″ each,

These openings date back 40 years, but were most worked in 1857 and '58. During the 60 years previous to 1865, there must have been 120,000 tons of ore taking from the numerous Irishtown run workings.

The balls at the top of the stope face arrange themselves sometimes in two or three layers, and will yield variously from one and a half to five tons to a ten foot area; whereas the bottom ore will yield one and a half to two tons per square yard of stripping.

3. The *Lower Limestone;* one plate six feet thick; silicious; Mr. Pechin gives the following analyses of these beds:

	1.	2.	3.
Carbonate of lime	74.89	87.69	70.68
Carbonate of magnesia	2.03	2.76	0.52
Sesquioxide of iron	2.03	——	——
Oxide of iron and alumina	——	1.13	1.84
Silica	15.02	——	——
Alumina	5.26	——	——
Insoluble matter	——	7.46	26.32
Water and loss	.64	.96	.64
Phosphoric acid	.13	——	——

Phosphorus seems confined, therefore, to the upper plates, which contain an abundance of animal remains.*

Catskill Rocks.

The Catskill Gray Sandstone, No. X, forms the arch of cliffs next below the narrow shelf or terrace of XI, on both sides of

* The "Mountain Limestone" of No. XI, above described, has been quarried not only on Chestnut Ridge but on Laurel Hill, and on the Allegheny mountain, in Somerset county. Mr. Young's report of it (1875) around Confluence and Ursina, is to this effect:

In Addison township, six and a half miles south-east of Confluence, J. M'Cartney's new quarry shows four feet ("18" feet in another place) of greenish and sometimes reddish rock, *highly fossiliferous*, making a much esteemed lime. It lies on at least twenty feet of flaggy sandstone. Under this lie "18" feet of calcareous sandstone, (used for macadamizing the National pike.) Under this lie 20 feet of sandy limestone, making poor lime. None of the other quarries in Addison township, seem to be on the Upper or Fossiliferous beds. One of them is at the base of a hill 300 feet high, the top of which is covered with pieces of supposed Conglomerate No. XII.

Seven miles north of Confluence, on Laurel Hill, and in Fayette county, is a cliff of flag stone, (15 feet;) 50 feet under which, lie two feet of limestone in thin layers, interleaved with olive shales crowded with fossils. The next lower five feet of limestone is also very fossiliferous. The red and green shales of XI, occupy the next 150 feet, (by barometer,) and under them lie five feet of greenish, grey, compact silicious limestone.

At the summit of the Allegheny mountain, one and a half miles south of the Clay pike, are seen—

Red and green shales of No. XI. (Umbral)	160′
Limestone, *fossiliferous;* interleaved shales	20′
Shales	20′
"Red marble"	10′
Interval, concealed	150′
Hard blue sandstones of No. X. (Vespertine or Gray Catskill.)	

The western slope is covered with blocks of XII. But none are to be seen on the eastern slope; showing how complete has been the erosion caused by the dissolution of these limestone and shale outcrops.

the gorge of the Youghiogheny through Chestnut ridge; the lower steeps and talus being made by the Catskill Red Sandstone, No. IX, in which none of the fish remains have yet been found which characterize this remarkable "Old Red" Formation all through the northern states;* as will be described in the Reports of Progress for 1875, by Mr. Carll and Mr. Sherwood. If search were made among the fallen pieces in the middle of the gap, where the lowest rocks come up on the crown of the arch, the whitish pasty coating of fish-bone tissue, or perhaps head plates, teeth or fin-spines, would be discovered.†

The Catskill Gray Sandstone No. X, in the gorge is really a pebble rock, or true conglomerate; which the Conglomerate proper, No. XII, is not. This is a noteworthy fact, having an important bearing on the geology of the Coal Field far into Ohio, and agreeing with the recent doubts thrown upon the identity of the Ohio Conglomerate with that of Middle Pennsylvania.

No. IX is 1,000 feet thick in Bedford and Somerset counties, 60 miles to the eastward, but is known to thin westward, and may not be more than half that thickness under Connellsville.

Chemung Rocks.

The Olive Sandstones of No. VIII, the Chemung Formation of the north, does not appear above water level in the gorge of the Youghiogheny. The centre line of the flattened arch of the mountain crosses the river half a mile below the lower salt well, just under the old Bear Wallow ore drifts; and the gorge of Elk run at or a little below the steam saw-mill; the salt well standing 500 feet lower than the saw-mill.

The Chemung Oil Sands, if present, must lie but a few hundred feet beneath the river bed in the gap. Two salt wells have been bored, which must have penetrated the Chemung Oil Rocks. Tradition says oil was found in both, and it is even asserted that one of these old salt wells was abandoned because of the quantities of petroleum which issued along with

* See also Hugh Miller on the Old Red of Scotland.

† See Dr. J. S. Newberry's descriptions, in his Geology of Ohio, Vols. I and II.

the brine. The depth of these old wells is not known, but it is thought that neither of them is more than 300 feet deep. As considerable quantities of oil have come up through some of the old salt wells of Westmoreland county, and as the West Virginia Oil Field has yielded largely, there seem to be no strong reasons to urge against the supposition that oil sand belts may be discovered in Formation VIII, at depths varying from 2,000 to 4,000 feet beneath the Youghiogheny Coke Region. It is even possible that the coke manufacture may have a gas-fuel future before it.

NOTE.—Recent studies of the Upper Kenawha valley by Professor Fontaine, of the W. Virginia University at Morgantown, have greatly aided in clearing up our ideas of the composite nature of the Seral Conglomerate, No. XII. He finds it there made up of a top gravel bed and a bottom gravel bed, with a whole system of intermediate coal measure shales, clays and coal beds. These he proposes to call the *Inter-Conglomerate Coal Measures*, a very good name; or, the New River Coal Measures, New River being the name of the upper part of the Kenawha. This last designation is, however, not admissible, because it is already occupied for a still older Coal Measures in Montgomery county, Va., *underlying* the Red Shale of XI.

Prof. Fontaine's Conglomerate is 1,200 feet thick, coal and all. No. XII is just that thick at Pottsville, without any coal beds. But heavy coal beds appear in it at Lykens Valley, and Shamokin in the Anthracite Field. The Sharon Coal Series of North-western Pennsylvania (the Block coal of Ohio) seems to be also locked up *in* the Conglomerate. In the chapter just closed it will be noticed (page 26 L, 27 L, above) that with the ores a small coal bed occurs, and others might be found in the intervals.—[J. P. L.]

SECOND GEOLOGICAL SURVEY OF PA.

1875

CONNELLSVILLE BASIN

UPPER PRODUCTIVE COAL MEASURES

IN

WEST VIRGINIA

SEE PAGE 33. L.

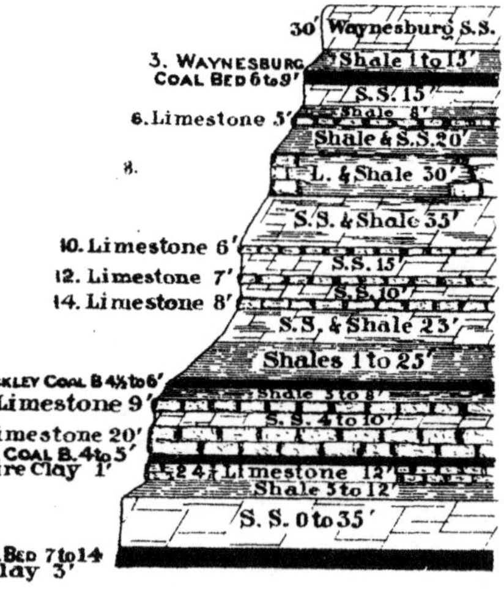

30' Waynesburg S.S.
3. Waynesburg Coal Bed 6 to 9'
Shale 1 to 13'
S.S. 15'
6. Limestone 5'
Shale 8'
Shale & S.S. 20'
8.
L. & Shale 30'
S.S. & Shale 35'
10. Limestone 6'
S.S. 15'
12. Limestone 7'
S.S. 10'
14. Limestone 8'
S.S. & Shale 23'
Shales 1 to 25'
17. Sewickley Coal B 4½ to 6'
Shale 3 to 8'
19. Limestone 9'
S.S. 4 to 10'
21. Limestone 20'
22. Red Stone Coal B. 4 to 5'
Fire Clay 1'
24. Limestone 12'
Shale 3 to 12'
S. S. 0 to 35'
27. Pittsburg Coal Bed 7 to 14
Fire Clay 3'

O.B. HARDEN. DEL

PHOTO-ZINCOGRAPH, by F. A. WENDEROTH & CO., 1328 Chestnut Street, Philada.

CHAPTER III.

The Coal Measures of the Connellsville Basin in West Virginia.

The following generalized section of the Coal Measures south of the Virginia State line, is taken from Prof. J. J. Stevenson's memoir published in 1872, by the American Philosophical Society, at Philadelphia, in its transactions, second series, Vol. XV, Article 2.

It is given a place here for comparison with what has been stated in chapters I and II above, and as a succinct and authentic guide to the rocks of the Connellsville Coal Basin.

Upper Productive Coal Measures.

(*Monongahela River Series.*)

No.	Stratum	Thickness	Mean thickness.
1.	Waynesburg Sandstone	30′ to 40′	35′
2.	Shale	1′ to 15′	
3.	*Waynesburg Coal Bed*	6′ to 9′	
4.	Sandstone	15′	195′ (Nos. 4–16)
5.	Shale	8′	
6.	*Limestone* (*a*)	5′	
7.	Shales and sandstone	20′	
8.	*Limestone* and shale	30′	
9.	Sandstone and shale	35′	
10.	*Limestone*	6′	
11.	Sandstone	15′	
12.	*Limestone*	7′	
13.	Sandstone	10′	
14.	*Limestone*	8′	
15.	Sandstone and shales	23′	
16.	Shales	1′ to 25′	
17.	*Sewickley Coal Bed* (*b*)	4½ to 6′	
18.	Shale	5′ to 8′	45′ (Nos. 18–21)
19.	*Limestone*	9′	
20.	Sandstone	4′ to 10′	
21.	*Limestone*	22′	
22.	*Redstone Coal Bed* (*c*)	4′ to 5′	
23.	Fire-clay	1′	40′ (Nos. 23–28)
24.	*Limestone*	12′	
25.	Shale	5′ to 12′	
26.	Sandstone (*d*)	0′ to 35′	
27.	*Pittsburg Coal Bed*	7′ to 14′	
28.	Fire-clay	3′	

(*a*) Prof. Stevenson *in this memoir* calls all the limestone beds below the

Waynesburg Coal, "Pittsburg Limestone," making 100′ of limestone in 350′ of measures; but he has seen good reasons for assigning this name distinctively to the limestone beds between the *Sewickley* and *Redstone Coal beds*, in his Report of Progress on Washington and Greene counties, 1875.—All the limestones are non-fossiliferous in this region.

(*b*) Sometimes divided by a layer of cannel coal, 2″ to 6″ thick.

(*c*) The clearest and purest coal in the basin, but neglected on account of the proximity of the Great Pittsburg Coal Bed.

(*d*) This sandstone which Mr. Stevenson calls the "Pittsburg Sandstone," crops out over the coal, for at least thirty miles along Chestnut ridge in West Virginia; but thins to nothing west of Morgantown.

(*e*) Protocarbonate ore, called locally "Olyphant Blue Lump," because worked by Mr. Olyphant, at Fairchance furnace, Uniontown, Fayette county, Pa. The deposit does not spread north of Fairmount.

(*f*) This good coal has sometimes been worked, where the owners were quite ignorant of the close neighborhood of the Pittsburg Bed.

(*g*) Contains large nodules of iron ore but not enough to mine.

(*h*) Same as at Pittsburg. The upper part has a curiously shattered look where exposed, due to the decomposition of nodules of impure iron ore.

(*i*) A curious stratum of limestone, sandstone and iron ore fragments, varying in size from a grain of sand to a man's head, usually rounded, as if by currents during deposition. Thin layers of homogeneous sandstone or shale may be traced to a considerable distance; and at one point there is a layer of iron ore one foot thick. The extent of this Conglomerate is unknown, but Mr. Stevenson doubts its existence west of the Monongahela river. It seems impossible to derive its materials from anywhere but the anticlinal range of Chestnut ridge. But if so, then the limestone fragments ought to be carefully compared with specimens from No. XI, and from the Lower Productive Coal Measures. Were they of No. XI, the conclusion would be inevitable, that the Ridge was elevated and deeply eroded long before the Pittsburg Coal Bed was laid down. Our present knowledge seems to forbid such an idea in the most absolute manner.

(*j*) Locally important east of the Monongahela. Slaty; impure cannel; sometimes "distinctly conchoidal, and of the color of lignite;" sometimes resembling the Grahamite of Ritchie county, West Virginia, or the Albertite of New Brunswick, to a wonderful degree. Ignites slowly, lasts longer and produces an intense heat, giving off not enough soot to coat the pipes; contains a considerable amount of free sulphur; ash bulky, light, no cinders. Many horse-backs and mud seams in the bed. This bed corresponds signally to the large Barton bed of the Cumberland Coal Field; for the Barton lies 180′ below the Pittsburg bed, and 200′ above the Upper Freeport. See Tyson's section, corrected by Mr. Jones, in 1875.

(*l*) An interesting group here, is thus described:

Shale, calcareous, blue, gray or black	3
Shale, dark, with many small iron ore nodules	12
Calcareous nodules	1′
Shale, olive	4′
Shale, brown, (not a persistent layer)	6′

All except the brown shale, are richly fossiliferous, and the following is Prof. Stevenson's list of recognized species:

Hemipronites crassus.

Chonetes Smithii; C. granulifera.

SECOND GEOLOGICAL SURVEY OF PA.

LOWER PRODUCTIVE COAL MEASURES IN W. VIRGINIA.

SEE PAGE 37. L.

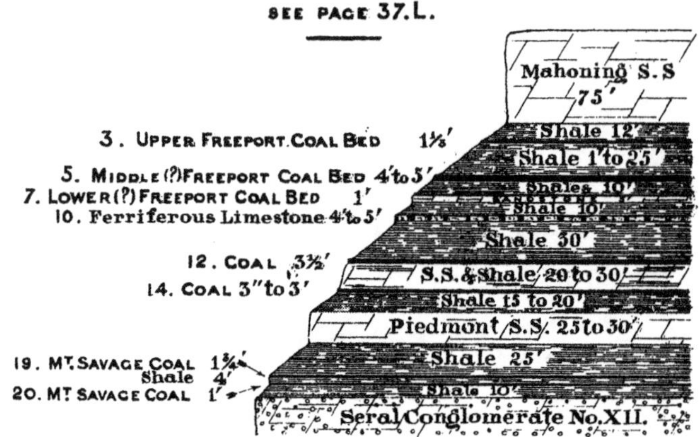

CONNELLSVILLE BASIN

LOWER BARREN MEASURES IN W. VIRGINIA

SEE PAGE 35. L.

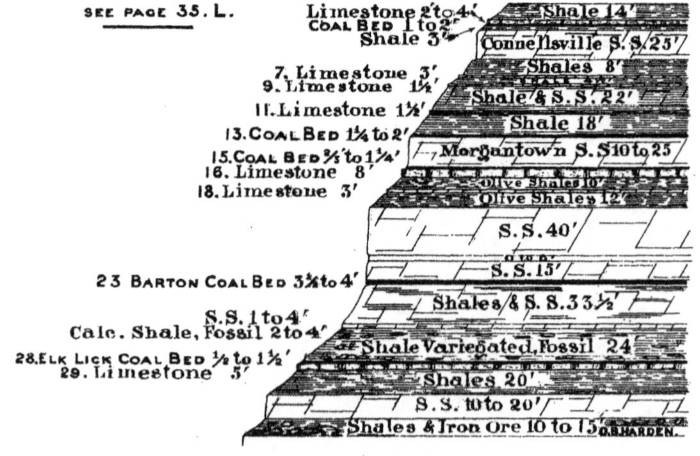

PHOTO-ZINCOGRAPH, by F. A. WENDEROTH & CO., 1828 Chestnut Street, Philada.

Lower Barren Group.

(*Barren Measures.*)

No.		Stratum	Mean thickness.	
1.		Shale with iron ore (*e*)..........	14'	17'
2.		*Limestone*........................	2' to 4'	
3.		*Coal Bed* (*f*)....................	1½ to 2'	
4.		Shale..............................	3'	
5.	*Connellsville*	Sandstone..........................	25'	
6.		Shales.............................	8'	
7.		*Limestone*........................	3'	
8.		Shale with iron ore................	4½	86½
9.		*Limestone*........................	1½	
10.		Shales and shaly sandstone (*g*),	22'	
11.		*Limestone*........................	1½	
12.		Shale..............................	18'	
13.		*Coal Bed*..........................	1¼ to 2'	17
14.	*Morgantown*	Sandstone..........................	10' to 25'	
15.		*Coal Bed*..........................	⅔' to 1¼	
16.		*Limestone*........................	8	
17.		Shales, olive......................	10'	
18.		*Limestone*........................	3'	
19.		Shale, olive.......................	12'	90'
20.		Sandstone (*h*)....................	40	
21.		Conglomerate (*i*).................	0' to 6'	
22.		Sandstone..........................	15'	
23.	*Barton Coal*	*Bed* (*j*)..........................	3½ to 4'	
24.		Shales and some sh. ss..........	33½	
25.		Sandstone..........................	1' to 4'	60
26.		Shale, *Calc. fossil* (*l*)............	2' to 4'	
27.		Shale, *Vari. fossil* (*l*)...........	24'	
28.	*Elk Lick? Coal*	*Bed*..............................	⅓' to 1½	
29.		*Limestone*........................	5'	
30.		Shales, varigated, ferrug. (*m*)...	20'	65'
31.		Sandstone..........................	10 to 20'	
32.		Shales, with iron ore (*n*)........	10' to 15'	

Productus Nebrascensis; P. Prattenanus; P. semi-reticulatus, (*here, probably identical with the American variety of P. costatus.*)

Orthis carbonarea.

Athyris subtilita.

Spirifer planoconvexus; S. cameratus.

Lima retifera.

Aviculopecten carbonarius: A. occidentalis.

Nucula parva; N. ventricosa; N. (?) anodontoides.

Nuculana bellistriata.

Yoldia carbonaria; Y. Stevensoni.

Edmondia Aspenwalensis.

Astartella concentrica.

Macrodon obsoletus.

Solonomya radiata.

Macrocheilus primigenius; M. ventricosus.

Euomphalus rugosus.

Bellerophon Montfortianus; B. percarinatus; B. carbonarius; B. Stevensanus; B. Meekianus.

Pleurotomaria Grayvilliensis.

Orthoceras cribrosum.

Nautilus occidentalis,

Petalodus Alleghaniensis.

Myalina,
Pleurophorus,
Edmondia,
Deltodus,
Lophodus,
Ctenoptychius, } *Undetermined Species.*

Fish teeth, very rare.

Crinoidal stems,
Bryozoans, } *A few near the top.*

Fossils are found not in very good condition in several good exposures along Decker's creek.

Excellent preserved specimens of nearly all the above species can be gathered in Mr. Williams' ravine, five miles north of Morgantown.

NOTE.—Here a small variety of *Chonetes granulifera* entirely replaces *C. mesoloba* which does not occur.

Some of these species are dwarfs; most of them are smaller than in the west. See also Mr. F. B. Meek's Report to the Regents of West Virginia University, 1870.

(*m*) Two layers of iron ore:—Upper layer nodular, not enough to mine; lower layer irregular, moderately good, occasionally calcareous; averages about 6'' inches. Both layers sometimes disappear suddenly.

(*n*) An irregular band of low grade nodules near the bottom of the mass; but used to be mined for mixing at Decker's Creek Old Furnace.

(*o*) The Mahoning sandstone, is for the most part, a massive rock, with alternating coarse and fine layers, the former sometimes conglomerate, and the latter overlying them pitted on the other side as if with rain-marks. Sometimes it is flaggy. There are also good quarries of building stone yielding blocks 6' to 8' thick. Indistinct vegetable impressions are not infrequent. Four miles south of Morgantown, it makes bluffs of 75 feet in height, weathered into large rounded cavities, or strangely honey-combed.

(*p*) Under the Mahoning sandstone on Decker's creek, near Morgantown, a dark shale, 12' thick, contains, near its middle, a band of nodular iron ore about 2' thick, holding an interesting group of fossils, of which the following are most numerous:

Lophophyllum proliferum.

Zeacrinus mucrospinus.

Ersocrinus.

Cyathocrinus (?)

Hemipronites crassus.

*Productus Nebrascensis**; *P. Prattenanus.**

*Athyris subtilita**.

*Aviculopecten carbonarius**; *A. Hertzeri.*

*Nucula ventricosa**.

Nuculana arata.

*Yoldia carbonaria**.

Lower Productive Coal Measures.

Allegheny River Series.

No.	Stratum	Mean thickness.	
1.	Mahoning Sandstone (*o*)	75′	87′ (1–2)
2.	Shale (*p*)	12′	
3.	(*Upper Freeport ?*) *Coal Bed* (*q*)	$1\frac{1}{3}$	
4.	Shales	1′ to 25′	12′
5.	(*Middle Freeport ?*) *Coal Bed* (*r*)	4′ to 5′	
6.	Shale	10′	10
7.	(*Lower Freeport ?*) *Coal Bed* (*s*)	1′	
8.	Sandstone	5′	50′ (8–11)
9.	Shale	10′	
10.	*Ferriferous Limestone* (*t*)	4′ to 5′	
11.	Shale	30′	
12.	*Coal Bed*	$3\frac{1}{2}$′	
13.	Sandstone and shale	20′ to 30′	25
14.	*Coal Bed* (*u*)	3′ to 3′	
15.	Shale	15′ to 20′	70′ (15–17)
16.	(*Piedmont*) *Sandstone* (*v*)	25′ to 30′	
17.	Shale	25′	
18.	*Mt. Savage* { *Coal Bed*, } (*w*)	$1\frac{3}{4}$	4 (18–20)
19.	*Mt. Savage* { Shale, } (*w*)	4′	
20.	*Mt. Savage* { *Coal Bed*, } (*w*)	1′	
21.	Shale (*x*)	10′	10′
22.	(Seral) Conglomerate, No. XII, (*y*.)		

*Astartella concentrica**.
*Maerocheilus primigenius**; *M. ventricosus**.
Polyphemopsis peracutus.
*Enomphalus rugosus**.
*Bellerophon Montfortianus**; *B. carbonarius**; *B. percarinatus**.
*Pleurotomaria Greyvilliensis**; *P. speciosa*; *P. carbonaria*; *P.* (?) *tumi-a*; and others undetermined.
*Orthoceras cribosum**.
Phillipsia Sangamonensis.

*Myalina**,
Schizodus,
Allorisma, } Undetermined Species.
Nautilus,
*Deltodus**,

Note.—Those marked * are found in the list given above in note (*n*).

On Booth's and Coburn's creek, this shale under the Mahoning sandstone dwindles to a black band 4″ (inches) thick, overlying 20′ (feet) of thinly laminated shale containing numerous fragments of

Neuropteris,
Sphenopteris,
Annularia,
Sphenophyllum,

and is not considered by Prof. Stevenson as a persistent stratum in Ohio or Pennsylvania, (*i. e.* across the Virginia line.)

(*q*) A good 15″ coal bed underlies this shale on Decker's creek, but does not appear on Booth's creek ; but is 3′ thick on the Baltimore and Ohio railroad, south of Fairmount.

(*r*) This is the important and persistent bed of the group. On Tibb's run, it is overlaid by a conchoidal bituminous shale, (cannel, poor,) sometimes mined with coal, which is friable.

This coal bed *immediately underlies the Mahoning sandstone* at W. Howell's, seven miles from Morgantown, and is nearly 8′ thick, divided by two thin clay shale partings into three benches. In the shales under the coal, fine fossils may be got by breaking nodules of iron ore.

(*s*) A very local coal bed.

(*t*) The Ferriferous limestone is frequently double; divided by several feet of shales. Towards the top it contains cavities with ochre, is very ferruginous, and has been mined as calcareous ore at one or two localities. It spreads for twenty miles south of the State line, but is not seen on the Baltimore and Ohio railroad, south of Fairmount, (Nizum's mill.) It is used for flux near Morgantown, and should be extensively burned by farmers.

(*u*) Called Brookville Coal Bed by H. D. Rogers. Called locally "Blacksmith's Vein," because free from pyrites, and friable.

(*v*) Instead of calling this the *Tionesta* sandstone, as Prof. Stevenson has provisionally done in his memoir, merely to suggest its relationship to No. XII, and the rocks of north-western Pennsylvania, the name *Piedmont* may be used with advantage. For this is the great "upper member" of the basal formation of the Productive Coal Measures, which marks the Cumberland Coal Basin with ranges of cliffs along the Potomac and its branches. It might be called the "Cumberland sandstone," were not the name "Cumberland" given not only to the Maryland Coal Field, but the Lower Silurian Valley of Middle Pennsylvania, and to the range of the Allegheny mountain in Virginia and Tennessee. "Piedmont" is as noted a place on the Potomac, as Connellsville is on the Youghiogheny, and the cliffs of this great sandstone surround the place.

It may be a long time before we can prove that the sandrock of the Tionesta valley, in M'Kean county, Pennsylvania, is this Piedmont sandstone.

Prof. Stevenson describes it as varying in texture from moderate coarse conglomerate to fine grained sandstone. On the Baltimore and Ohio railroad it weathers in huge chambers. The compact layers are very refractory and have been used for furnace hearths. A small coal bed (3″ to 4″) occurs in this rock on Decker's creek.

Mr. Howard Grant Jones, in a memoir on the Cumberland Coal Basin in 1875, says: "The most prominent feature is the sandstone lying over the "three feet" seam of coal already referred to as lying upon the Conglomerate proper at Piedmont.

"This rock has been alluded to as the "Upper Conglomerate." In places it is found somewhat conglomerate near the base, but in general, it outcrops as a pure, hard, coarse, gray sandstone, changing sometimes to yellowish red. We have seen it between Piedmont and Bloomington, disintegrated, in broken slabs of a dirty ferruginous color.

"In the northern part of the basin, on the Pittsburg and Connellsville railroad, this sandstone is 30′ to 40′ thick. Under it is a 3′ coal, with a fire-clay floor of 8′ to 9′, on shales and thin sandstones. The Mt. Savage fire-brick is made from clay from this bed 200′ up the mountain side. South of Piedmont, the vertical outcrop of this sandstone makes a wall 60 feet high; some admixture of shale is noticeable. The whole is one mass, substantially a gray coarse sandstone, a little ironstained, with a cubical cleavage. Further up the Potomac, on the north side of Lost Land Run, there is a floor of this sandstone, split into immense cubes, in position, but separated by vertical fissures from one to two feet wide and 30′ to 40′ deep, the surface clothed with vegetation, a dangerous labyrinth of pit-falls. Further up the river, the probable thickness of No. XII, is 60′ to 80′.

"No. XII, where Stony run enters, forms the bed of the Potomac, and its floor is studded with pebbles the size of a pigeon's egg.

"The base of the Coal Measures, (Mr. Jones resumes,) always presents the features of a bold, coarse, white or reddish sandrock, towering above a broken mass of Conglomerate, and running like a great white wall along the base of the hill slopes."

(*w*) This is the coal bed which lies at water level of the Potomac under Piedmont, in Allegheny county, Md., in the Cumberland Coal Basin, and the fire-clay of which is worked at Mt. Savage. Near Morgantown it is separated by 4′ (feet) of sandstone into an upper group of thin layers:—

Coal	8″	1′ 9½″
Shale	4″	
Coal	1½″	
Shale	2″	
Coal	1″	
Shale	1″	
Coal	4″	

and a lower bed of good solid coal 1′ thick. On Booth's creek only one bed is seen (18″). At Nizum's mill, on the Baltimore and Ohio railroad, the bed is seen 3′ thick, thinning to nothing over a thickening fire-clay floor.

(*x*) Two bands of persistent iron ore, impure, extensive deposits overlie the shale at Nizum's mill. See for these ores Prof. W. B. Rogers' Pridevale Iron Works Report.

(*y*) The Great Conglomerate is nowhere measurable in the Monongahela region, the gaps and ravines being filled with its immense fragments, some of which must weigh a thousand tons. Its quartz pebbles are often three-quarters of an inch in diameter; but some of its strata are finegrained. Mr. Stevenson estimates the total thickness of No. XII, on the Monongahela, in W. Virginia, at about 350 feet.

CHAPTER IV.

CONNELLSVILLE COKE TRADE.

The region in which the Pittsburg Coal Bed is opened and worked for coking purposes, and from which the famous Connellsville coke is shipped, has been examined from the new Fairchance Iron Works, six miles south-east of Uniontown, Fayette county, to the farthest openings and ovens to the north-east at Spring Grove station, Fayette county. All the openings in this whole distance, making in all a basin thirty miles long by an average of three miles wide, have been carefully examined by Mr. Young, and the facts in reference to them will be given in detail. The appended map (Plate VI) compiled from the county maps, shows the position of these mines and ovens, and gives the outline of the basin. The key-list of mines and companies enables the geographical position of any of the works to be easily located.

It is not necessary to give sections of the different exposures of the Pittsburg Bed, though the thickness of the coal and any features of geological or practical importance will be noted in each case. Speaking generally for the region, the Pittsburg Coal Bed in this Connellsville Coke Basin is a magnificent bed, ranging from eight to eleven feet in thickness, with one small slate, the "bearing in slate" eighteen inches above the floor. The roof is good, the floor even and quiet, and the coal of remarkably good and uniform character.

All discussions of character of coal, &c., will be included under the Chapter on Coking, where they properly belong.

Fayette County Branch of Pittsburg and Connellsville railroad.

The new Fairchance opening of Mr. Oliphant is on the Pittsburg Coal Bed, six miles south-east of Uniontown. The furnace was not yet quite completed September, 1875. As the railroad now stops at Uniontown the works are not connected with the railroad system, though a road has been graded from Uniontown up to and beyond the furnace, but the iron has never been laid down.

The coal and underlying iron ore at Oliphant's mine show as follows :—

Fig. 3.

Pittsburg coal	10′ 0″
Clay and slate	2′ 6″
Blue lump iron ore	1′ 0″
Slate containing 2″ of flag ore	3′ 0″
Big Bottom ore	0 10″

On the line of the Fayette branch of the Pittsburg and Connellsville railroad, Messrs. Ewing, Boyd & Co., have their coke ovens at Lemont station, three miles north of Uniontown.

The coal bed and iron ores show thus:

Slate roof. *Fig. 4.*

Coal	6′ 6″
Slate	1″ to knife edge.
Coal	3′ 0″
Slate and unseen measures	4′ 6″
Iron ore reported	1′ 8″

There are one hundred and seven Beehive Bank Ovens, with material on the ground for thirty to forty more. The ovens are one-half 12′×6′, and one-half 11′×6′.

One hundred bushels of coal are charged into an oven. None of the gases are utilized either here or at any other coking establishment in the region.

The coal is roasted for forty-eight hours, except the Friday and Saturday charges, when an extra amount of coal is charged and the roasting is continued for seventy-two hours.

There is a decided increase in bulk in coking ; 100 bushels of coal yielding an average of 120 bushels of coke. With the coal at 76 pounds and coke at 40 pounds to the bushel, the yield of pounds of coke to pounds of coal is 63 per cent, or as it is commonly and conveniently stated in figures, 13 to 8. The works employ in all eighty-five men.

Messrs. F. H. Frost & Son are operating at Frost Station.

They mine the Pittsburg Coal Bed in its full thickness, and with its regular roof and floor. The mine is worked for lump coal, of which ten to fifteen cars a day are shipped to Connellsville for use on the Pittsburg and Connellsville railroad. Thirty-six men are employed at the mine.

There are twelve Beehive Bank Ovens, charged with mine slack; the amount of charge being the same as at the other works.

The coal is roasted for twenty-four hours, the time being increased for Friday and Saturday coke.

Messrs. Hogsett, Watt & Co. are operating at Mt. Braddock station.

The Pittsburg Coal Bed is worked. The mine gives the following section of the bed:—

Coal left in roof. *Fig. 5.*

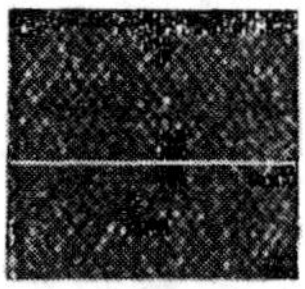

Coal	4′
Slate	1″
Coal	3′

Fire-clay floor.

There are some horseback and clay veins, but none of any consequence. But seven feet of coal are mined; the top slate forming but a poor roof, and coal being left for roof. The mine produces 180 tons of coal daily.

There are one hundred and twenty-seven Beehive Block Ovens, in size 11′×5½′ The charge is one hundred bushels, and one hundred and seventeen bushels on Friday and Saturday. The coal is roasted for forty-eight hours, except the Friday and Saturday charges, which yield seventy-two hour coke.

The production is 6,300 bushels daily, and an additional 945 bushels per diem (2 days) for the ovens charged on Friday and Saturday.

No coal is shipped from the mine, all of it being used in the ovens; and the coke is shipped to Wheeling, St. Louis, &c., and as far as Salt Lake City.

Eighty men are employed in all, in the mine and coke yard.

Messrs. Hogsett, Beal & Co. are located at Ferguson's station, one mile north of Mt. Braddock.

They work the Pittsburg Coal Bed, ten feet thick, but of which only seven feet are mined the balance being left in the roof. Small bone coal in roof and floor. The mine gives this section:—

Slate roof. *Fig. 6.*

Bony coal		2″
Coal	6′	10″
Slate		3″
Coal	2′	7″
Bony coal		2″

Fire-clay floor.

There are seventy Beehive Bank Ovens; the charge being the same as the average.

The ovens are run on forty-eight hour coke, with the seventy-two hour coke of Friday and Saturday charges. The production is 4,500 bushels daily, and the works supply Dunbar Furnace.

Messrs. Paull, Brown & Co., are operating one mile west of Dunbar furnace.

They mine the Pittsburg Bed of Coal, nine feet thick, with the usual bearing in slate three feet above the floor. Seven feet of coal are mined.

There are one hundred Beehive Block Ovens, in two rows; the production from which is 6,000 bushels daily for four days, and 7,000 bushels daily for two days. The coke is shipped to Youngstown, Ohio.

Messrs. Henderson & Co., are operating half a mile north of this last place. They work the Pittsburg Bed, nine feet thick, and take it all from top to bottom. The small bearing in slate is in its usual place.

There are seventy Beehive Bank Ovens, 12′×6′, and they are charged and worked as is usual with these Beehive ovens. The ovens yield 4,200 bushels for four days, and an increased yield for two days. The coke is shipped west. There are thirty-seven men employed in all in the mine and coke yard.

Messrs. W. T. Watt & Co., are operating at Watt's station. They mine the Pittsburg Coal Bed, ten feet thick, showing here the following section:

Fig. 7.

Coal in roof.	
Coal....................	.... 4′ 0″
Very thin slate.	
Coal....................	.... 2′ 0″
Non-persistent slate.	
Coal....................	.... 3′ 0″
Fire-clay and concealed measures..............	.... 4′ reported.
Iron ore reported. Thickness unknown.	

There are sixty Beehive ovens, in size 11½′×5½′. They are charged and worked as usual, and produce 22,800 bushels of coke a week, most of which is shipped to Ohio. Fifty men are employed.

The Connellsville Gas Coal Company operate at Fayette station. They work the Pittsburg Coal, nine feet thick.

There are one hundred Beehive Bank Ovens, in size 11½′×6′, charged and worked as usual, and yielding 36,000 bushels of coke every week. One hundred men are employed.

The table below gives the main facts in the above works:

Resumé of Coke Works on Fayette County branch of Pittsburg and Connellsville Railroad.

NAME OF FIRM.	No. of ovens....	Kind of ovens.	Weekly production in bushels,	Number of men employed.....	Where shipped.
Boyd, Ewing & Co....	107	Beehive bank...	38,000	85	Chicago, St Louis, and west.
Hogsett, Watt & Co...	127	Beehive block..	39,700	80	Wheel'g, Salt Lake City, Omaha.
Hogsett & Beale.....	70	Beehive bank...	28,800	40	Dunbar Furnace.
Paul, Brown & Co....	100	Beehive	33,000	50	Youngstown, O.
R. Henderson & Co...	70	Beehive bank...	26,600	37	West.
W. T. Watt & Co....	60	Beehive bank...	22,800	50	Ohio.
Connellsville Gas Coal Company..........	100	Beehive bank...	36,000	100	St. Louis, Salt Lake City, Johnstown.
Total....	634		224,900	442	

South-west Pennsylvania Railroad..

On the line of the South-west Pennsylvania railroad, near Connellsville, the Pittsburg and Connellsville Gas Coal and Coke company, Mr. John F. Dravo, agent, are operating largely.

The Pittsburg Coal is mined nine to ten feet in thickness, of which seven to eight feet are taken out and all coked.

There are two hundred and fifty-three Beehive Bank Ovens, in size $11\frac{1}{2}' \times 6'$. The usual charge at these ovens is one hundred and ten bushels of coal; and the coal is roasted for forty-eight hours, except the Friday and Saturday charge, which is roasted seventy-two hours. These ovens produce one hundred and twenty-two cars of coke weekly. Each car averaging 625 bushels, or 76,250 bushels of coke weekly.

Some of the coke is shipped to Newcastle; some to Johnstown, but the larger part of it goes to Etna station, on the West Pennsylvania railroad. Ninety-two men are employed.

John Moyer was building, September, 1875, forty Beehive Bank Ovens, of the size $11\frac{1}{2}' \times 6'$.

A mine was then being opened on the Pittsburg Coal Bed.

Messrs. Dillinger, Sherrick & Co. are operating at Pennsville station. The Pittsburg Coal Bed is worked, nine feet thick, with a slate binder at four feet above floor. Eight feet of the coal are taken out:

Fig. 8.

Black slate.

Coal with bands of fire-clay	4′
Fire-clay shale	1′ 6″
Coal	5′
Slate binder	Thin.
Coal	4′

Fire-clay floor.

Bank ovens, in size $11\frac{1}{2}' \times 6'$. The charge is four wagons to each oven, or one hundred and forty wagons daily. The ovens are worked as usual, and yield 4,800 to 5,400 bushels of coke daily. Forty-two men are employed.

Messrs. Willson, Boyle & Playford are operating at the Valley coke works, Valley Works station. They work the Pittsburg Coal Bed, averaging nine feet in thickness, but in some places running as high as eleven feet.

Fig. 9.

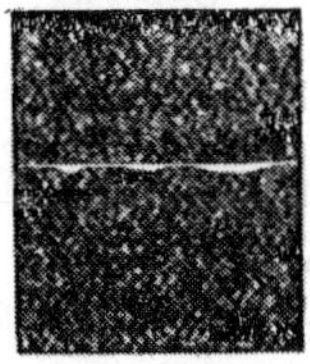

Slate roof.

Coal	4′ 0″
Slate parting.	
Coal	5′ 0″

Fire-clay floor.

There are one hundred and two Beehive Bank Ovens, in size 11½′×6′. The charge is three and a half to four wagons, and the ovens are worked as usual, yielding eleven cars (6,875 bush.) daily, which is shipped both east and west. Eighty men are employed.

Messrs. Serrick, Rice & Co., are operating one-third of a mile above Valley Works station. They work the Pittsburg Bed, nine feet thick, with a small and non persistent middle slate at about four feet above the floor.

Fig. 10.

Slate roof.		
Coal........................	....	5′ 0″
Slate parting, not persist't.		
Coal........................	....	4′ 0′
Fire-clay floor.		

Eight feet of the coal are taken out and all used in the ovens.

There are twenty Beehive Bank Ovens, in size 11⅓′×5½′. The charge is three wagons, and the ovens are worked as usual, making forty-eight hour coke, except the Friday and Saturday charges which are roasted for seventy-two hours. Twelve cars are shipped weekly (7,500 bushels) east and west.

Messrs. Dillinger & Suttle are operating the Enterprise Works at Hawk Eye station. They work the Pittsburg Coal Bed, nine feet thick, with the small slate binder three feet above the floor. The coal is all taken out and is used in the coke ovens, except some little custom coal. The coal lies here one hundred feet above the railroad, and is sinking gently to the south-east.

There are forty-one Beehive Bank Ovens of the usual size. The charge is three wagons for four days, and three and a half wagons for two days, and the ovens are worked as usual, making forty-eight hour coke, except the seventy-two hour Sunday coke. Twenty-four cars are shipped weekly, (in all 15,000 bushels,) mostly to Pittsburg.

Messrs. Hurst, Stoner & Co., are operating at Stonersville. They work the Pittsburg Coal Bed, nine feet thick, with an irregular slate binder three feet above the floor. Seven feet of the coal are mined; the coal all going into the ovens.

There are thirty Beehive Bank Ovens, and forty Beehive Block Ovens—seventy in all; in size 11⅓′×5½′. The charge is three wagons, increased slightly on Friday and Saturday, and making forty-eight hour coke, with the usual amount of seventy-two hour "Sunday coke." Forty-eight men are employed.

Samuel Warden & Co. are also operating close by Stonersville. They work the Pittsburg Bed, nine feet thick, with no regular slate partings. They mine the coal the whole thickness of the bed, and use it in their ovens.

There are eighteen Beehive Bank Ovens, in size 11¼'×6¼' The charge is three wagons, and the ovens are operated as usual, giving 6,300 bushels weekly of coke, forty-eight hour coke, with the usual seventy-two hour Sunday coke. The coke is shipped to Chicago and points west of it. Twelve men are employed.

Messrs. Stoner, Hitchman & Co. are operating at Farr's station. They work the Pittsburg Coal Bed, nine feet thick, with no regular slate parting. Eight feet of coal are mined, some of which is sold as custom coal, the greater part however going into the ovens.

There are sixteen Beehive Bank Ovens, and fourteen more are to be built. The ovens are 10'×5½', are charged and worked as usual, and yield 6,300 bushels of forty-eight and seventy-two hour coke. Twelve men are employed.

The table below recapitulates the main facts concerning the coke works on the South-west Pennsylvania railroad for convenient reference:

Resumé of Coke Works on South-west Pennsylvania Railroad.

NAME OF FIRM.	No. of ovens....	Kind of ovens.	Number of men employed.....	Production per week—cars....	Where shipped.
P. & C. G. C. & C. Co.—John Dravo, agent..	203	Bank...........	92	122	Johnstown, N. Castle, Etna, W. P. railroad.
Dillinger, Sherrick & Co..................	70	Bank...........	42	50	According to order, no general place.
Valley Coke Works—Willson, Boyle and Playford...........	102	Bank...........	80	66	East and west.
Sherrick, Rice & Co...	20	Bank......	11	12	According to order.
Enter'se Coke W'ks—Dillinger & Suttle..	41	Bank...........	15	24	Pittsburg.
Hirst, Stoner & Co....	70	30 bank, 40 block,	48	50	
Sam'l Warden & Co..	18	Bank...........	12	10	Chicago and west.
Stoner, Hitchman & Co	16	Bank...........	12	10	
Total	540		312	344	

Mount Pleasant Branch Railroad.

Messrs. Frick & Co. are operating at Broad Ford station, on the Mount Pleasant Branch of the Pittsburg and Connellsville railroad, and two miles north of Connellsville. They are working the Pittsburg Coal Bed, nine feet thick of clean coal, without slate or bone coal, except that small binders are found at three feet and at five feet above the floor. The binder at three feet is found, though very rarely, five inches thick. The rider of coal which is found overlying the Pittsburg Coal Bed at varying distances is, at this mine, almost incorporated into the bed, there being less than a foot of fire-clay between the top of the main coal and the bottom of the rider. It is here three feet thick; the coal being very good for house use, and cokes fairly well. It is sometimes mixed with coal from the main bed in charging the ovens.

Fig. 11.

Slate roof.	
Coal rider	3′ 0″
Fire-clay	11″
Coal	4′ 0″
Slate binder.	
Coal	2′ 0″
Slate binder	1½″ to 5″
Coal	3′ 0″

From seven and a half to eight feet of clean coal are mined from the main bed, all used in the ovens.

There are one hundred and one Beehive Bank Ovens, in size 11′×5½′. The charge of the oven is three wagons for four days of the week, and three and a half wagons for Friday and Saturday. The ovens are worked in the usual way, and yield of forty-eight hour daily coke and seventy-two hour Sunday coke, eleven cars daily, or 6,875 bushels. This is shipped to Milwaukee, Chicago, Salt Lake City, and other points in the west. Sixty-one men are employed.

Messrs. Morgan & Co. are operating only one-fourth of a mile north of Frick & Co.'s works. They are working the Pittsburg Coal Bed, showing here also nine feet of coal, and at places ten feet, with the small slate partings at three feet and five feet above the floor. Eight feet of this coal are taken out and used in their ovens.

There are one hundred and eleven Beehive Bank Ovens, in size 11′×6′. The charge is one hundred and ten bushels of coal for four days in the week, and one hundred and twenty-five bushels on Friday and Saturday. They burn forty-eight and seventy-two hour coke; shipped mainly to the west, some of it having gone as far as California; and since the strike in the anthracite region (in 1874) a certain amount of the coke continues to come east to the Susquehanna and Lehigh valleys. Eighty men are employed.

Messrs. Strickler & Lane are operating at Morgan station, on the Mount Pleasant branch of the Pittsburg and Connellsville railroad. They are mining the Pittsburg Coal Bed, which is here in the same condition as at Morgan & Co.'s, nine feet of clean coal.

There are forty-four Beehive Bank Ovens, in size 11½′×6′. The charge of the ovens and working are the same as at Morgan & Co.'s works, and of the forty-eight hour and seventy-two hour coke twenty-eight cars (17,500 bushels) are shipped weekly. Thirty men are employed.

Messrs. Hutchinson & Co., are operating north of Morgan station. They are working the Pittsburg Coal Bed, which shows as described above.

There are seventy-nine Beehive Bank Ovens of the usual size. They are charged with three wagons, (100 bushels,) worked in the usual way and yield of forty-eight and seventy-two hour coke thirty-eight cars, (23,750 bushels,) which are shipped west usually. Forty-five men are employed.

Messrs. Markle, Sherrick & Co., are operating north of Morgan station. They mine the Pittsburg Coal Bed, nine feet thick.

There are eighty Beehive Bank Ovens, in size 11′×5½′. They charge 100 bushels of coal, with the usual increase on Friday and Saturday, and produce forty-eight and seventy-two hour coke. The product, fifty cars weekly (31,250 bushels) of coke is shipped west. Six men are employed in the yard.

Messrs. Hirst, Moore & Co., are operating the Summit mines, one mile north of Morgan station. They mine the Pittsburg

Coal Bed, nine feet thick of coal, with a slate binder showing at three feet and another at five feet above the floor. These binders are irregular, the thickness changing rapidly, but are never large. Seven and a half feet of coal are taken out and used in the ovens.

Fig. 12.

Slate roof.	
Coal	4′ 0″
Slate, irregular.	
Coal	2′ 0″
Slate, irregular.	
Coal	3′ 0″
Fire-clay floor.	

There are one hundred and one Beehive Bank Ovens, in size 11½′×6′, charged and worked as usual, yielding of forty-eight hour and seventy-two hour coke, sixty-six cars (41,250 bushels) weekly, which is shipped by Morgan & Co. Seventy-five men are employed.

C. H. Armstrong & Son are operating one-half mile north of Summit mines. At date, (December, 1875,) they had twelve Beehive Bank Ovens built, and intended to build seventy-three more; size 11½′×6′. They were opening a mine on the Pittsburg Bed.

Charlotte Furnace is operating coking ovens opposite Scottdale station, on the South-west Pennsylvania railroad. They mine the Pittsburg Coal Bed, nine feet in thickness. The regular slate binders show at three feet and five feet above the floor. They are irregular and vary in size from six inches down to a knife edge.

Fig. 13.

Slate roof.	
Coal	4′ 0″
Slate	6″ to 0″
Coal	2′ 0″
Slate	6″ to 0″
Coal	3′ 0″
Fire-clay floor.	

There are fifty Beehive Bank Ovens, charged and worked as usual, yielding of forty-eight and seventy-two hour coke 3,000 bushels daily, which is used at the furnace.

Messrs. Keifer & Co. are operating at Fountain Mills station, on the Mount Pleasant Branch of the Pittsburg and Connellsville railroad. They mine the Pittsburg Coal Bed, nine feet thick, with its middle slate five feet above the floor, ranging from five inches down to nothing. Eight feet of coal are mined, all of which is used in the ovens.

There are ten Beehive Bank Ovens, in size 12′×6′, charged and worked as usual, yielding of forty-eight hour and seventy-two hour coke one car (625 bushels) daily, which is shipped to Pittsburg and Harrisburg.

Messrs. Ihmsen, Lake & Co. are operating the Fountain mines, near Fountain Mills station. They mine the Pittsburg Coal Bed, nine feet thick, carrying the binders three feet and five feet above the floor, both very irregular. Eight feet of coal are mined, all used in the ovens.

There are fifty Beehive Block Ovens, in size 11½′×6′, charged and worked as usual; the charge three to four wagons, yielding of forty-eight hour and seventy-two hour coke thirty-three cars (20,625 bushels) weekly, shipped mainly to the west; a small part to the east. Thirty-five men are employed.

Messrs. J. R. Stauffer & Co. are operating the Dexter mines, one mile north of Fountain Mills station. They mine the Pittsburg Coal Bed, nine feet or more in thickness; the upper part of the bed markedly hard. There is no regular slate parting, but in some parts of the mine there are two half inch slate binders four inches apart, and four feet above the floor.

There are forty Beehive Ovens, in size 11½′×6′, charged with three and a half to four wagons, worked as usual, yielding twenty-six cars weekly (17,250 bushels) of forty-eight hour and seventy-two hour coke, which is shipped east and west to order. Thirty men are employed.

Messrs. Painter & Co. are operating at West Overton station. They mine the Pittsburg Coal Bed, which shows here nine feet of coal, as at the Dexter mines.

There are seventy Beehive Bank Ovens, in size 11′×5½′. The charge is three wagons (100 bushels) for four days, and four wagons for two days. The ovens yield of forty-eight hour and seventy-two hour coke, forty cars (25,000 bushels) of coke weekly, most of which is shipped west. Thirty-one men are employed.

Messrs. Lomanson and Sauft are operating half a mile north of West Overton station. They mine the Pittsburg Coal Bed, nine feet thick, showing itself about the same as at Dexter mines.

There are thirty Beehive Bank Ovens, in size $11\frac{1}{2}' \times 6\frac{1}{2}'$. The charge is three and a half wagons of coal for four days, increased to four wagons to the charge on Friday and Saturday. The yield of forty-eight hour and seventy-two hour coke is twenty cars (12,500 bushels) weekly, which is now shipped east. Fifteen men are employed.

Messrs. A. S. R. Overholt & Co., are operating at the West Overton mines. They mine the Pittsburg Coal Bed, nine feet in thickness, with two small persistent slate binders, rather irregular in thickness, four feet above the floor.

Fig. 14.

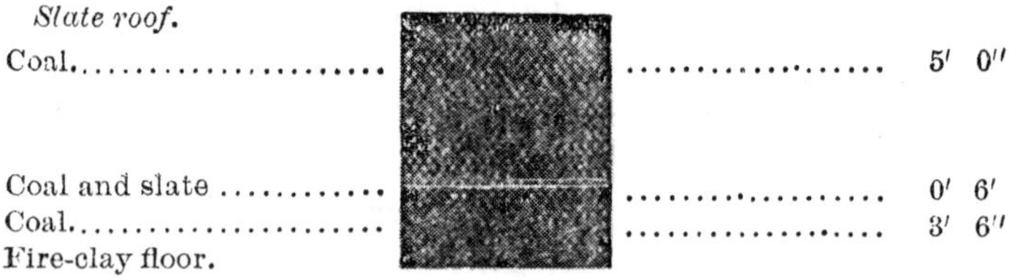

Slate roof.

Coal	5′ 0″
Coal and slate	0′ 6′
Coal	3′ 6″

Fire-clay floor.

The rider is about three to four feet above the main bed. Of the main bed, seven feet are taken out, all used in the coking ovens.

There are sixty-two Beehive Bank Ovens, in size $11\frac{1}{4}' \times 6\frac{1}{2}'$. The charge is one hundred bushels, increased on Friday and Saturday, yielding of forty-eight and seventy-two hour coke thirty-six cars (22,500 bushels) weekly, which is shipped west. Fifty men are employed.

Messrs. Markle & Co., are operating at the Rising Sun coke works, one-third of a mile north from Iron Bridge station. They mine the Pittsburg Coal Bed, nine feet thick. At three feet above the floor there is a double slate binder, the same as at the West Overton mines, and at six feet above the floor there is a slate binder one inch thick. The sulphur is usually in the lower bench, and there is a one and a half inch binder of slate and iron pyrites in the floor of the coal.

Fig. 15.

Rider coal.	
Slate	3′ 4
Coal	3′ 0″
Slate	0′ 1″
Coal	2′ 6″
Riders and coal	0′ 6″
Coal, including bone and pyrites binder at base..	3′ 1½″
Fire-clay floor.	

The rider is three to four feet above the main coal bed. The coal is sinking to the north-west.

There are seventy Beehive Bank Ovens, in size 11½′×6′. The charge is three to three and a half wagons of coal, yielding of forty-eight hour and seventy-two hour coke forty-six cars (28,750 bushels) weekly. Sherrick, Markle & Co., ship all the coal from these works. Forty-five men are employed.

Mr. I. F. Overholt is operating just opposite to the Rising Sun coke works. He mines the Pittsburg coal, of the same thickness, nine feet, and with the same partings.

There are thirty-six Beehive Bank Ovens charged and worked the same as the ovens above named, yielding of forty-eight hour and seventy-two hour coke, thirty-six cars (22,500 bushels) weekly, shipped by Messrs. Lake & Co. Twenty men are employed.

Messrs. Cochran & Ewing are operating the Buckeye coke works at Bridgeport station. They mine the Pittsburg Coal Bed, nine feet thick, with the small slate binders at three feet and five feet above the floor. A small slate, carrying much iron pyrites, shows at two feet above the floor; but though showing generally, it is not invariably persistent.

Fig. 16.

Slate.	
Coal	1′ 0″
Slate	1′ 0″
Coal	1′ 6″
Fire-clay shale	2′ 6″
Coal	4′ 0′
Slate, thin.	
Coal	2′ 0″
Slate, thin.	
Coal	3′ 0,′
Fire-clay floor.	

The coal is dipping to the north 35° west.

There are sixty Beehive Bank Ovens, in size $10\frac{1}{2}' \times 5'$ The charge is 100 bushels of coal, increased to 115 on Friday and Saturday. The ovens are worked as usual, yielding of forty-eight hour and seventy-two hour coke thirty-eight cars (23,750 bushels) weekly, shipped to the west. Thirty-six men are employed.

Messrs J. F. Stauffer & Co. are operating at Bridgeport station. They mine the Pittsburg Coal, which is here nine feet thick, and with partings as described at the Buckeye mines.

There are twenty Beehive Bank Ovens, in size $11\frac{1}{2}' \times 6'$. The charge is three and four wagons. The ovens are worked as usual, and the yield is of forty-eight hour and seventy-two hour coke thirteen cars (8,125 bushels) weekly, shipped west. Twelve men are employed.

Mr. Wm. D. Mullin operates north of Bridgport station. He mines the Pittsburg Coal Bed, nine feet thick, and showing similarly to the section described at the Buckeye mines.

There are sixty Beehive Bank Ovens, in size $11' \times 5\frac{1}{2}'$. The charge is three and a half to four wagons. The ovens are worked as usual, and the yield is of forty-eight hour and seventy-two hour coke thirty-six cars (22,500 bushels) weekly, shipped west by Messrs. Sherrick and Markle. Thirty-five men are employed.

Messrs. Boyle and Hazlett are operating on the west side of the railroad, opposite to Mullin's works. They work the Pittsburg Coal Bed, which is here twenty-three feet below the railroad level, and sinking to the north-east. The coal is nine feet thick, and shows its partings as at the Buckeye mines.

There are one hundred and seventy-one Beehive Bank Ovens, in size $11\frac{1}{3}' \times 6'$. The charge is three to four wagons of coal. The working of the ovens is as is customary, and the yield is of forty-eight hour and seventy-two hour coke twenty cars (12,500 bushels) daily, or 75,000 bushels weekly. The coke is shipped to Chicago. One hundred and twenty-five men and boys are employed.

Messrs. Duncan & Bro. are operating at the north terminus of the Mount Pleasant Branch of the Pittsburg and Connellsville railroad. They mine the Pittsburg Coal Bed, nine and a half feet thick, without any slate binders. The rider is, as usual, made up of coal and slate layers.

The Superintendent states that the mine shows the following structure:—The coal is reached at a depth of 220 feet, by a slope 550 feet long. It strikes the coal within 25 yards of a point from which the coal rises in all directions. At Bridgeport, one mile south, the coal comes up to day-light, and it also comes out about one mile north, one mile east and one mile west. Eight and a half feet of the coal are mined, all for use in the ovens.

There are twenty-five Beehive Block Ovens, in size $11\frac{1}{2}' \times 5\frac{1}{2}'$. The charge is four wagons. The ovens are run upon seventy-two hour coke, of which they yield thirteen cars (8,125 bushels) weekly, which is shipped west.

There is to be an increase of the number of ovens to fifty, whenever the condition of the coke business warrants, the foundations of the extra ovens being already laid. They are to be built in a block. Twenty men are employed.

The hill-side, at Duncans, shows the following section:

Soil	10′
Limestone	12′
Shaly limestone	5′
Parted coal bed	2′
Ferruginous shale and sandstone	32′
Limestone	8′
Fire-clay	1′
Blue slate with iron ore	35′
Parted coal bed	4′
Slate and sandstone	85′
Pittsburg coal bed and rider	15′
Limestone and ore.	

Resumé of Coke Works on the Mt. Pleasant Branch of the Pittsburg and Connellsville Railroad.

NAME OF FIRM.	No. of ovens....	Kind of ovens...	Number of men employed.....	Weekly production—cars.....	Where shipped.
Frick & Co..................	101	Bank..	62	66	Chicago, Milwaukee and Salt Lake City.
Morgan & Co	111	Bank..	80	70	West as far as California.
Strickler, Lane & Co........	44	Bank..	30	28	
Hutchinson & Co...........	63	Bank..	45	38	West, on order.
Markle, Sherrick & Co......	80	Bank..	60	50	West.
Summit Mines—					
Hurst, Moore & Co........	101	Bank..	75	66	Morgan & Co.
Charlotte Furnace..........	50	Bank..	35	30	Furnace.
Keifer & Co	10	Bank..	8	6	Pittsburg & Harrisburg.
Fountain Mines—					
Ihmlen, Lake & Co.......	50	Block,	35	33	East and west, to order.
Dexter Mines—					
J. R. Stauffer & Co	40	Bank..	30	25	East and west, to order.
Painter & Co...............	70	Bank..	32	40	West.
Lomanson & Stauft.........	30	Bank..	15	20	East.
Markle & Co................	70	Bank..	45	46	Sherrick, Markle & Co.
J. F. Overholt	36	Bank..	20	36?	Lake & Co.
West Overton—					
A. R. S. Overholt & Co ...	62	Bank..	50	36	East.
Buckeye Mines—					
Cochran & Ewing.........	60	Bank..	36	38	West.
J. T. Stauffer & Co..........	20	Bank..	12	13	West.
William D. Mullin	60	Bank..	35	36	Sherrick, Markle & Co.
Boyle and Hazlett..........	171	Bank..	125	120	Chicago.
Duncan & Bro	25	Block,	20	13	West, to order.
Total....................	1,284		870	700	

Pittsburg and Connellsville Railroad.

Messrs. Frick & Co. are operating at Broad Ford, on the Pittsburg and Connellsville railroad. They mine the Pittsburg Coal Bed, nine feet thick, with the usual small slate binders at three feet and five feet above the floor. Seven and a half to eight feet of coal are taken, all for use in the ovens.

There are one hundred Beehive Block Ovens of the usual size. The charge is three wagons, increased on Friday and Saturday, and the yield of forty-eight hour and seventy-two hour coke is sixty-six cars (41,250 bushels) weekly, shipped by Messrs. Morgan & Co. One hundred and thirty-seven men are employed in all.

Messrs. S. Cochran & Co. are operating the Washington

mines, one-third of a mile west from Broad Ford. They mine the Pittsburg Coal Bed, in full size of nine feet thick.

There are thirty-five Beehive Bank Ovens, in size $10' \times 5\frac{1}{2}'$. The charge is eighty-five to ninety bushels of coal, and the ovens are run upon forty-eight hour coke. The product, three cars (1,875 bushels) daily, is shipped west. Sixteen men are employed.

Messrs. Laughlin & Co., are operating the Tyrone mines.—They mine the Pittsburg Coal Bed, nine feet thick, with its double small slate binder at three feet above the floor; the slate binder at five feet above the floor is not persistent. A knife-edge of slate and iron pyrites, is found eighteen inches above the floor:

Slate roof. *Fig. 17.*

Coal	4′ 0″
Slate thin, not persistent.	
Coal	1′ 6″
Slate and coal	6″
Coal	1′ 6″
Slate and pyrites binder.	
Coal	1′ 6″
Fire-clay floor.	

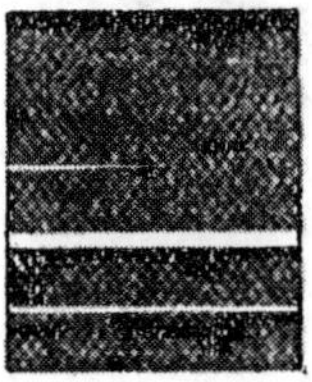

Seven feet of coal are taken out, all for use in the ovens.

From this mine on to Jackson the coal is nearly level; at the lower end of the Jackson works it dips under the railroad, not going deep however.

There are one hundred and five Beehive Bank Ovens, and eleven Beehive Block Ovens, one hundred and sixteen ovens in all. Of these, fifty ovens are in size $10' \times 5\frac{1}{2}'$, and sixty-six are in size $11' \times 6'$. The charge is three wagons of coal for the large, and two and a half wagons for the small ovens, increased on Friday and Saturday. When examined (July, 1875) the ovens were running on seventy-two hour coke; generally they make forty-eight hour coke. The production is sixty-three cars (39,375 bushels) weekly. Fifty-five men are employed.

Messrs. Brown & Cochran are operating the Stirling mines. They mine the Pittsburg Coal Bed, nine feet thick, parted as described above at the Tyrone mines.

There are one hundred and fourteen Beehive Bank Ovens and forty-three Beehive Block Ovens, in all one hundred and fifty-seven ovens, in size $10\frac{1}{2}' \times 5\frac{1}{2}'$. The charge is three wagons and increase on Friday and Saturday. The ovens were working for seventy-two hour coke, but run on time to order. The product, fourteen cars (8,750 bushels) daily, is shipped to Pittsburg. Ninety men are employed.

Messrs. John M. Cochran & Co., are operating the Jackson mines. They mine the Pittsburg Coal Bed, nine feet thick, the usual slate binder at five feet above the floor being very thin. They work the whole thickness of the bed, the coal taken out going into the ovens.

Fig. 18.

Slate Roof.	
Coal	4′ 0″
Slate binder.	
Coal	1′ 6″
Slate and coal	0′ 6″
Coal	3′ 0″
Fire-clay	1′ 0″
Black slate with ore	1′ 6″
Limestone	3′ 0″
Slate and shale	4′ 0″
Limestone	2′ 6″
Carbonate iron ore	1′ 0″
Black shale, with irregular 6″ coal seam	2′ 0″
Limestone	2′ 0″
Calcareous and siliceous shales	10′ 0″
Calcareous shales	4′ 0″
Coaly black slate	1′ 0″
Limestone with shale	4′ 0″
Slate and shale.	

There are sixty-three Beehive Bank Ovens; sixteen are in size 12′×6′, and forty-seven are in size 10′×5½. The charge is ninety and one hundred and five bushels of coal in the small ovens, one hundred and twenty and one hundred and thirty-five bushels in the large ovens.

The Fayette Coal Company are operating the works at Sedgwick station. They mine the Pittsburg Coal Bed, in full size of nine feet.

There are one hundred Beehive Bank Ovens, in size $10' \times 5\frac{1}{2}'$. The charge is two and a half wagons of coal, increased on Friday and Saturday. The ovens are run on forty-eight hour coke, and yield fifty-five cars (34,375 bushels) weekly. It is shipped to Pittsburg, to Graff, Bennett & Co., and Shoenberger, Blair & Co. Seventy-five men are employed.

Messrs. Cochran and Keister are operating the Spring Grove mines, on Hickman's Run siding of the Pittsburg and Connellsville railroad. They mine the Pittsburg Coal Bed, nine feet thick, with the usual slate binders at three feet and five feet above the floor; the latter one sometimes running up to five inches in thickness. Four inches of slate and iron pyrites are in the floor of the mine.

The rider coal three feet in thickness, sub-divided by a six inch slate, is less than two feet above the main bench of the coal:

Fig. 19.

Slate.	
Coal	1′ 6″
Slate	6″
Coal	1′ 6″
Slate	2′ 0″
Coal	4′ 0″
Slate binder.	
Coal	2′ 0″
Slate binder.	
Coal	3′ 0″
Slate and pyrites	4″
Fire-clay floor.	

There are one hundred Beehive Bank Ovens; forty in size $10' \times 5\frac{1}{2}'$, and sixty in size $11\frac{1}{4} \times 6'$. The charges are three and four wagons, and the ovens are run on forty-eight hour coke. The product, sixty-three cars (39,375 bushels) weekly, is shipped to Pittsburg. Seventy-five men are employed.

Messrs. Brown and Cochran are operating the Jimtown mines. They mine the Pittsburg Coal, nine feet thick, parted as last described.

There are one hundred and seventy-seven Beehive Bank

Ovens, and one hundred and five Beehive Block Ovens, in all two hundred and eighty-two ovens. The size is 11′×5½′, and the charge is four wagons of coal. The coke is burned to order, but usually the ovens are run upon forty-eight hour coke. The product, forty-five cars (28,125 bushels) daily, is shipped to the Shenango Valley, Ohio. One hundred and sixty men are employed.

Resumé of Coke Works on Pittsburg and Connellsville Railroad.

NAME OF FIRM.	No. of ovens....	Kind of ovens...	Number of men employed.....	Weekly production—cars.....	Where shipped.
Frick & Co................	100	Block...	65	66	Morgan & Co.
S. Cochran & Co..........	35	Bank....	16	18	West, to order.
Tyrone mines............	......	11 block,			
Laughlin & Co..........	116	105 bank,	55	63	Laughlin & Co., Pitts'g.
Jackson mines—					
John M. Cochran & Co..	63	Bank....	35	38	West, to order.
Stirling mines...........	.....	114 bank,			
Brown & Cochran.......	157	43 block,	90	84	Pittsburg.
Fayette Coal Company...	100	Bank....	75	65	Pittsburg.
Spring Grove—					
Cochran & Kiester......	100	Bank....	75	63	Western Pennsylvania.
Jimtown mines...........	......	105 block	160	270	
Brown & Cochran.......	282	177 bank,	....	....	Shenango Valley, Ohio.
Total	1,053		471	667	

CHAPTER V.

COKING.

The detailed description has already given the character and capacity of the different coke works in the Connellsville basin, and the condensed tabular statement given below shows that there are in all 3,578 ovens, producing when run on full time on forty-eight hour coke, 1,302,600 bushels weekly, equal to 2,171 cars, or 26,000 tons weekly.

Recapitulation of Connellsville Coke Region tables.

NAMES OF DISTRICTS.	No. of works....	No. of ovens....	Weekly shipm'ts in cars, 600 bu..
Fayette County branch, Pittsburg and Connellsville R. R.,	7	646	375
South-west Pennsylvania railroad	9	630	374
Mount Pleasant branch, Pittsburg and Connellsville R. R.,	21	1,349	860
Pittsburg and Connellsville R. R., Hickman Run branch,	8	953	562
Total for region....................................	45	3,578	2,171

Perhaps the most surprising feature of this enormous business is its sudden and recent growth; nearly all of these ovens having been built within the last ten years. Before 1865, the trade was small, the market chiefly local to the Pittsburg region, the reputation of the coke much less wide spread, and the number of coke ovens growing slowly. Since that time the increase of the business has been amazing. Other coking districts have enlarged their capacities also; much coke, and of good quality too, now coming from the line of the Pennsylvania railroad from Blairsville to Pittsburg; but the growth of their trade has been slow, compared to that of the Connellsville region. Such a difference pre-supposes some special adaptability of the Pittsburg coal at Connellsville for coking; and this is undoubtedly the case. In the tests made for strength and efficiency, the only coke which closely approaches the Connellsville coke, is that made at Bennington station, on the Allegheny mountain. And as the Connellsville Basin shows the Pittsburg Coal Bed in specially fine condition for coking, and the area of the condition limited, so the Bennington coke works show the "Miller" Coal Bed, bed B of the Lower Productive Coal Measures, in unusually fine condition for coking, and this condition existing over an area not specifically defined as to its limits but undoubtedly of moderate extent.

The paper of Mr. Fulton, appended to this report, treats of most of the main points in reference to coking, some of them quite fully. And to avoid repetition, in so far as it has been found possible, this chapter will either treat very briefly or avoid entirely subjects which are sufficiently discussed in his paper in this same volume.

In coking coal, the object is to drive off the water, the hydrocarbons and the volatilizable sulphur, and leave in the coke the fixed carbon, ash and such part of the sulphur as may not be volatilizable. The object to be attained is, at the lowest possible cost, to make a coke which shall be silvery, with metallic ring, cellular, capable of bearing a heavy burden, and as free as possible from impurities; a compound of fixed carbon and ash, with the coke structure and without water, sulphur or phosphorus.

Two main points at once present themselves, the character of the coal to be coked, and the method of coking. To the latter of these points has been given the chief part of the attention bestowed upon coking of late years; but the facts when carefully gathered seem most decidedly to intimate that the character of the coal itself must be made the most important factor in any coking operations. No oven can make a first class coke out of impure coal and one not suited to coking, and it may also be said that under no system of coking will a good coking coal fail to yield a fair coke.

The Connellsville coal, calling by that name all of the Pittsburg Coal Bed in the region marked on the sketch map (Plate VI of this report) as the coking coal region, is unusually and exceptionally a fine coking coal. A specimen from the mine of Messrs Frick & Co., at Broad Ford, yielded on analysis by Mr. M'Creath, at the Laboratory of the Survey in Harrisburg:

Water	1.260	
Volatile matter	30.107	
Fixed carbon	59.616	
Sulphur	.784	
Ash	8.233	
	100.000	
Color of ash, reddish gray.		
Coke per cent, 68.633.		
Sulphur left in coke		0.512
Per cent sulphur in coke	.746	
Per cent ash in coke	11.995	
Per cent carbon in coke	87.259	
	100.000	

The coal is bituminous, with dull resinous lustre generally, with seams of bright shining crystalline coal, for the most part coated with a yellowish silt. It contains numerous partings of mineral charcoal and slate, also small crystals of pyrites. The coal is generally hard and compact, some of it having a tendency to break up into cubes.

This may be taken as a fair sample of the Connellsville Coking Coal. It must be remembered that the coke yield as given above, 68.633 per cent is only the laboratory yield, while it will be shown hereafter that in coking on a large scale in Beehive Ovens, the usual yield is 63 per cent of coke. Moreover, the expelled sulphur is also the result of a test of a small quantity in the laboratory.

With reference to the different methods of coking coal, the reader is referred to the appendix, p. 122, where the three methods are figured and plainly described.

The Beehive Oven, which is in universal use in the Connellsville Basin, has undergone no change of any consequence in the past fifty years.

This oven is eleven or twelve feet in diameter and five and a half to six feet high. The working is very simple. The coal is dumped into the oven from a hole in the top, and spread evenly on the floor; the front opening is closed with bricks, luted with clay, and sufficient opening is left at first to supply the needed air; then, after sufficient heat is developed, these openings are closed, and finally the roof opening is closed.

The average time of coking is forty-eight hours, with seventy-two hour coke for that burned over Sunday. Twenty-four hour coke is also made occasionally. The seventy-two hour coke is a firmer and better coke than either of the others.

When the coke is thoroughly burned, the door of the oven is taken out, and water is thrown in from a hose on to the red hot coke. This apparently primitive system answers its purpose most admirably for the character of the coke, and it comes out of the oven firm, tough, silvery, pure and especially dry and free from water.

The burning of coke in the open rick is the oldest method of which we know, running back in England certainly to the seventeenth century. The method is simple. (See p. 122 for illustration.)

"Beginning on a base of fourteen feet wide, coal is spread to a depth of eighteen inches. On this base the flues are arranged. The flues are made of refuse coke and lump coal, and are covered with billets of wood. Fire is applied to the base of the vertical flues, igniting the kindling wood at each alternate flue.

"When the burning of the gaseous matter has ceased, the heap is carefully closed with dust or duff, and nearly smothered out in this way. The final operation is the application of a small quantity of water down the vertical flues, which is quickly converted into steam, permeating the whole mass."

The above description is given by Mr. Fulton of the open rick coking as done by the Cambria Iron Company at Bennington Station, on the Allegheny mountain.

In burning coke in the open ricks the time of coking varies, ranging from five to eight days at Bennington, and five to seven days in some ricks southwest of Connellsville; and Prof. Walter R. Johnson, in coking some Cumberland coal for the purpose of testing the power of the coal and coke, burned his coal in the open rick for ten days.

Under the heading of the Belgian Coking Oven are included many varieties, all using, however, the same main ideas, viz: to utilize the gases expelled in the process of coking, and to push out the coke in one mass and cool it outside of the oven, thereby saving labor and keeping the oven from being cooled by water thrown in.

The Belgian Ovens are explained and illustrated on p. 124.

Two varieties of the improved ovens, the Appolt and Coppeé Ovens, are now extensively used.

*"The Appolt Oven is practically a large brick chamber, about seventeen by twelve feet and thirteen feet high, divided by thin partition walls into twelve independent compartments or retorts, about four feet long and one foot six inches wide, having a free open space around each, in which the gases expelled in the process of coking are burnt, the resulting heat being transmitted through the walls of the chambers to the coal contained in them. The coking operation lasts twenty-four hours; at the expiration of that time the bottom plate of the compartment or retort is removed, the charge falls out of its own weight, and is cooled by throwing water on it.

The Coppeé Oven has obtained great favor in Europe, where, even in 1873, there were 600 or 700 in Belgium, and 1,400 to 1,500 in Germany. It consists essentially of a series of rectangular prisms, thirty feet long, fifteen inches wide, and about three or four feet high. The heat for coking is communicated, as in the Appolt system, through the thin walls which separate the oven from the gas flues.

This oven is less costly than Appolt's, and to a great extent attains the same objects. The manipulation of the charges is done by machinery, a ram pushing the entire charge out of the oven when sufficiently coked. The process of emptying and refilling the oven need not occupy more than eight minutes, and at the Ebbw Vale works, in Wales, the total cost of coking is one shilling a ton, the contractor taking the crushed and wasted coal from the bins, finding all the labor for filling and discharging the ovens, (including the working of the coke ram,) and filling the coke into trains. The oven is not adapted to coking any but fine coal, so for this reason, and also to be able to get rid of the impurities, the coal is crushed and washed.

It is stated that the coke quenched outside of the oven, as in the Coppeé system, contains more water than that from the Beehive Oven; in the former case, at the Ebbw Vale Works, six per cent of water was found in the coke, while but 0.8 per cent remained in that quenched inside the Beehive Oven."

* Engineering and Mining Journal.

If this latter statement be accurate it is a matter of very great moment; for not merely is the six per cent of water a dead loss, but it requires to be driven off, using up carbonaceous matter for this purpose and lowering decidedly the general calorific effect of the coke.

The comparative cost of making coke by these different methods has been the subject of a great deal of discussion, much of it of a decidedly acrimonious nature; frequently, however, with a minimum of facts, and those naturally biased and distorted by the advocates of the different ovens.

One true test would be to coke a sufficient quantity of coal from the same mine by all three methods, the open rick, the Beehive and the Belgian ovens; but not to confine the test to one coal, but to test several varieties of coal, ranging in composition from the Cumberland or Broad Top coal holding about 17 per cent of hydro-carbons, up to the coking and gas coals with from 30 to 35 per cent of hydro-carbons. No such complete test has been made.

The Cambria Iron Company using in their extensive operations both the open rick and the Belgian oven for coking, has afforded an opportunity for a partial test of this matter. On p. 126 of this volume, the facts as gathered by Mr. Fulton are detailed. Without repeating his facts, it is only needful here to say that after making allowances for interest on plant, repairs, &c., he makes the cost of coking thus: Open pits, 2.37$\frac{3}{5}$; Beehive oven, 2.33$\frac{3}{5}$; Belgian oven, 2.06$\frac{3}{4}$.

These conclusions as to cost of coking by the different methods, as well as the tables showing the varying loss of carbon in coking in the open pit, Beehive and Belgian oven, while containing valuable facts, must be taken as simply approximations, and not as the complete and definite figures which would be furnished by a thorough testing.

For example: the Miller coal at Bennington and the Connellsville coal, analyze thus:

	Miller	Connellsville.
Water	......	1.260
Fixed carbon	68.500	59.616
Ash	8.000	8.233
Volatile matter	22.380	30.107
Sulphur	1.120	.784
	100.000	100.000

The Miller coal when coked in open pits at Bennington, yields 59.1 per cent coke. Comparing the theoretical and actual coke:

	Theoretical.	Actual.
Ash	8.00	8.00
Sulphur, (two-thirds)	.75	.75
Fixed carbon	68.50	50.35
	77.25	59.10

In this the sulphur of the coke is assumed to be two-thirds of the sulphur of the coal, one-third probably having been volatilized.

The fixed carbon, therefore, of the coal and coke stand to each other thus:

68.50 : 50.35 :. 100 : 73.5

showing that 26.5 per cent of fixed carbon have been lost in this open rick coking.

The Connellsville Coal, coked in the Beehive Oven, yields 63 per cent of coke. This percentage is not derived from a complete series of figures, but from the general statement of the works as to their coal output and coke yield.

Comparing the theoretical and actual coke yield—

	Theoretical.	Actual.
Ash	8.233	8.233
Sulphur	.512	.512
Fixed carbon	59.626	54.255
	68.361	63.000

The fixed carbon, therefore, of the coal and coke are thus proportioned:

59.616 : 54.255 : : 100 : 91

Showing a loss of nine per cent of fixed carbon in coking Connellsville Coal in a Beehive Oven.

These figures are valuable, but only partially aid in answering the question, *What would have been the loss of fixed carbon in coking the Miller Coal in a Beehive Oven?*

Or the question, *What would be the extra loss of fixed carbon if the Connellsville Coal were coked in open pits?*

Upon this latter point there are some facts.

Assuming the loss of fixed carbon in the open rick coking at Bennington to be a fair average, and applying it to the Connellsville Coal, the percentage of coke would stand thus:

	Theoretical.	Supposed.
Ash	8.233	8.233
Sulphur	.512	.512
Fixed Carbon	59.616	43.817
	68.361	52.662

At Oliphant's New Furnace, six miles South-west of Uniontown, the (Pittsburg) Connellsville Coal is being coked in open ricks; but the works were only just started when examined, and no close statement could be procured.

The Superintendent of the Fairchance Iron Works, two miles South-west of this place, had for many years coked the Connellsville Coal in open ricks, and gave about 100 bushels of coke to 100 bushels of coal as an average yield. Other authorities placed the yield at from 100 up to 110 bushels of coke to 100 bushels of coal.

Assuming 100 bushels of coke as an average, the figures are,

	Pounds.
100 bushels of coal	7,600
100 bushels of coke	4,000

An average yield of 52.6 per cent, or with a loss of carbon the same as given by the Miller coal when coked in open ricks.

If 105 bushels of coke to 100 bushels of coal be taken as an average, and perhaps this is fairer, the average yield of coke is 55 per cent, and the loss of carbon is 24 per cent.

With reference to the comparison of the open rick coking and the Belgian Oven, the statistics of the Cambria Iron Company of the large amount of coke made at Bennington in open ricks, and at Hollidaysburg in Belgian Ovens, afford a full and fair means of comparison, the coal used being from the same mine in both cases.

The coke yield of the Belgian Ovens, using the Miller coal from Bennington, shows thus:

	Theoretical.	Actual.
Ash	8.00	8.00
Sulphur (two-thirds)	.75	.75
Fixed carbon	68.50	61.25
	77.25	70.00

The proportion, therefore, of fixed carbon in the coal and coke are:

68.50 : 61.25 : : 100 : 89.4

Showing a loss of 10.6 per cent of fixed carbon in coking the Miller coal in Belgian Ovens.

Leaving out the quality, therefore, and considering only the quantity of coke made, the open pit makes only 59.1 pounds to the Belgian Oven 70 pounds; and the open pit loses 26.5 per cent of carbon, while the Belgian Oven loses only 10.6 per cent

It should be noted that a part of this loss of carbon is inevitable in any case, and is directly connected with the constitution of the coal.

But this difference in the loss of fixed carbon, and when the loss is heavy the marked decrease in the yield of coke and increase in cost of production, is of greater or less consequence directly according to the cost of the coal. Where coal is transported to iron works and coked there, costing, say one dollar and fifty cents a ton delivered in the coke yard, a saving of ten per cent is a matter of moment. But where, as in the Connellsville Region, the coal is run out from the mine directly on to the bank of ovens, and where the cost of cutting coal is one cent a bushel (twenty-eight cents a ton) or less, the matter of saving five to ten per cent of carbon is secondary to other matters of economy in managing the works. And especially such very moderate saving as economy of fixed carbon would effect in the last case is entirely subordinate to the most important feature, the character of the coke.

The physical character of the coke depends largely on the percentage of volatile matters in the coal from which it is made; highly bituminous coals, which swell when roasted, leave behind a hard, metallic ringing, tenacious coke, strong either hot or cold, and bearing heavy pressure. The open or block coals, on the contrary, do not swell in roasting, keep almost perfectly their original form, and yield a less tenacious coke, much less able to bear the burden in an high stack.

Mr. Peelor, assistant engineer of the Cambria Iron Company, has prepared, under Mr. Fulton's directions, a table showing the relative strength of Pennsylvania cokes, their burden bearing power, their cell capacity, &c. This table will be found in full on page 129 of this volume. The experiments were conducted by Mr. Peelor with great care and ingenuity, and make a valuable contribution to our knowledge of Pennsylvania cokes.

Without reproducing the table in full, but only the conclusions, the Pennsylvania cokes stand thus:—

	Compres. strength per cub. inch in lbs. ¼ ultimate str'ngth.	Height of furnace charge, which can be supported without crushing......
Beehive ...Connellsville, 72 hour........................	284	114
Open Pit...Bennington (Miller coal)....................	281	112
Belgian ....Hollidaysburg (Miller coal)	259	104
Beehive ...Connellsville, 48 hour.........................	249	100
Belgian ....Gap Furnace (Miller coal)....................	248	100
Belgian ....Johnstown..	245	99
Beehive ...Kemble, C. & I. Co., Broad Top.............	240	96
Open Pits..Broad Top..	220	88
Open Pits..Rockhill, C. & I. Co., Broad Top............	200	80

The Connellsville coke, made from the Pittsburg Coal Bed in the Beehive Oven, stands first on the list, closely followed by the coke made in open pits from the Miller Coal Bed, bed B of the Lower Productive Coal Measures, at Bennington station on the Allegheny mountain.

The weakest coke on the list of those tested, the open pit coke made by the Rockhill Coal Company from washed Broad Top coal, is capable of bearing the burden in an eighty foot stack; and the greater part of the cokes tested will stand up in an one hundred foot stack. With reference to our present iron making, the burden bearing power of cokes may be dismissed with the general statement, that about all of our cokes can stand up in the present stacks, and most of them have much more than the needed strength.

That is of course of the Pennsylvania cokes, for there are undoubtedly cokes made from dry burning coals which are entirely unequal alone to bearing the burden of an eighty foot stack. Many a bad working furnace is simply worried by a too tender coke. The coke mashing slowly under the burden, makes a closely compacted mass through which the blast cannot penetrate, and the combustion is necessarily imperfect. It is mainly to keep this mass from compacting, that furnace men use a proportion of coke with their raw coal. The coal has abundant heat producing power by itself, but it will not hold shape.

Sulphur is the constituent, always present in greater or less quantities in the coal, that the coke manufacturer desires to drive off. Furnace men do not now attach anything like so much importance to the presence of a moderate amount of sulphur in a coal, coke or iron ore as formerly, but even yet the expelling of sulphur is an important element in coke manufacture.

In making our ordinary illuminating gas for domestic use, the object of course is to procure the gas as pure as possible and leave the sulphur in the coke. In coking, however, the converse is the case; the sulphur as far as practicable is to be expelled with the volatile matters and the coke to be left free from sulphur.

As the washing and scrubbing of illuminating gas to free it from impurities is attended with considerable expense, much time, attention and ability have been given in many places to procuring an illuminating gas free from sulphur; while much less attention has been given to the sulphur question in coke making, it receiving usually slight consideration in discussing the value of different ovens and different systems of coking. The two processes of coking or making gas for domestic use being thus the converse of each other, it would seem as though exactly what was advisable in the one case must necessarily be decidedly inadvisable in the other. Thus in gas making it is said "it is almost needless to say, that the coal should be dry before being used, and that it should be stacked under cover. When a quantity of moist coal is thrown into a retort, the outer surface, after undergoing for some time the action of the fire, is converted into coke, and the bisulphuret of iron into proto-sulphuret of iron, over which latter the steam from the interior of the mass of coal passes, with, of course, the same result as if this proto-sulphuret of iron were purposely subjected, at a red heat, to the action of the vapor of water; that is to say, the two compounds mutually decompose each other, and give rise to oxide of iron and sulphuretted hydrogen, so that by mismanagement of this, the whole of the sulphur contained in bituminous coal may be made to pass off into the gas, and thus double the labor and expense of purifaction."

Again, with reference to gas making, Prof. Chandler says: "As the heat continues, these outer layers of coal become converted into coke, which is soon raised to a red heat. In the meantime the heat reaches the interior of the charge, and the vapors produced, passing through the red hot layers of coke, are in turn converted into fixed gas. As each such successive portion of vapor has to pass over a large surface of red hot coke, it is more and more completely decomposed, and its percentage of carbon, and consequently its illuminating power, reduced. For this reason the quality of the gas deteriorates as the process of distillation continues, till, finally, little besides hydrogen is evolved. At the last stages of the process the sulphur contained in the coke is said to form bi-sulphide of carbon, which is a most objectionable impurity."

Now these very points which are mentioned as being so injurious in making gas, should be, as far as possible, embodied in the process of coking.

It is not possible by any of the processes of coking now in use to drive off all the sulphur; but the incomplete figures concerning the subject show that very varying proportions of sulphur are expelled, and that these variations are caused both by the method of coking and also by the condition of the sulphur in the coal.

As to this condition of sulphur in the coal there is still much obscurity. Prof. Wormly, of the Ohio Geological Survey, publishes numerous analyses showing how small a percentage of the sulphur contained in the specimens of coal analyzed could have existed in combination with iron, in some cases not more than one-tenth of it existing as iron pyrites.

Mr. M'Creath, Chemical Assistant of the Pennsylvania Geological Survey, has also given his attention to this subject, but the facts gathered so far do not seem to justify any definite conclusions on these points:

1. What are the combinations in which the sulphur exists in the coal? and

2. To what extent its existence as iron pyrites, or in some other combination, is favorable or unfavorable to its expulsion in coking.

For instance, the Connellsville coal, as analyzed by Mr. M'Creath, contained .784 per cent of sulphur, with .567 per cent of iron. This iron requires .648 per cent of sulphur to form $Fe S_2$, iron pyrites. Therefore .136 per cent of the sulphur exists not as iron pyrites; a small portion may exist as calcium sulphate.

Now, in coking this coal in the laboratory, of the .784 per cent. of sulphur there remained .512 per cent in the coke, or 35 per cent of the sulphur was expelled in coking.

Again, a coal coked in the laboratory, containing 3.88 per cent of sulphur, all as iron pyrites, lost in coking 1.66 per cent of sulphur, so that 2.22 per cent remained in the coke; or 43 per cent of the sulphur was expelled in coking.

Again, a coal coked in the laboratory, containing in all 8.35 per cent of sulphur, of which 4.25 per cent. were not in combination with iron, and 4.10 per cent existed as iron pyrites, lost 3.84 per cent of sulphur; or 46 per cent of sulphur was expelled in coking.

Now, therefore, if 35 per cent of sulphur is expelled when six-sevenths of the sulphur exists as iron pyrites and only one-seventh in other combinations unknown, and 43 per cent of sulphur is driven off when all the sulphur exists as iron pyrites, and 46 per cent of sulphur is expelled when the sulphur is nearly divided equally between iron pyrites and unknown combinations, it would seem to be necessary to await more facts before discussing the effect of the condition of the sulphur in the coal.

In one case, however, where the sulphur exists in the coal as gypsum, it is clear that little or none will be expelled in coking. In gas coal the presence of the thin films of carbonate of lime which frequently occur, are of service, as the impure gas turns it into sulphuret of calcium, and it remains with the coke. But to the coke manufacture it is a decided injury.

But while this condition of the sulphur in the coal is of consequence where the coal is coked directly as it comes from the mine, it becomes of the utmost importance where coke is made from washed slack coal, as is done in many cases along the Youghiogheny and Monongahela rivers, or from washed coal, as at Blairsville and in the Broad Top Region. The coal is crushed, and the pure coal, being lighter, is floated off, the slate and pyrites sinking and being thrown away. It is plain that where the sulphur exists as iron pyrites in segregated masses, as "sulphur balls," the greatest amount of sulphur will be removed in washing; a lower percentage where the iron pyrites as small crystals is scattered through the mass of the coal, and least of all where the sulphur is in other form than as iron pyrites.

Mess. Carnegie & Co. are now washing slack coal near Pittsburg successfully.*

In examining the coke from the Belgian Oven the marked difference between the top, the middle and the bottom layers is apparent. The bottom coke is heavy, dense, and not of a nature to work kindly in a furnace. The same difference between the top and the bottom of the coke, when made in Beehive Ovens, exists, but to a much smaller extent.

The bottom layers of the Belgian Oven coke are also said to be more sulphurous; and from this is drawn the conclusion that in all coking ovens shallow charges are the best. Yet in charging the Beehive Ovens for the "Sunday coke," the ovens

*The slack coal is purchased from neighboring gas coal mines at a merely nominal price, and, after passing through a revolving conical screen, 6′ long and from 4′ 6″ to 5′ 6″ diam., is washed in jigging machines of the old Hartz type, in which the bottoms are fixed and the water forced up through them from an adjoining water cylinder where a piston works. The clean coal is removed from the jig box by the blades of a revolving scraper, which carries a little of the coal out of the box at each revolution; the shale and pyrites accumulate in the bottom of the jig box till the man in attendance notices some of these impurities passing out along with the coal. The jig box is then emptied and the operation is recommenced. This somewhat crude arrangement, though very ingenious in many of its details, presents several objections; it is wasteful of coal, for a portion is thrown away in emptying each jig box; it allows a certain amount of impurities to go out with the coal, an amount depending on the vigilance of the attendant; its operation is intermittent, and yet its results are, on the whole, satisfactory.

There are four jig boxes, each 7′ 6″ long x 3′ 6″ wide, worked at Messrs. Carnegie's work, and, we are informed, 400 tons of slack coal can be washed on them in a day of nine hours. The plunger is worked at the rate of 80 strokes a minute, the stroke being four inches; the power required to drive the whole apparatus is provided by a small engine, 12″x24″, which is found much more than sufficient when working with a steam pressure of forty pounds.

As the slack comes from the mine it contains about one per cent of sulphur, with a considerable quantity of shale; the washer removes about ten per cent of the charge, some coal being thrown away with the shale, and the coke made from the washed coal contains about one-third of one per cent sulphur. The cost of washing is stated to be about one-half cent per bushel, say twelve cents per ton of 2,000 pounds. The total cost of the four washers and machinery for working them is about $5,000.—*Engineering and Mining Journal.*

are charged deeper, and unless the extra time of burning could be supposed to overcome the injury inflicted by a deeper charge, the seventy-two hour Sunday coke should be more sulphurous than the forty-eight hour coke. Yet as a matter of fact, (there are no specific analyses,) the seventy-two hour coke is apparently firmer, better in all respects and is preferred and bought by steel works. There are clearly other important features in the case, besides depth of charge, and too much stress should not be laid on that one point.

In Mr. Fulton's paper, appended to this report, he has collected the statistics of the working of several iron furnaces, some of them using coke and some anthracite coal, and after the needed reductions and calculations to bring similarity in the cases, the average efficiency of coke as compared with raw bituminous coal or anthracite coal is deduced. Mr. I. Lowthian Bell's statement can be safely accepted, that the iron master is doing well who can make one ton of No. 3 iron with 2,408 pounde of coke, taking an average of Durham coke and Cleveland iron stone.

And this practical testing is in this case especially needful, for the various investigations into the calorific effects of coal have demonstrated some very remarkable facts, in some cases the total calorific effect exceeding the proper total of the combustion of the elements, and in other cases coals similar in analysis yielding widely different calorific effects.

In Prof. Walter R. Johnson's careful series of investigations into the power of coals, made for the United States Navy Department, he considered and tested three cokes: 1. Coke made by him from Cumberland coal. 2. Coke from the Richmond, Virginia Basin, (Midlothian mine:) and 3. Natural coke from the Virginia Coal Field. The summing up of Prof. Johnson, of the value of these cokes as compared with anthracite coal and semi-bituminous coal, is given below, simply in tabular form, thus:—

	Relative evaporative power for equal weights.
Cumberland coal—(Neff's)	.882
Cumberland coke—(Neff's)	.840
Lehigh coal	.835
Midlothian coke	.807
Natural coke	.792

And again:—

	Relative rapidity of ignition.
Cumberland coke—(Neff's)	.427
Cumberland coal—(Neff's)	.298
Natural coke	.287
Midlothian coke	.250
Lehigh coal	.153

The above tables, made from experiments conducted on a large scale, and with the use of considerable quantities of the fuel, probably give a fair average of the calorific effects. The experiments were made with the utmost care. From the boat load of Cumberland Coal (Neff's mine) used in testing the Cumberland Coal, Prof. Johnson made the coke needed for testing. He constructed a coke heap of 22,340 pounds of coarse and 6,160 pounds of fine coal, and coked it for ten days.

The coke weighed 82.72 per cent of the coal used; the loss therefore of weight was 17.28*. And as the weight of the coke was 31.57 pounds per cubic foot, while the weight of the coal was 54.287 pounds per foot, the enlargement of bulk on coking must have been 42.25 per cent. (In the Connellsville region, in the Beehive Ovens, it has been shown that the enlargement of bulk is about 20 per cent.)

Prof. Johnson's conclusions are: "On comparing the evaporative power of the pound of coke with that of the same weight of Neff's coal, it will be observed that the latter was 9.742, and the former 8.997. As the waste from coal was, on the day of the first trial alluded to, 11.792 per cent, and 13.515 for the coke, the evaporative power in the unit of combustible matter in coal is 11.044, and in coke 10.381. Thus it appears that the combustible matter in the coke is 5.8 per cent less effective, pound for pound, than that in the coal."

The comparison of the coke with that from Midlothian coal and with the Natural coke, will make it evident that the evaporative power of the combustible matter in each, was almost exactly the same, being 10,381 for Neff's Cumberland coke, 10,343 for Midlothian coke, and 10,389 for Natural coke. But while, as just seen, the coke of Cumberland coal is 5.8 *less* effective in its combustible constituents than the coal, in the

* It is remarkable that this open rick coking could have been thus thoroughly done, burning ten days, without loss of fixed carbon.

Midlothian, the reverse is true; the coke is 5.005 per cent *more* efficient in the action of its combustible part than the original coal is in that of its compound of fixed and volatile combustibles. The time required by this coke to bring the boiler to steady action was 1.166 hour.

In the preceding article it has been seen that the Midlothian coal lost of its weight in coking, 19.14 per cent and gained in bulk 18.37 per cent. And as it was found that when submitted to rapid distillation in a close vessel, specimens of the coal from which it was produced lost about 30.2 per cent, it is evident that of this quantity there remained in the coke 11.06 parts. If the water proved to have been imbibed by the coke, (2.81 per cent of its weight,) be added to the apparent diminution by coking, it will give 21.41 per cent as the quantity of volatile matter expelled, leaving only 8.79 parts remaining in the coke when first raked from the heap. This is but little more than two-thirds as much as in the Natural coke already described, which by an average of seven trials, contained 12.86 per cent of volatile matter. As above stated, the Cumberland coal lost of its *weight* 17.28 per cent, and gained in *bulk* no less than 42.25 per cent."

The cost of coking coal in the Connellsville region can only be given approximately, there being slight differences in the cost at each bank of ovens. Taking however, the ovens of Mr. J. F. Dravo, as well located and carefully managed as any in the region, as the example of economical production of coke, the statement as furnished by Mr. Davidson, the superintendent, is as follows:

One hundred bushels of coal, mining cost, - - - -	$1 00
Hauling and putting in oven, - - - - - -	1 00
Drawing and loading, - - - - - - - -	70
One hundred and twenty bushels of coke yielded for	2 70

or 2¼ cents per bushel.

This estimate is made on the basis of forty-eight hour coke, with seventy-two hour "Sunday coke." To run solely on twenty-four hour coke should reduce slightly the cost of coking; to run on seventy-two hour coke exclusively should slightly increase it; the cost of the permanent employés and interest on the plant remaining the same with the larger and smaller output respectively.

The above, however, is the minimum cost of making coke at well situated ovens, and with the present low prices for labor; but the basin is so even and regular, and the coal runs so undisturbed and so thick, that the average cost of making coke in the Connellsville Basin will be about as given above.

The area of the Connellsville Coal Basin proper, is thirty miles by three miles. The coal lies most favorably situated for mining over the greater part of the whole area; and the low cost of production, combined with the keen competition in the trade, have extended the use of the coke more and more widely with each year. It is used now from the valley of the Lehigh to the Rocky mountains and the shores of the Pacific ocean; and wherever it obtains a foothold, it is likely to remain until forced out by some very strong competitor.

In the discussion relative to the amount of sulphur volatilized in coking, the amount of fixed carbon lost, &c., the nature of the Connellsville coke as compared with Bennington coke, Broad Top coke and others, has already been presented.

The coke used as Connellsville coke in those discussions, was the coke made in the Laboratory at Harrisburg from a quantity of Connellsville coal; and to be more certain that the coke was a fair average, Messrs. Frick & Co. of Broad Ford, Fayette county, were requested to forward a quantity of their coke to the Laboratory at Harrisburg for examination. This was done, and an analysis made of the average of this specimen; about thirty to fifty pounds of coke making the specimen.

For all practical estimates the analysis of this coke of Frick & Co. may be taken as an average, the coke being thoroughly burned, and as well made as can be produced by any coke works in the Connellsville Basin. The analysis shows (M'Creath):—

The coke is exceedingly coherent and compact, with silvery lustre and containing some little slate.

Water at 225°	.030
Volatile matter	.460
Fixed carbon	89.576
Sulphur	.821
Ash	9.113
	100.000

Color of ash, reddish brown.

It has been stated that the object in coking is to expel the water, the volatile matter, and such of the sulphur as may be volatilizable, retaining the fixed carbon and ash as coke. The above analysis shows how closely that object has been accomplished.

For purposes of comparison with the Connellsville coke, it was desired to test carefully some other cokes in addition to those from Bennington, Johnstown, Hollidaysburg and the Broad Top. For this purpose, the Snow Shoe Coal Company, the Diamond Gas Coal Company, at Reynoldsville, in Jefferson county, and the Fairmount Coal Company, at Fairmount, in Clarion county, were requested to forward specimens of their coal and coke, the coal to be the run of the mine and the coke an average of the open rick burning done by them at their mines.

The Snow Shoe coal and coke were not received in time for testing.

The Fairmount Coal Company forwarded from their mine in Clarion county, specimens of their coal and coke. The coal, however, was not the run of the mine, but the slack coal, and represents therefore the lower bench of the coal, below the bearing in slate.

The analysis of this coal from the Freeport Coal Bed of the Fairmount Company in 1874, showed a very high percentage of volatile matters, the specimens for analysis then representing the whole thickness of the coal bed.

The specimen of slack coal representing only the bottom bench of the coal bed shows on analysis, (M'Creath :)

The coal is bituminous slack coal, containing considerable pyrites and a large amount of slate.

Water at 225°	2.375
Volatile matter	32.565
Fixed carbon	49.955
Sulphur	1.960
Ash	13.145
	100.000

Coke per cent, 65.060.

Ash, dirty grey with red tinge.

Iron	1.673
Sulphur as Fe S_2	1.912
"Free" sulphur	.048

Sulphur left in coke.......	Coke made in laboratory from the above coal.........	.960
Per cent of sulphur in coke,		1.479
Per cent of ash in coke....		20.200

The Fairmount Coal Company also forwarded a box of the coke made from the above coal in open ricks at their mine. The coke analyzed, (M'Creath:)

The coke is porous but coherent, dirty and very slaty, containing a large quantity of loose particles of slate.

Water at 225°	2.045
Volatile matter	1.961
Fixed carbon	80.600
Sulphur	1.111
Ash	14.283
	100.000

Ash, red with white specks.

The Diamond Gas Coal Company forwarded from their mine at Reynoldsville, Jefferson county, specimens of their coal and coke for testing.

The coal was analysed at the laboratory of the Survey in Harrisburg, and shows (M'Creath):

Bituminous coal, compact, shining, containing numerous small partings of charcoal, pyrites and slate.

Water at 225°	1.550
Volatile matter	34.500
Fixed carbon	57.386
Sulphur	1.118
Ash	5.446
	100.000

Coke per cent, 63.950.
Color of ash, cream.

Iron in coal		.812
Sulphur as $Fe\ S_2$		.928
"Free" sulphur		.190
Sulphur left in coke........	Coke made in laboratory from the above coal.........	.683
Per cent of sulphur in coke,		1.070
Per cent of ash in coke......		8.520

The coke forwarded by the Diamond Gas Coal Company as representing the average coke made at their mine, shows on analysis as follows (M'Creath):

Coke, shining lustre, rather porous, very slaty and not very coherent.

Water at 225°	.520
Volatile matter	.575
Fixed carbon	86.056

Sulphur	1.027
Ash	11.822
	100.000

Color of ash, red with white specks.

Of the above cokes, the Fairmount coke cannot be accepted as a fair sample of what the coal can make. The coke shows over two per cent of water and nearly two per cent of volatile matters remaining in it, and the coke has not been completely burned. It is clear that the coal is capable of making an excellent coke, if the coking were carefully and skillfully done.

The coke of the Diamond Gas Coal Company from Reynoldsville, Jefferson county, is well burned, moderately tough, and in general character may be classed as a very good coke. Taking the Connellsville coke analysis (p. 78) as the typical good coke, it is easy to compare at a glance the above cokes with it, and see how favorably the Diamond coke shows alongside of it.

Mr. Jno. Fulton, General Mining Engineer of the Cambria Iron Company, kindly consented to examine into the physical qualities and test the burden bearing power of these cokes by means of his apparatus designed for the purpose, at his office in Johnstown. The results of his examination are embodied in the table and description given below.

[A.]

TABLE *exhibiting the physical properties of coke, submitted by Franklin Platt, Esq., Assistant, Second Geological Survey of Pennsylvania.*

LOCALITY.	GRAMMES IN 1 CUBIC INCH.		POUNDS IN ONE CUBIC FOOT.		PERCENTAGE.		Compressive strength per cubic inch in lbs (¼ ultimate stregth)...	Height of furnace charge which can be supported without crushing	Order in cellular space..	Remarks.
	Dry	Wet	Dry...............	Wet	Coke	Cells				
Pittsburg and Connellsville Coke Co. taken as a standard for comparison	12.46	20.25	47.47	77.15	61.53	38.47	284	114	I.	Very good furnace coke.
Diamond Gas Coal Company, Jefferson county, Pa	15.00	20.67	57.26	78.85	72.42	27.57	252	101	II.	Coal requires cleansing to give a good coke.
Frick and Company, Connellsville, Fayette co., Pa..	12.73	19.93	48.51	76.62	62.98	37.02	217	87	I.	Very good furnace coke.
Fairmount Coal Company, Clarion county, Pa	12.57	19.63	47.89	76.23	62.23	37.76	54	22	I.	Requires careful washing to produce a good coke.

Frick & Co.'s Coal and Coke.

The Connellsville Coal is peculiarly adapted to coking. It holds a sufficient volume of volatile combustible matter to supply the necessary heat in coking, thus preserving its carbon, the loss of which is only nine per cent. The amount of slate or "ash" in coal and coke is too high; five per cent in the latter is regarded as the maximum of purity. Few cokes, however, attain this low percentage of ash. The sulphur has been reduced by volatilization in coking, 34.57 per cent, (see table B,) leaving in the coke .821 per cent of sulphur, which is about an average of coke from this region.

No data have been furnished showing the percentage of coke obtained from this coal, but the inquiries made in the Connellsville Region showed 63 per cent of coke in the Beehive Ovens.

The physical structure of this coke is shown in table A. At the head of it are placed the determinations of the coke from the *Pittsburg and Connellsville Coke Co. for a standard of comparison.*

By carefully comparing these it is manifest that they are so nearly alike that no especial distinction should be made. The cell space in Frick & Co.'s coke is somewhat less than the standard, but this could readily be induced by the use of a piece of coke more *dense* than the average. Why it sustains less burden than the standard is not yet definitely settled. In addition to the large cellular structure inherited by the Connellsville coke, which facilitates its combustion in the furnace, it has also a columnar structure induced in coking by planes, vertical to the floor of the oven, slicing it into slender pieces, also contributing to its ready combustion and energy as a furnace fuel.

Fairmount Coal Company.

This coal is low in carbon and high in ash and sulphur. It holds a good proportion of combustible matter, which would make large cells in the structure of the coke.

The coal requires to be washed to prepare it for use in coking.

This can be readily performed by one of the many methods now in use.

The coal should produce in a Beehive Oven 60 per cent. But if washed the percentage would be somewhat reduced by the consumption of heat in driving off the moisture of the coal from the washing process. This is true in all coals requiring washing.

In the coking process 51.02 per cent of the sulphur has been volatilized. This is corroborated by Mr. M'Creath's analysis, which shows that the bisulphide ($Fe\ S_2$) of the coal has been reduced to a mono-sulphide ($Fe\ S$) in the coke. In other words, one part of sulphur has been removed in coking. But the percentage of sulphur is still too high, and, as all the reduction that can be made in the coke oven in this coal is a little over 50 per cent, it is evident that a further reduction must be looked for in the washing of the coal alone. In the process of crushing and washing considerable pyrites are thrown out bodily; this will reduce the sulphur very materially, and it is the only way in which it can be accomplished.

The very friable nature of this coke is due to the presence of slate discs thickly scattered through the coke, destroying its tenacity.

A thorough cleansing of this coal would give a coke of first class physical structure, and I believe desirable in many respects for furnace use.

Diamond Gas Coal Company.

This coal approaches the Connellsville in general chemical structure. It has nearly an equal amount of carbon, more volatile matter and less ash. It should give a purer coke, with the single exception of sulphur.

The coke exhibits capacity for bearing furnace burden nearly equal to the Connellsville, but it lacks somewhat in cellular space.

The coal of the Diamond Gas Coal Company, as well as the coal of the Fairmount Coal Company, require thorough cleansing to produce a pure, clean coke for use in blast furnaces.

The general relationship of Connellsville coke to other Pennsylvania cokes, and its decided average superiority, have been sufficiently brought out in the different comparisons made in various parts of this chapter.

The enormous thickness of the Pittsburg coal bed in the Connellsville coke basin is as astonishing as its exceptional coking character. It yields from eight to eleven feet of clean coal, 13,000 to 17,000 tons of coal to the acre, of which gross amount probably 10,000 to 12,000 tons to the acre are or easily can be won out. Even with the heavy output of coal needed to supply the coke ovens of the Connellsville Region, the area of coal annually consumed is comparatively small; and years more of such a yield, or even an increased one, will scarcely affect materially the gross capacities of the basin.

It is not necessary here to retabulate the Western coals and cokes, some of which will be found in the appendix, (p. 121.) It may be safely stated that the West has produced as yet, in quantity, no coke equal in character to the Connellsville Coke, and the Western market must extend year by year.

The shipments of Connellsville coke to the iron furnaces in the Central and Eastern parts of Pennsylvania have only grown up within a few years past, and as yet the trade is small. At the present rates of anthracite coal and Connellsville coke there is no economy to the anthracite furnace in the use of coke, but the furnace men report that the "admixture of some coke with anthracite makes the furnace work better."

The economical utilization of the enormous waste heaps of slack coal of the anthracite region stands in the way of an extensive increase of shipments of coke to the eastward.

The method of Mr. Loiseau has been repeatedly described in full, and is well known.

For purposes of comparison, a description is given below of the method now employed in Wales to utilize the waste heaps of fine coal dust by coking it up with bituminous coal and pitch. The description is from a paper read by W. Hackney, B. Sci., before the Iron and Steel Institute of Manchester, England, and reprinted in the *American Manufacturer*. It is safe to say that if even a part of the valuable results claimed by Mr. Hackney are realized in practice, the question is of importance as affecting decidedly the question of eastern shipments of coke in the future.

The materials used are any quality of anthracite or semi-anthracite, if free from shale or stones, good bituminous or binding coal and pitch, in the following proportions:

Anthracite	60
Bituminous coal	35
Pitch	5
	100

Specimens are on the table of coke made of Messrs. Brock & Sons' anthracite, from Cwmllynfell colliery, near Cwm Amman; of a mixture of this with Yniscedwyn anthracite, and of culm or semi-anthracite from Birch Rock colliery, near Pontardulais. The bituminous coal used in making all the samples exhibited is that from Tyrissa colliery, near Swansea.

The materials are passed, together, through a Carr's disintegrator, to crush and mix them; the proportions in which they are mixed being regulated by supplying the feeding hopper of the disintegrator by three elevators, one carrying up each constituent, and each provided with buckets of such size and number as to bring up the relative quantity required. Samples are shown of the anthracite, bituminous coal and pitch, in the condition in which they are supplied to the disintegrator, and of the crushed mixture produced.

The ovens used are of the oblong shape generally employed in South Wales, 15 feet long by 5 feet 7 inches wide at the back, and 6 feet 2 inches in front, and 4 feet 4 inches high to the under side of the arch. Each oven is charged through a hole in the roof, with about four tons of the crushed mixture; this is levelled by a rabble put in through the door at the end, and a small quantity of bituminous coal, sufficient to form a layer about 2 inches thick, is thrown in and spread uniformly over the surface. The oven is then lighted by throwing a few shovelfuls of hot embers on the top of the charge, immediately inside of the door, and the coking is managed as in working an ordinary charge of bituminous coal. The object of covering the charge with a layer of bituminous coal is to prevent the burning away of the pitch, and its use appears to be essential for the production of a hard and strong coke. Ordinary slack, of the same quality as that in the mixture, is used for the covering; this is mostly very small, but it is not specially crushed.

Rather more than two charges per week are made in each oven; the coke is watered in the oven, and is then drawn out in one mass by a chain and hand winch.

The yield of coke is eighty per cent. of the weight of the charge. The coke is steel gray in color, and very much harder than the anthracite from which it is made; so hard, indeed, that it scratches glass with comparative ease. In a common fire, or under the action of a blast, it burns away without showing any tendency to crumble or decrepitate. It is about twenty-three per cent. heavier than the best coke made from Welsh bituminous coal; so that in sending a cargo abroad, recently, a vessel that could not carry more than two hundred and forty tons of ordinary coke, was able to take in as much as three hundred and ten tons of anthracite coke. Another valuable consequence of the dense compact character of the coke, in addition to the saving in cost of carriage is, that even if soaked in water it takes up very little, only from 1.5 to 2 per cent. of its weight; while many kinds of ordinary coke absorb readily ten per cent. or more. The coke is harder, and more dense, the finer the materials are crushed and the more intimately they are mixed.

In practical use, both in the cupola and in the blast furnace, the coke, so far as it has been tried, has given remarkably good result. These are probably due in part to its hardness and density, or rather to the high temperature required to set it on fire, which brings the zone of combustion closer to the tuyeres, and diminishes the waste of fuel in the upper part of the furnace, caused by the transformation of $C O_2$ into $C O$; and in part to its freedom from water, and the small amount of ash that it contains.

In a small foundry cupola, in which one pound of good Welsh coke, that from Bryndu, near Bridgend, melts ten pounds of iron, one pound of anthracite coke melts sixteen pounds, and the metal is hotter when tapped out; and in a trial carried out at Messrs. Tangye's works near Birmingham, anthracite coke melted well with twenty-five per cent more burden than that placed on ordinary coke, and would probably have done more, but the managers were unwilling to run any risk of deranging the working of the cupola, and did not push the experiment further.

In a trial made in one of the blast furnaces at Landore, working on spiegeleisen, the burden, in using anthracite coke, was increased twenty-eight and one-half per cent, and the economy might probably have been raised to thirty per cent or more, but the stock of coke in hand was not sufficient to admit of carrying on the experiment. The Landore Company are, however, so satisfied of the value of the coke, that they have nearly completed preparations for making it in all their ovens, and using nothing else in their two blast furnaces.

The cost of anthracite coke is about the same as that of the best ordinary coke made in the district. Anthracite in Wales is about two shillings a ton cheaper than bituminous coal—an economy in one constituent that balances the extra cost of the pitch; and in making best ordinary coke, the coal used is ground, at a cost of about six pence a ton, just as in the case of coke from anthracite. The yield of eighty per cent in coking anthracite, against seventy per cent or less in coking bituminous coal, is a gain in favor of the former.

The cost of the crushing and mixing arrangements, to grind 1,000 tons a day, is estimated by the inventors at from £2,000 to £2,500. This would include a six foot three inch disintegrator, with driving powers, elevators and shed.

The process has been carried on near Swansea for about nine months, and though it was suspended for some time, during last winter, on account of the colliers' strike, between 2,000 and 3,000 tons have in all been made.

CHAPTER VI.

YOUGHIOGHENY GAS COAL TRADE.

In the Connellsville coke region described in chapter IV, the coal mined is used almost exclusively for coking purposes, only a very fractional percentage being for steam coal, gas coal and house use.

In the Gas Coal Region now to be described, though the most of the coal is shipped to market for gas coal, yet there are also numerous accompanying coke ovens.

The Waverly Coal Works at Smith's Mills station, on the Pittsburg and Connellsville railroad, are mining on the Pittsburg Coal Bed. The coal shows six feet one inch thick, with two small bearing in slates at one foot above the floor, and bone coal of irregular thickness, varying from four inches to one-tenth of an inch, at four feet above the floor of the coal.

The rider of coal is very much parted by clay layers. It is two feet six inches thick and is separated from the main bed by one foot of clay. The floor shows slate, with iron pyrites.

Slate. *Fig. 20.*

Layer	Thickness
Rider	2′ 6″
Clay	1′ 0″
Coal	2′ 1″
Bone coal, irregular.	
Coal	2′ 9″
Slate and coal	0′ 3″
Coal	1′ 0″
Slate and pyrites in floor.	

The coal when mined is screened at the tipple; the lump coal being used for gas and steam purposes, the nut coal for steam and foundry uses, and the slack for coking.

The coal is mostly shipped as gas coal, and principally to Locust Point, Baltimore. The daily output of the mine is forty cars, four hundred and forty tons. One hundred and sixty-five diggers and eight haulers are employed.

There are also at these works twenty Beehive Block Ovens. The charge is one hundred and twenty-five bushels of slack coal, and they are run on seventy-two hour coke. As the slack contains the bearing in slate and its pyrites, greater proportions of these are found in this coke than from coke made from the run of the mine.

The Youghiogheny National Coal Company, at West Newton, work the Pittsburg Coal Bed. The coal is developed by a shaft seventy-eight feet deep, making the coal about fifty-five to sixty feet below the level of the Youghiogheny river. The coal bed is over six feet thick, of which five feet six inches are mined, one foot of sulphurous coal being left in the floor. There is a bearing in slate, but the usual slate at four feet above the floor of the coal is absent.

Fig. 21.

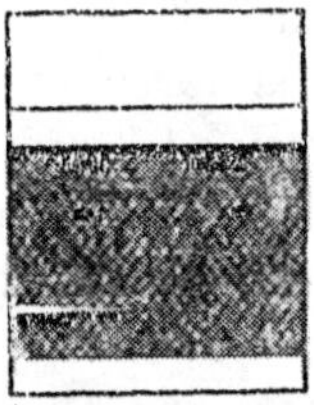

Slate.		
Rider	2′	6″
Soft fire-clay	1′	0″
Coal	4′	3″
Bearing in slate.		
Coal	1′	3″
Sulphurous coal	1′	0″
Fire-clay.		

The rider of coal is found above the main coal and separated from it by one foot of soft fire-clay. Ten to twelve cars of lump coal for gas purposes, are shipped daily from this mine to Locust Point, Baltimore. Four men are employed outside.

Messrs. Heath and White, White Heath station, Pittsburg and Connellsville railroad, are working the Pittsburg Coal Bed.

The coal is from thirty feet to forty feet below the Youghiogheny river level, the small overlying limestone coming to daylight a short distance above the works. The coal measures six feet in thickness; the lower one foot is sulphurous, and is not worked, and five feet of coal are taken out. There are two small bearing in slates, three inches apart, one foot above the bottom of the worked coal. The face of the coal is N. 70° W.; S. 70° E.

The shipment of coal from these works is twenty cars daily, (220 tons,) for gas making purposes entirely. Some of the coal goes to Baltimore, but the bulk of it is shipped to New York via Baltimore. Ninety men are employed.

The Black Ball Coal Works are located one mile below White & Heath's.

They mine the Pittsburg Coal Bed, but were not working at the time of the examination. Their capacity is about three hundred to four hundred tons daily.

Messrs. Markle & Son are operating about one-fourth of a mile below the mouth of the Big Sewickley creek. They mine the Pittsburg Coal Bed, and their mine has a capacity of twenty to thirty tons daily. Their coal goes to the paper mill at West Newton. The coal at their mine is seventy feet above the Youghiogheny river level.

The Penn Gas Coal Company have a siding running up the Big Sewickley creek to Irwin's Station, on the Pennsylvania railroad.

They have Youghiogheny mines Nos. 1, 2, 3 and 4, opened on the Pittsburg Coal Bed. They mine four feet six inches of coal; the face of the coal is north 65° west, and south 65° east.

Mine No. 3 is not yet opened for shipment.

They ship (September, 1875,) 25 cars (275 tons) daily, all for gas making purposes. Two-thirds of this amount go via the Pennsylvania railroad to Greenwich Point, and one-third to Pittsburg and Cumberland, via the Pittsburg and Connellsville railroad.

It is calculated to ship 150 cars daily from these works when run to their full capacity.

Two hundred and fifty men are employed.

Mr. Thomas Moore is operating the Ocean Mines at Moore's Station, on the Pittsburg and Connellsville railroad.

He works the Pittsburg Coal Bed, here about forty to fifty feet above the level of the Youghiogheny river, and rising gently to the northwest. The mine shows six feet of coal, with the usual bearing in slates; the lower one foot carries too much iron pyrites, and is not worked, the mine yielding therefore five feet of clean coal.

Fig. 22.

Fire-clay roof.	
Coal	3′ 9″
Bearing in slate.	
Coal	1′ 3″
Pyritous coal	1′ 0″
Fire-clay.	

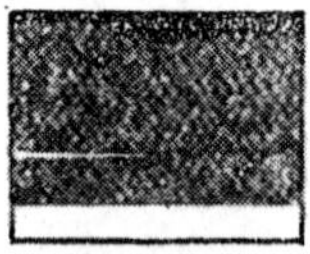

The mine was yielding in August, 1875, seventy cars, or seven hundred and seventy tons daily, and the operator intended to raise the output to one hundred cars daily. The coal is shipped for gas making purposes, and goes chiefly to New England via Baltimore. Three hundred and ten men are employed.

Messrs. C. H. Armstrong & Son are operating north of Moore's Station. They are mining on the Pittsburg Coal Bed, which shows here also as described above. The coal lies seventy feet above the Youghiogheny river level.

The mine shipped 8,830 tons of coal in June, 1875, nearly all for gas making purposes, but some little of it for steam coal. It goes both east and west of Pittsburg. One hundred and fifty-five men are employed.

The Youghiogheny Coal Hollow Coal Company are operating at Shaner's station, on the Pittsburg and Connellsville Railroad. They are mining on the Pittsburg Coal Bed, which is here fifty-five feet above the level of the Youghiogheny River; the coal shows a section similar to that already described at Moore's station.

The company ships forty cars (440 tons) of coal daily, all for gas making purposes. Of this amount, three-fourths goes to Baltimore and the balance to Cumberland to ship by water. Two hundred and thirteen men are employed.

In the coke works attached there are twenty Beehive Bank Ovens, in size 12′×6′. The charge is one hundred bushels of coal slack, with the usual Friday and Saturday increase. The ovens are worked as usual and are run upon forty-eight hour coke, shipped to Sharon and Newcastle. The product is two cars (1,250 bushels) daily.

At this mine the coal slack is washed before coking.*

Mr. N. J. Bigley is operating the Bigley Mines at Alpsville station, on the Pittsburg and Connellsville Railroad.

* Mr. Young describes the washing machinery at these works as follows: "The slack coal falls from the tipple screen into a hopper, from which it is carried by an elevator of the kind used in flouring mills, to a screen with four sized mesh, which separates the slack into different grades.

"Each grade of slack falls upon a dasher liberally supplied with water. The impurities, as they are removed, fall upon a valve worked by hand power; the coal is carried by the water to the drying apparatus, a cylinder of brass wire gauze. From this cylinder the coal passes into the hopper, whence it is removed by an elevator similar to the former one to the hopper from which the larry is charged.

"The resultant coke is a very beautiful article."

The mine is opened on the Pittsburg Coal Bed, which is here over two hundred feet above the level of the Youghiogheny river. The coal shows as before described, yielding five feet of clean coal. The output is forty cars daily of lump coal, and twenty cars daily of slack coal; half of which latter is shipped, the rest being coked.

The coal is shipped by rail to a point on the Youghiogheny river, several miles below the mine, where it is transferred to barges and shipped to points along the Ohio and Mississippi rivers, some of it going as far as New Orleans. Occasionally some coal is shipped east to Baltimore.

There are thirty-five Beehive ovens attached to these works, ten of them at the wharf. The size of the oven is $11' \times 5\frac{1}{2}'$. The charge is of coal slack, and the ovens are worked as usual, running on forty-eight hour coke. The product is three cars (1,875 bushels) daily.

The coal slack at this mine is washed previously to coking, as at Shaner's station. Two hundred men are employed.

Messrs. C. H. Armstrong & Son are operating at the Osceola Coal Works, Osceola station, on the Pittsburg and Connellsville Railroad. They work the Pittsburg Coal Bed in its average size and purity in this region. The output of their mine is fifteen to eighteen cars daily of lump coal, and fifty per cent. of slack coal. This is all used in the mills, puddling furnaces, &c., being shipped by rail to Pittsburg. One hundred and fifty men are employed.

Messrs. Cornell & Werling are operating at Ellrod station, on the Pittsburg and Connellsville Railroad, the works being on the west bank of the Youghiogheny river. They work the Pittsburg Coal Bed in full size, and here about one hundred and twenty-five feet above the river. The product is 14,000 bushels of lump coal, 3,500 bushels of nut coal, and 3,500 bushels of washed slack coal daily, all of which is shipped for gas making purposes to Cincinnati. Two hundred miners, fifteen laborers and six rivermen and washers are employed.

Mr. James Neil is operating his mine about one-fourth of a mile north of Ellrod station. He is working the Pittsburg Coal Bed, and the product of his mine is 8,000 bushels of lump coal and 1,000 bushels of slack coal daily, all of which is shipped as gas coal to Pittsburg by river. One hundred and fifty men are employed.

Mr. John Penny is operating his mine one mile above M'-Keesport. [No statistics were furnished.]

Messrs. Stone Brothers have their works at the confluence of the Monongahela and Youghiogheny rivers. They work the Pittsburg Coal Bed, which yields here four feet five inches of clean coal, with the usual bearing in slate. The output of the mine is 12,000 bushels of coal daily, which is shipped by river to Cincinnati, St. Louis and other river ports. There are five Beehive Bank Ovens of the usual size. The charge is 125 bushels of unwashed slack coal, increased on Friday and Saturday. The ovens are run upon twenty-seven hour coke, which is shipped to Cincinnati, to mills, furnaces, breweries and to the M'Keesport rolling mills. One hundred and sixty men in all are employed.

Mr. William Neal is operating opposite M'Keesport. He is mining on the Pittsburg Coal Bed, which yields its average of four feet six inches of clean coal. The output of the mine is 8,000 bushels of lump coal, and 1,500 of coal slack and nut coal, the latter of which is shipped. The coal is sent down the river to Cincinnati and beyond. There are four Beehive Ovens, in size 12′×6′, charged and worked as usual; they run on forty-eight hour coke, which is shipped with the coal. Seventy-five men are employed.

Messrs Neal & Oliver are operating just north of the William Neal mine. They work the Pittsburg Coal Bed, of the average size, and two hundred feet above the river. The output of the mine is 11,000 bushels of lump coal, and 1,200 bushels of nut coal daily; the slack coal is not used. The coal is shipped by water down the Ohio and Mississippi rivers. One hundred men are employed.

Mr. W. H. Brown is operating at Saltzburg station, on the Pittsburg and Connellsville Railroad.

The mine is on the Pittsburg Coal Bed, which is of full size and in excellent condition.

These lower works put out 12,000 bushels of lump coal daily.

There are twenty-four Beehive Bank Ovens. The charge is one hundred and twenty-five bushels of coal slack, and the coal is burned to order. Both the coal and coke are shipped to the river ports. One hundred and seventy-two men in all are employed.

The upper works run the same.

The Braddock's Field Gas Coal Company are operating at Braddock's Station. They mine the Pittsburg Coal Bed, four and one-half feet thick; the output of the mine being one hundred and sixty tons of lump coal and six hundred bushels of nut coal. The slack is hauled away.

The coal is shipped by the Pennsylvania Railroad Company to Pittsburg to the company's yards and to the Pittsburg Forge and Iron Company, where it is used mainly for steam coal. Forty diggers and ten laborers are employed.

Messrs. Corey & Co. are operating at Braddock's. They mine the Pittsburg Coal Bed of full average thickness. The mine output, when running full time, is twenty-five cars (275 tons) of lump coal daily and 15 per cent of nut coal. The coal is shipped to Pittsburg for gas making purposes.

There are forty Beehive Bank Ovens. The charge is one hundred bushels of unwashed coal slack, and the ovens are run upon seventy-two hour coke, or to order. The coke goes to J. F. Dravo.

Messrs. Redmond & Fawcett are operating on the West of the Monongahela river, opposite Braddock's. They work the Pittsburg Coal Bed, here about two hundred feet above the river. The bed yields four feet five inches of good coal, which is worked, and one foot eight inches of poor coal in floor, which is not lifted. The output of the mine is 10,000 bushels of lump coal and 25 per cent of nut and slack coal daily, all of which is shipped to Louisville and New Orleans. One hundred and twenty miners and twenty laborers are employed.

Messrs. M'Kinney & Bro. are operating just above, on the Pittsburg Bed, in the same condition and of the same size, and ship 6,000 bushels of coal daily.

Messrs. H. B. Hays & Bro. are operating at Hays' Station, on the Pittsburg, Virginia and Charleston Railroad. They work the Pittsburg Coal Bed, four feet six inches of coal, and put out from the mine 11,000 bushels of coal daily. This is shipped by river to Cincinnati and Louisville. The nut and slack coal are sold. One hundred and ninety men in all are employed.

The Beck's Run Company are operating one mile north of Hays'. They mine the Pittsburg Coal Bed, of average size, the output of the mine being 14,000 bushels of coal daily. Some of this is shipped by rail, the balance Messrs. Simpson, Harker & Son take by river to New Orleans. Two hundred and ten men are employed.

The total amount of this gas coal shipped from the Valley of the Youghiogheny is very great, and though the increase of shipments are temporarily checked by the stagnation in business and consequent economy in the use of materials of all kinds, yet the growth of the gas coal shipping has been so steady and for so many years, that it is safe to say that when business is again in its normal condition the growth of the trade will go on at about the same rate as before.

The region is well situated for shipment of coal, either east, west or south-west. The mines are opened directly on the slack water navigation of the Youghiogheny river, thence on to the Monongahela, the Ohio and the Mississippi rivers, these rivers to-day being the greatest single coal bearer of the world. And the water shipment has the great advantage, moreover, that the trade is capable of sudden and great increase when the shipments are needed.

But in addition to the shipments by this great water avenue to the west and south-west, extensive shipments are made east to Baltimore, by the Pittsburg and Connellsville Railroad via. Cumberland, and from there to other points in the east; and also east by the Pennsylvania Railroad.

The coal is well known and highly esteemed for its excellent character, and it is used as a gas coal at points widely scattered over the United States.

It must be borne in mind that the amount of volatile matter as expressed by a chemical analysis of different coals, by no means expresses exactly their relative powers as gas producing coals. When the water in the coal is simply given as a part of the volatile matters, and included in them, it must be noted that the oxygen in passing off, partly combined with hydrogen as water, and partly with carbon as carbonic oxide and carbonic acid gas, not merely reduces the nominal amount of useful volatile matter, but actually neutralizes a part of the gas producing element of the coal.

But even where the water is given separately and the useful volatile matters given together, there are striking differences in the amount of illuminating gas yielded by coals having almost the same chemical analysis. The laboratory of the Pennsylvania Geological Survey has not yet conducted any researches into this matter, and the conclusions of Prof. Wormley, as condensed in the Ohio Geological Report for 1873, are given below, more especially as his investigations included also examinations of these Youghiogheny gas coals. The report says:

"A coal which contained only 27.70 per cent of volatile combustible matters evolved 3.32 cubic feet of fixed gas per pound, whilst another, which contained 38.80 per cent of volatile com bustible matter, evolved only 3.03 cubic feet per pound. Of fourteen samples tested, the average volatile combustible matter was 33.54 per cent, and that of the fixed gas in cubic feet per pound of coal was 3.306. Gas works practically obtain more gas per pound than the chemists, doubtless through a re-distil lation of tarry matters and their conversion into permanent gas." Prof. Wormley also suggests, "that at such works, the measurement is taken at a higher temperature; a difference of five degrees changing the volume of gas about one per cent. From a fair average sample of Youghiogheny coal, Prof. Wormley obtains only about three and a half cubic feet per pound, whereas in the ordinary manufacture of illuminating gas, this coal as is well known, yields about four cubic feet per pound of coal."

There rests, however, no uncertainty upon the capacity of the Youghiogheny gas coal for furnishing illuminating gas; it has been practically tested in hundreds of gas works, and its powers are well known. The illuminating power of the gas furnished is high, about fourteen candles; not indeed so high as some other coals, for in rare instances the gas furnished will average eighteen candles, but higher than the average of gas coals.

Already in the previous chapters the quantity of sulphur present with the coal, and its condition have been sufficiently dwelt upon; the sulphur percentage, as already shown, ruling much below the average for coals.

The gas coal trade rests upon a well assured basis. The natural gas, as far as we now have it, possesses only a moderate illuminating power. At present there seems nothing to look forward to except a steady growth of the gas coal trade, a growth proportioned to the increased population and wealth of the regions to which this Youghiogheny coal now goes as a gas coal

CHAPTER VII.

Iron Ores and Fire-Clays.

The general geology of the Youghiogheny Valley, as already given, notes where the Lower Productive Coal Measures are the country rock, and gives sections showing these measures as exposed along Dunbar creek, Mount's creek and Jacob's creek.—(Figs. 1 and 2. Plate III.) These vertical sections show the rocks below the Seral Conglomerate of XII, the measures between the Seral Conglomerate and the Mahoning Sandstone, and the Barren Measures between the Mahoning Sandstone and the Pittsburg Coal Bed.

There are two marked and productive horizons of iron ore in the Youghiogheny Valley and its subordinate branch valleys: 1. The iron ores just under the Pittsburg Coal Bed, and, 2. The iron ores underlying the Seral Conglomerate. Besides these there are intermediate iron ores developed on Jacob's creek; there is an iron ore bed of some regularity in the Freeport Group at other points, and there are other iron ores in the Barren Measures. For the region on Dunbar creek, in fact from Connellsville to six miles beyond Uniontown, the iron ores below the Pittsburg Coal and below the Seral Conglomerate are the ores now worked for furnace use.

The Fairchance Iron Works, in Fayette county, six miles south-west of Uniontown, have run for many years on the iron ores just below the Pittsburg Coal Bed, using them alone, without admixture of Lake Superior iron ores, and making a brand of iron well and widely known for its high character. These works are not now running, but the same measures are opened up two miles north-east of Fairchance, and four miles south-west of Uniontown, at Oliphant's New Furnace. The only iron ores worked at this place are those just below the Pittsburg Coal Bed; the iron ores under the Seral Conglomerate, it is reported, not being either in quantity or quality to justify working.

The openings for the furnace are on the eastern outcrop of

the Pittsburg Coal Bed, at the west foot of Chestnut Ridge Mountain. The measures lie nearly horizontal, and the Pittsburg Coal has over an area of some acres at the outcrop only a few feet of cover over it. But the roof is firm and tight and keeps the coal in perfect order, and it is stripped and quarried, instead of mining. A vertical section of the Pittsburg Coal Bed and the underlying iron ores measured at Oliphant's Furnace, shows thus:

Fig. 23.

Pittsburg Coal Bed	9′ 0″
Clay and slate	2′ 6″
Iron ore, "Blue Lump"	10″ to 1′ 0″
Clay and interval, holding a 2″ iron ore, the "Condemned Flag ore."	2′ 9′
Iron ore. "Big Bottom"	1′ 0″
Interval	1′ 9″
Iron ore "Red Flag"	0′ 2″

In addition to these ores there is an iron ore bed, apparently regular though small, opened up in the meadow east of the Furnace. This ore, which is here about sixty feet below the Pittsburg Coal Bed, is called, locally, the "Yellow Flag" ore.

Specimens of these iron ores were forwarded to the Laboratory of the Survey in Harrisburg.

Complete analyses of the Blue Lump and the Big Bottom iron ore yielded as follows (M'Creath):

The Blue Lump ore is a clay carbonate iron ore, exceedingly hard and compact, and minutely crystalline, bluish gray with conchoidal fracture.

The Big Bottom ore is a clay carbonate iron ore, hard and compact, with small seams of limonite, and with conchoidal fracture.

	Blue Lump.	Big Bottom.
Protoxide of iron	49.500	44.742
Sesquioxide of iron	.700	.818
Bisulphide of iron	.020	.272
Alumina	1.153	2.795
Protoxide of manganese	1.636	1.053
Lime	1.859	3.119
Magnesia	2.018	3.870

	Blue Lump.	Big Bottom.
Phosphoric acid	.204	.096
Sulphuric acid	Trace.	Trace.
Carbonic acid	34.900	34.450
Water	1.395	1.090
Carbonaceous matter	.730	.640
Insoluble residue	5.790	7.450
	99.905	100.401
Iron	39.000	35.500
Sulphur	.011	.145
Phosphorus	.089	.042

In addition to these ores above, specimens of the Blue Lump Flag ore, the Red Flag ore and the Yellow Flag ore were forwarded to the Laboratory of the Survey, and yielded on analysis (M'Creath):

The Blue Lump Flag ore is a carbonate ore, blue, hard and compact, with a sub-conchoidal fracture.

The Red Flag Ore is a carbonate ore, hard, compact, reddish gray, and showing small crystals of pyrites.

The Yellow Flag Ore is a carbonate ore, hard and compact, crust hematitic, outside surface yellowish brown, fresh fracture bluish gray. Structure, flaggy.

	Blue Lump Flag Ore.	Red Flag Ore.	Yellow Flag Ore.
Iron	37.500	35.800	35.400
Sulphur	.041	.047	.319
Phosphorus	.505	.083	.069
Insoluble residue	5.670	9.560	10.450

The limestone overlying the Pittsburg Coal Bed about seventy-five feet, which makes all through this region an excellent flux for furnace use, is opened up for the use of Oliphant's Furnace. A specimen of the limestone forwarded to the laboratory of the Survey yielded on analysis (M'Creath):

Limestone hard and compact, of a very dark color, minutely crystalline, and spotted with pyrites.

Carbonate of lime	80.647
Carbonate of magnesia	2.217
Carbonate of iron	1.657
Bisulphide of iron	1.125
Alumina	.543
Sulphuric acid	.052
Phosphoric acid	.066
Water	1.010
Carbonaceous matter	1.250
Insoluble residue	10.770
	99.337

Iron	1.300
Sulphur	.621
Phosphorus	.029

A specimen of what is known as the "Limestone Ore" was also forwarded by the Superintendent of the Furnace, and yielded on analysis (M'Creath):

Limestone ore, hard and compact, bluish gray, showing considerable pyrites.

Iron	11.100
Sulphur	.313
Phosphorus	.018
Carbonate of lime	43.285
Carbonate of magnesia	2.747
Insoluble residue	26.090

These ores show a freedom from phosphorus rather remarkable in carbonate iron ores; the only one showing any considerable percentage of it, the Blue Lump Flag ore, with .505 per cent, is a condemned ore and not used in the furnace.

Special attention has been given to this ore deposit on account of the excellent grade of iron which they produce, and the regularity with which they accompany the Pittsburg Coal Bed through this part of the basin. Lying moreover as they do, directly under the floor of the coal bed, and in clay, which affords easy mining, they are taken out cheaply. The coal bed, worked at the same time, affords the best quality of coal for coking.

This valley therefore presents an unusually favorable location for making cheaply a good grade of iron. At the Fairchance iron works, the superintendent states that the regular mixture of the ore was one-third Blue Lump ore, one-third Big Bottom ore, and one-third Red Flag ore. Three tons of ore going to make one ton of pig metal.

"Ninety-five bushels of coke were estimated to the ton of iron; and coking Connellsville coal (Pittsburg Bed) in open ricks, it yielded about 50 per cent of coke."

If the above statement with reference to coking be accurate, it shows great waste in the open rick coking. In the Beehive Oven the same coal yields (as shown in chapter V) to every one hundred bushels of coal (7,600 pounds) one hundred and twenty bushels of coke, (4,800 pounds;) but the 50 per cent average, as stated above, would yield to one hundred bushels of coal, (7,600 pounds,) only ninety-five bushels of coke (3,800 pounds.)

The new furnace and mines are on a railroad route, located and graded, but not yet ironed. But the South-west Pennsylvania, starting at Greensburg, on the Pennsylvania railroad, running parallel with the Uniontown branch of the Pittsburg and Connellsville railroad, from Connellsville to Uniontown, is intended to continue on from the latter place to Fairmount on the Monongahela river, thus bringing to a market this eastern outcrop of the Pittsburg coal and its underlying ores for many miles.

Preliminary estimates of the cost of making iron in any region are notoriously delusive, it seeming to be inevitable that there shall be in them some sins either of omission or commission which render them inaccurate in practical working. The statements below are of contracts made and in operation at the Oliphant furnace.

Coal in coke yard, 100 bushels at ½ cent	$0 50
Ninety-five bushels of coke, 1½ cents for coking	1 42
Iron ore, 3 tons at $2	6 00
Limestone, 1 ton at 40 cents	40
	8 32
Labor, furnace expenses, &c	8 00
	16 32

The latter item for labor, &c., ($8 per ton,) is estimated; the other figures are given by the Superintendent as exact.*

Going north-east from Oliphant's Furnace there are no openings in the iron ore below the Pittsburg Coal now being worked, (July, 1875,) for furnace use until reaching Dunbar Furnace Mines. But the iron ore is shown in numerous places where the coal is mined.

Messrs. Ewing & Boyd, at Lemont Station, on the Uniontown branch of the Pittsburg and Connellsville Railroad, have opened for their new furnace an iron ore bed lying about three hundred and fifty feet below the Pittsburg Coal Bed.

The ore ranges in thickness from one foot to two and one-half feet, and averages about two feet. It lies in a deposit of blue shale, the floor having a talcose feel.

The Dunbar Furnace Company have developed thoroughly not only the Pittsburg Coal Bed and the ore underlying, but

*It must be noted, that it has been stated above, that the measures at this place afford unusual opportunities for mining cheaply the iron ores and coal.

also the iron ores below the Seral Conglomerate; and the manager, Mr. E. C. Pechin, has had made at the furnace laboratory, for his own use, sufficiently full and complete analyses to enable the character of the ores to be stated very certainly.

A remarkable difference is at once seen in the ores underlying the Pittsburg Coal Bed at Dunbar when compared with the section at Fairchance and Oliphant's, the distance between the points being sixteen miles.

At Dunbar the Big Bottom ore and the Red Flag ore, most important ores in the Fairchance section, are found only as limestone, with streaks of iron ore; and the Blue Lump ore has come down to an inch in thickness. But about four feet below the bottom of the coal an iron ore is found of very peculiar appearance. This same ore is found underlying the coal for ten miles south-west of Dunbar, as far as Uniontown. This ore has been fully described on page 18.

Two limestones are opened at Dunbar, one seventy-five feet, and the other one hundred and twenty feet above the Pittsburg Coal Bed.

The Dunbar Furnace Company work extensively the "Mountain ores," the ores underlying the Seral Conglomerate, the mines being in the Chestnut Ridge mountain. The size and distances apart of these ores have been thoroughly developed by the company; and the beds have been fully described on page 27 of this report, with complete analyses furnished by the Laboratory of the Furnace.

These ores are strikingly similar to each other in character by the analysis; but Mr. Pechin states, that "in practice the kidney and honey-comb ores make the best iron." But they are all excellent ores, and show how it was possible for the furnace to make the good record of a year's work given below.

Year ending August 1, 1875, Dunbar Furnace, Fayette county, Pennsylvania:

Product.	Tons.
No. 1, Foundry	371
No. 2, Foundry	699
No. 1, Mill	11,953
No. 2, Mill	337
Mottled	95
White	39
Total tons of 2,268 pounds	13,494

Average consumption of Connellsville coke to one ton of iron, eighty-eight and seven-eighth bushels; average consumption of ore to one ton of iron, two and one-half tons; average consumption of limestone to one ton of iron, one and one-third tons.

Mixture of iron ores: one-twelfth Lake Superior ore, one-fifth mill cinder, and the balance the native carbonates, the analyses of which have been given.

The "Mountain ore," the ore below the Seral Conglomerate is worked for furnace use at the Mount Vernon mines, seven miles north of Connellsville.

The ore is used in Charlotte furnace, at Scottdale; being carried for three miles by the Green Lick Narrow Gauge Railroad to the Mount Pleasant Branch Railroad, and then three miles more by that road to the furnace. The ore is mixed at the furnace with hematite ore from Bloomfield mines in Blair county, Pennsylvania, and with Lake Superior ore, and the furnace product is excellent metal.

The ore averages eighteen inches in thickness, in two plates separated by a small clay slate layer; and about two feet above this, also in clay slate, is the small four inch ore called the Pin vein, an unusually rich and pure iron ore.

An average of analyses of several specimens of the main bench of ore is furnished by the company, as follows:

Water		0.93
Silicic acid		14.83
Peroxide of iron	1.16	
Carbonate of iron	67.20	
Metallic iron		33.60
Alumina		6.44
Carbonate of lime		5.84
Carbonate of magnesia		2.83
Phosphoric acid		0.25
Sulphate of lime		0.54

The above analysis represents an excellent character for the ore.

A specimen of the main bench of this ore was forwarded to Harrisburg for analysis and yielded (M'Creath):

Iron	31.20
Sulphur	.253
Phosphorus	.129
Insoluble residue	21.930

The ore is a carbonate, hard and compact, dark bluish gray, brittle, somewhat slaty.

A specimen of the Pin Vein Ore on top yielded on-analysis (M'Creath):

Iron	41.00
Sulphur	.191
Phosphorus	.120
Insoluble residue	6.810

The ore is a carbonate, compact, brittle, bluish gray, minutely crystalline, with small crystals of iron pyrites.

The iron ore underlying the Pittsburg Coal Bed is seen at the mines of Frick & Co., at Broad Ford; at the mines at West Overton; and at the works of Duncan Brothers, at Mount Pleasant. At all of these places the exposures are only such as are necessarily made in working the coal bed for the coking ovens, and in no case is the ore mined for shipment.

The next important point where the iron ores have been opened up and worked is on Jacobs' Creek.

The description of the geology of the Jacobs' Creek Valley in chapter I, shows that the country rock for a considerable area is made of the lower productive coal measures. The Pittsburg coal does not come into the hilltops along the creek, and the ores underlying that coal are therefore wanting at this point.

There are several different iron ores open along the creek.

The "Furnace Vein" is opened on the north side of the creek, three miles above the mouth, and one-half mile above the old furnace. It shows:

1. Sandstone roof.
2. Slate of varying colors, from red to black, in all nine feet thick, holding fourteen to sixteen inches of iron ore, mainly in two layers, but also with some scattered lumps.
3. Iron ore, six to eight inches.
4. Slate, clayey, underlying.

This ore has been benched for two miles up the creek for use in the old furnace, and is said to have shown somewhat larger in the workings on the south side (Fayette) of the creek, than on the north (Westmoreland) side.

The ore was used unmixed, and made an iron which was worked up in the old forge into bar, horse-shoe and nail iron.

A specimen of this Furnace Vein ore yielded, on analysis, (M'Creath):

Protoxide of iron	51.271
Sesquioxide of iron	.943
Bisulphide of iron	.515
Alumina	2.050
Protoxide of manganese	2.352
Lime	1.344
Magnesia	.814
Sulphuric acid	.007
Phosphoric acid	.537
Carbonic acid	33.980
Carbonaceous matter	.710
Water	.910
Insoluble residue	5.120
	100.553
Iron	40.750
Sulphur	.278
Phosphorus	.229

The ore is a carbonate, compact, but exceedingly brittle; color, bluish gray; structure somewhat flaggy; seamed with white crystalline carbonate of lime.

The Forge vein is opened not far from the Furnace vein, and underlies it by fifty feet. It shows—

1. Sandstone, massive.
2. Coal, one and a half feet.
3. Clay, two and a half feet.
4. Ore, two feet.
5. Fire-clay, five feet, with some ore nodules.

A specimen of this ore forwarded to the Laboratory of the Survey yielded, on analysis (M'Creath):

The ore is a carbonate, compact and sandy, bluish gray, with conchoidal fracture, and shows small specks of pyrites:

Iron	28.300
Sulphur	.079
Phosphorus	.137
Carbonate of lime	13.680
Carbonate of magnesia	7.870
Insoluble residue	13.885

The "Coal Bank" ore is opened up on the south bank of Jacob's creek, two miles above the mouth. The ore shows sixteen to twenty inches thick, resting on limestone. A specimen yielded on analysis (M'Creath):

Carbonate ore, surface hematitic, on fresh fracture bluish gray, conchoidal fracture and showing considerable calcite:

Iron	26.500
Sulphur	.090
Phosphorus	.046
Carbonate of lime	23.120
Carbonate of magnesia	5.600
Insoluble residue	13.810

This ore, like the Forge ore described above, though not rich in metallic iron, is very low in sulphur and phosphorus and would make good iron.

A specimen of this ore underlying the coal was analyzed in 1866, by Dr. Otto Wuth, who reports the analysis as follows:

"Silicic acid	8.060
Alumina	2.250
Carbonate of iron	75.040
Carbonate of lime	8.300
Carbonate of magnesia	4.910
Manganese	.850
Organic matter	.590
	100.000

The ore is free from phosphates and contains only 0.006 per cent of sulphur, almost nothing. Roasted, it will yield from 50 to 55 per cent of iron. There is no reason to speak of the superior quality of this ore. The analysis shows it clearly."

A coal bed is opened up ten feet above the iron ore. It shows:

Roof, clay slate	5′ 0″
Black slate	0′ 9″
Coal	0′ 2″
Slate	0′ 1″
Coal	0′ 4″
Slate	0′ 1½″
Coal	2′ 4″
Slate, sulphurous	0′ 4″
Coal	9″ to 1′ 0″

And the bottom not seen. This coal, and the others of the Freeport group, were seen at other points on Jacob's creek, ranging from three to four feet in thickness. But while the Connellsville coal is so close, and the coke so cheap, it is not likely that these lower coals will be applied to any purpose in iron making, excepting perhaps the roasting of the ores.

Besides the ores described above, which are below the Mahoning sandstone, there were some smaller ore outcrops, some above the Mahoning sandstone. One of these is an iron ore, opened about one mile above the mouth of Jacob's creek, and near the water level, which shows about two feet of carbonate iron ore. A specimen of it yielded on analysis, (M'Creath):

Carbonate ore, part of the specimen hematitic, greenish gray, with conchoidal fracture, and very silicious.

Iron	24.680
Sulphur	.047
Phosphorus	.128
Insoluble residue	36.675

The greenish portion of the ore, analyzed separately, contained, (Forman):

Iron	22.90
Insoluble residue	40.92

Specimens of two of these less important beds of iron ore, the "Bridge Ore," and the "Barren Run Ore," opened up at the outcrop from one to one and a half miles south-east of Jacob's Creek station, on the Pittsburg and Connellsville railroad, yielded on analysis, (M'Creath):

	No. 1.	No. 2.
Iron	27 700	11.700
Sulphur	.160	.075
Phosphorus	.679	1.245
Carbonate of lime	7.640	56.353
Carbonate of magnesia	4.517	4.994
Insoluble residue	25.240	10.920

No. 1, "Bridge Ore" is a carbonate ore, hard and compact, crust hematitic; fresh fracture bluish gray; brittle; seamed with white crystalline carbonate of lime.

No. 2, "Barren Run Ore," is a ferriferous limestone ore; crust hematitic; color pearl gray; fracture conchoidal; specimen generally highly crystalline.

These analyses show sufficiently the general character of the ore deposits on Jacob's creek. The ores are not now mined for shipment, but their proximity to market, Jacob's Creek station being only forty miles from Pittsburg, and their excellent character must soon bring them into use.

But there is another feature in the connection of the Jacob's Creek valley and the manufacture of iron, which a few years ago would not have been worthy of mention, but is now a factor of very considerable consequence, and that is the presence of natural gas in apparently great quantities. The experiment of working iron with natural gas has proved a success, and it has also been shown that the gas can be piped for long distances without excessive leakage.

An old salt well, put down about one mile up Jacob's creek, and abandoned many years ago, has continued to yield gas constantly; and the gas now comes up through the bed of the creek in sufficient quantity to be lighted at any time.

Well No. 1 was put down close to the old salt well. There is no record except that there was much gas. The well was in all 1,100 feet deep.

Mr. Frank D. Howell, of Philadelphia, kindly furnished the following from the Report of the Superintendent in charge of the borings for oil on Jacob's creek:

"Aug. 19, 1865. No. 3 well, depth five hundred and eighty feet, have just bored through a red rock one hundred and twenty feet thick; now in a grey sandstone rock; large amount of gas in this well, etc.

"Sept. 23, 1865. Well No. 4, depth four hundred and thirty-five feet, white sand rock, a great deal of black gas.

"Oct. 21, 1865. Well No. 3 is seven hundred and forty feet deep; we have struck a crevice in this well in which the tools dropped or fell seven feet; when we struck this opening in the rock an immense amount of gas came up, etc.

"Dec. 22, 1865. Well No. 5 is progressing satisfactorily, and with no end of gas.

"Jan. 1, 1866. No. 5 well is two hundred and ninety-four feet deep, in the second sand rock. The boring of this well has been delayed somewhat by the large amount of gas.

"Jan. 6, 1866. No. 5 well is three hundred feet deep; the boring of this well has been delayed by the immense amounts of gas."

Mr. Howell furnishes the report of the Superintendent, under date of December 15, 1865, from which the following is taken verbatim:

"At well No. 5 we struck the red rock at a depth of one hundred and thirty feet; at the other wells we struck the same rock at a depth of five hundred and fifty feet; at the other wells the gas and salt water were found above the red rock, at No. 5 below it. All the strata of rock in No. 5 being entirely different from the others At No. 5 we have bored through one beautiful sandstone rock, and then soap stone and fire-clay; after that the red rock, which was twenty-five feet thick, and then soap stone. At a depth of about two hundred and twenty-five feet we struck a stratum of rock of a dark soft substance (*sic*) with a very strong smell, different from anything that I or any of the men had seen. After boring in this singular rock a short distance, and arriving at a depth altogether of two hundred and forty feet we struck salt water, after which we struck gas, and the whole thing came roaring up, and for four hours it continued pouring up gas and water the whole size of the conductor, clear up against the roof.

"It then subsided, and the men commenced boring, which was continued until the next evening, when the performances were repeated with a few variations, when it again subsided.

"The men commenced boring again, which was continued until the afternoon, when it came on again with tremendous force, and in spite of every exertion caught fire, and came near burning up some of the men. By great exertions we succeeded in smothering it out with blankets and dirt, and succeeded in getting the fire out without much damage. It was the most astonishing exhibition of gas that I ever heard of."

A statistical report on the Youghiogheny valley would not be complete without a statement of facts in reference to a matter so important at this time as a supply of natural gas.

In a report of the survey appended to this volume, the character of this natural gas, its efficiency in iron making, and the probabilities as to its permanency are discussed. The facts of the borings on Jacob's creek are therefore given here above, and without comment.

It should be added, however, that at the time the reports of the superintendent were made, natural gas was considered as a nuisance and a drawback, a fact which should be remembered in weighing the evidence as to the quantity of the gas.

In various parts of the Coal Measures, red hematite iron ore is found. It was found in Jefferson county, in the lower productive coal measures in the season of 1874, and in 1875 a piece was forwarded by Mr. Young from the Barren Measures underlying the Pittsburg Coal Bed. But in neither case, and in no other case where the ore has been observed in the Coal Measures of Pennsylvania, is there any evidence of sufficient regularity of deposit to give the ore a practical value.

The specimen from the Barren Measures in the Youghiogheny valley yielded on analysis, (M'Creath):

Exceedingly hard and tough arenaceous red hematite.

Iron	52.200
Sulphur	.131
Phosphorus	.080
Water	1.790
Insoluble residue	18.320

In addition to the coke, gas coal, iron and iron ore industries of the Youghiogheny valley, there are several other branches of manufacturing and mining, which though much smaller than the three chief branches named above, are yet of very considerable importance in the aggregate

Fire-clay works are located at numerous points in the valley, the enormous increase in the number of coking ovens requiring great quantities of brick and rather over stimulating the trade.

Messrs. Ewing, Boyd & Co., at Lemont station, on the Uniontown branch of the Pittsburg and Connellsville railroad, work a fire-clay bed ten feet thick in all, made up of layers of clay of various qualities. They run a one pan mill, with two kilns, and have a capacity of 4,500 daily.

The Cambria Fire Brick Works are at Braddock station, on the Uniontown branch of the Pittsburg and Connellsville Railroad. They work a fire-clay bed, about ten feet thick, blue, black and drab in color. They have a one pan mill, one kiln, bake four days, and have a capacity of forty-five to fifty thousand. These works had not yet started shipments when they were examined.

Messrs. Bliss, Marshall & Co., have fire-brick works at Dunbar, Fayette county. They work a fire-clay bed nine feet thick, and have a one pan mill with two ton rollers, three fifty thousand kilns, and burn four days. They manufacture bricks, arch, tiles, rings, &c., and pick and wash for rolling mill brick.

Messrs. Soisson & Co., have their fire-brick works at White

Rock station, on the Pittsburg and Connellsville Railroad. They work a bed of fire-clay, which shows thus:—

Soil	3′
Slaty coal	3′ to 5′
Soft clay	5′
Small lump hard clay	5′
Large lump hard clay	5′

The coal is five feet thick in one place but seems to be thinning down. It is of an entirely worthless character. They have a one pan mill, two forty-five thousand kilns, and burn seventy-two hours. The rollers are 4,600 pounds.

Messrs. Soisson & Glover have fire-brick works.

The mine is on the western slope of Chestnut Ridge. It shows thirteen feet of hard, small lump clay, free from iron ore where worked in an open cut. But twenty feet north of this, where a small drift has been put in, the clay needs picking to free it from iron ore. The floor is soft white clay, one foot of which was penetrated without reaching the underlying rock. They have a one pan mill, with two thirty-five thousand kilns, and burn ninety-six hours. They manufacture all articles in the fire-brick line, and ship to Pittsburg.

The fire-brick works of Messrs. Soisson & Co., at Oakdale station, on the Pittsburg and Connellsville Railroad, was not running when examined. There are two kilns. The clay was not mined at the works.

Messrs. Maxwell, Brady & Co., have the Diamond Fire-brick Works at Layton station, on the Pittsburg and Connellsville Railroad. They work a rather soft fire-clay bed nine feet thick, with a thirty inch coal resting on top. Some sand is mixed with the clay for use. They have a one pan mill, two fifty-five thousand kilns, burn three to four days, and make bricks, tiles and rings.

Two fire-clays from Jacob's creek, the "Furnace Clay" and the "Forge Fire-clay," yielded on analysis, (M'Creath):

	No. 1.	No. 2.
Silica	56.780	65.370
Alumina	26.890	24.870
Protoxide of iron	3.222	.756
Lime	.369	.168
Magnesia	.987	.234
Alkalies	3.920	.010
Water	8.380	8.970
	100.548	100.378

No. 1, "Furnace Clay," comparatively soft and brittle, somewhat sandy, with pearl gray to greenish color.

No. 2, "Forge Clay," hard and compact, with bluish gray color and conchoidal fracture. These clays are apparently in abundant quantity.

Messrs. M'Adams & Co., have at Mount Pleasant their kilns for burning lime. The quarry is on the hill north-east of the town, and within the limits of the borough. It shows twelve feet of gray and drab limestone now quarried, without the bottom being reached. "The bottom layer makes a fair cement." The limestone is of excellent quality, as is evidenced by the analysis below, made by Dr. Otto Wuth of Pittsburg:

Silicic acid	2.190
Alumina	0.240
Peroxide of iron } Phosphoric acid }	0.620
Carbonate of lime	95.230
Carbonate of magnesia	1.720
	100.000

The limestone is some three hundred feet above the Pittsburg Coal Bed. They work four kilns, two pots, two water flames, and burn 4,000 bushels of lime per week, drawing every twelve hours and using coal as a fuel. The lime is shipped to Pittsburg, for mortar, gas and glass works use. Seven men are employed in the kilns and twelve in the quarry. Page's patent kilns and M'Adams' patent breaker are used in the pot kilns, built in 1872.

The Youghiogheny Cement Company have their works one mile above West Newton. They work in all some fifty feet of rock, including in that the worthless layers which do not enter the kilns. This rock is about one hundred feet above the Pittsburg Coal Bed. They have three pot kilns, draw every twenty-four hours, have a capacity of eighty barrels daily, and ship chiefly to Pittsburg.

Mr. J. R. Smith has sand works at Dawson station, on the Pittsburg and Connellsville railroad. The material used is bank sand from the side of a Barren Measure hill west of the station. The sand is riddled and then washed in a series of four washers through which run shovel bearing belts. It is shipped to Pittsburg, and used in glass works and as packing for the bottom of puddling furnaces. The capacity daily is about thirty tons.

Messrs. Speer, Clarke & Co., have sand works at Layton station, on the Pittsburg and Connellsville Railroad. The sandstone is of two qualities, white and red; the white sand being superior and used in making fine glass.

The following description of the method of crushing the stone is given by Mr. Young: "The stone is crushed in a powerful steam crusher to lumps the size of a walnut, being brought from the quarry in pieces of about five pounds weight:

"From the crusher the stone goes to the grinder, a crushing roller revolving in a stationary pan. The sand and gravel are then placed in a screen revolving in a vertical plane, from which the sand is dropped into the washer and the gravel on to a table, from which it is again conveyed to the grinder.

"The washing is done in a series of three inclined troughs, slanting upward from the screen at a small angle. The water and sand are conveyed upward by means of a screw, a little water being added where the contents of one trough flow into another.

"At the top of the third trough, the highest in the series, the water is drawn off and the sand conveyed to the stock pile.

"The time occupied in the operation, from putting the stone into the crusher until the sand issues from the third trough, is ten minutes, the work all being done by machinery; four men are employed in the works and fifteen in the quarry."

The Bayard Salt works are half a mile below Ellrod station, on the Pittsburg and Connellsville Railroad. The well is three hundred and twenty feet deep, and was drilled in 1870. The works were not running when examined, but have a capacity of about ten barrels daily. The following is the record of the boring:

		Total depth.
0	Surface	0
58′	Sand and gravel	58′
82′	Bluish white rock	140′
6′	Coal	146′
57′	"Fire-clay"	203′
21′	Sharp grit rock	224′
	First salt at 215 feet.	

		Total depth.
38′	"Soapstone"	262′
43′	Black slate	305
26′	Hard white rock	331
17′	"Fire-clay"	348′
22′	Hard, dark oily slate	370′
25′	Hard white sandstone	395′
41′	Dark, heavy hard slate	436′
52′	Dark slate rock	488′
	Salt water 5° at 464 feet.	
20′	Hard fine white rock	508′
15′	Hard rock, coal appearance 2′	523′
57′	White rock	580′
16′	"Like soapstone"	596′
64′	Dark slate rock	660′
13′	Soapstone	673′
41′	Slaty rock, ending in bastard limestone	714′

Opposite Ellrod station, Messrs. Duncan & Lamb are boring (September, 1875) a salt well. They are now down nine hundred feet and are going deeper. The well at present would yield ten barrels daily.

Mr. C. W. Taylor has salt works at Long Run station on the Pittsburg and Connellsville Railroad.

The well is five hundred and eighty feet deep, and was drilled fifty or more years ago by Major Caven.

The works have a capacity of sixteen barrels per day, though there is water enough for twenty-five. The water is evaporated in open pans:—Twenty-four hours boiling; twenty-four hours settling and twenty-four hours crystallizing. It is boiled to 33°. Shipped mostly up the Pittsburg and Connellsville Railroad.

In the same building Mr. J. J. Deakey manufactures bromine. Mr. Young describes the process thus:—"He boils the bitter water to 45°, adds MnO_2 and SO_3, passes steam through and collects in a florentine receiver. He uses the bitter water mother liquor from Duncan and Lamb, the Bayard and the Long Run works. He has the capacity of eighteen barrels of bromine daily, if he could get the water." It is all shipped to Rosengarten & Sons, in Philadelphia.

Mr. J. A. Jameson has salt works at Salt Works station, on the Pittsburg and Connellsville Railroad. His well is over four hundred and seventy feet deep. Capacity of his works twelve barrels daily, mostly shipped to Pittsburg and up the river.

There are numerous brick yards for making common bricks at different points on the Youghiogheny, some of them notably large. They all use clay from the flats in the vicinity of their works.

APPENDIX A.

On the Methods of Coking Coal for Furnace Use; its Efficiency and Economy, as Compared with Anthracite Coal in the Metallurgy of Iron.

JOHN FULTON, E. M., GENERAL MINING ENGINEER, C. I. CO. 1875.

The State of Pennsylvania occupies the leading position in the production of pig iron, and in the magnitude and variety of its allied industries.

The ores of iron, the fuels and fluxes have been so liberally deposited in the Commonwealth as early to invite efforts in iron making and to stimulate it, until it has attained its present large proportions and momentum of progress.

With the clearing of the forests the period of charcoal, as a furnace fuel, must soon pass away. The attention of iron makers at the present time is mainly given to three varieties of mineral fuel—anthracite coal, coke from bituminous and semi-bituminous coal, and the dry or block coal of Mercer county.

Anthracite coal is a natural coke, produced under immense pressure, presenting the most dense and compact fuel known. It has, however, some disadvantages, as the purest variety decrepitates to such an extent in the blast furnace as to impede the blast, and hence cannot be used advantageously. A second class, somewhat banded with slate, is found more tenacious, and is generally used as a furnace fuel.

The chief supply of this coal in the State or United States is found in the Schuylkill, Lehigh and Wilkesbarre districts, aggregating four hundred and seventy-two square miles of coal measures.

From the limited supply of this fuel, and its constant increase in domestic uses, it is evident that its enhanced price will restrict its use to the furnaces on the Lehigh, Schuylkill and a few other favored localities.

It is also manifest *that coke is destined to become the leading fuel for blast furnaces, and to retain this position from its almost inexhaustible source of supply, its calorific efficiency, and its continued economy.*

The north-eastern portion of the Appalachian coal field covers the western portion of the State, from the Allegheny mountain crestline to the western border, breaking up in the northern counties into a number of terminal fingers and detached coal fields.

The Broad Top region is an eastern outlying basin of coal. The whole bituminous and semi-bituminous area of the State is over 12,000 square miles.

The area of the dry block coals of Mercer county is quite limited, embracing one workable seam, but the coal has an important place as a furnace fuel in the extensive iron works of western Pennsylvania and eastern Ohio.

As anthracite and the dry burning coals of Mercer county require no special preparation for use in smelting furnaces, the principal inquiry will be directed to the typical methods of coking coal as now practiced in this State.

In all coking operations the work to be accomplished is *to expel the gaseous elements of the coal,* retaining the carbon and ash which constitutes *the coke.*

It is thus evident that the quantity of coke obtained from any coal cannot exceed the sum of its carbon and ash.

On the other side it is rarely found that coke can be made without the loss of several units of carbon, depending on the quality of the coal and the method of coking it.

The minimum loss of carbon should be made in coals having a large volume of hydrogenous matter; in other words, holding a sufficient amount of gaseous product to supply the necessary heat for the operation of coking without using any of the carbon.

The maximum loss of carbon would result in coking a dry coal, or one holding a small percentage of gaseous matter, thus requiring the burning of carbon to supply the necessary heat.

These considerations lead in the outset to an inquiry into the requisite qualities in a good coal for coking.

It might be expected that all the bituminous and semi-bituminous coals would produce good coke. That such is not the fact is now becoming clear to those interested in this industry. The difficulty hitherto in getting light on the requirements of a good coking coal, and the principles of coking it, consisted in the loose statements of the advocates of the several kinds of ovens, who seem determined to make *them* the prime element in governing the quantity and quality of the coke produced. The quality of the coal used, or contemplated to be used, being regarded as an unimportant factor in this consideration.

There is, doubtless, great economy in the use of proper ovens in coking coal, but under all this *the character of the coal* is the *prime factor in determining the quantity, quality and structure of the coke. And this is true whether the coal is coked in the most improved oven or in the primitive open air "pits" or mounds.*

The value of ovens is confined rigidly to the economy of labor in the process of coking, and in the saving of carbon.

Blast furnaces demand the fuel to be pure, compact, tenacious, of uniform quality, and as free from moisture as possible.

It is evident that the calorific power of coke is derived from its carbon, and hence the purest coke will produce the greatest heat. This requirement of pure dry coke is the more evident when it is considered that all foreign matter and moisture not only do not contribute heat but require the expenditure of it, in disposing of the extraneous matter in the slag and vaporizing the moisture.

It is manifest that as *the character of the coke* is determined *by the quality of the coal used,* the latter should receive very careful examination before expending largely in plant for coking.

The first requirement in the production of good coke is a pure semi-bituminous coal—coal having small quantities of slate, sulphur or phosphorus.

The second requirement is, that it contains a sufficient proportion of volatile or gaseous matter to supply the necessary heat in coking, without the expenditure of carbon.

And thirdly, that the coal produces a coke of sufficient tenacity to sustain, without crumbling, the burden and blast of the furnace, and to inherit *an open cellular structure, to facilitate its impregnation and solution by the carbonic acid gas in the furnace.*

Three belts of semi-bituminous coals have been thoroughly tested in the production of coke for blast furnaces—the Connellsville coke region in the west of the State, Bennington, on the crest of the Allegheny mountain, and the outlying coal field of Broad Top in the east.

The Connellsville coke region in Fayette county embraces a zone twenty-five miles long by two and a half to three miles wide, containing sixty to seventy-five square miles; lying west of Chestnut ridge, divided near its middle, crosswise by the Youghiogheny river, on which the growing town of Connellsville is located.

This belt is underlaid with the Pittsburg coal seam from six to ten feet thick. The coal has sometimes a bright calcitic appearance, but generally a columnar structure, is rather soft and friable, containing an excess of bituminous matter and yielding a fair percentage of excellent coke.

The middle or Bennington zone is developed on either side of the Pennsylvania railroad tunnel, through the summit of the Allegheny mountain, by the Cambria Iron Company, for the use of its furnaces at Bennington, Hollidaysburg and Frankstown.

The coal bed is nearly three feet thick; is soft and friable, producing as it comes from the mine a sonorous, cellular and tenacious coke of great purity and calorific vigor. The seam is the second or B bed, locally known as the Miller seam. How large the belt is producing this superior coking coal is not yet defined.

Adjoining the mines of the Cambria Iron Company, at this place, are the mines and coke yard of Messrs. Porter, Dennison & Co., also producing an excellent quality of coal and coke.

The eastern or Broad Top field of eighty square miles affords two seams, (B C,) known locally as the Barnet and Kelly, both very good for the production of a bright, open, tenacious and strong coke.

These furnish the three types of the best qualities of coking coals of the State. The analyses of these typical coals are given as a means of comparison and standards of qualities in coking coals.

	CONNELLSVILLE. Pittsburg seam.	BENNINGTON. Miller.	BROAD TOP.	
			Barnet.	Kelly.
	a.	*b.*	*b.*	*c.*
Fixed carbon	59.62	68.50	74.65	71.12
Ash	8.23	8.00	7.50	7.50
Volatile matter	31.36	22.38	16.00	19.68
Sulphur	.784	1.12	1.85	1.70
	100.	100.00	100.00	100.00
Coke	68 per cent.	76 per cent.	81 per ct.	78 per ct.

ANALYSES OF OTHER COALS FOR COMPARISON.

	PITTS'G SEAM. Irwin's mines.	ENGLISH COAL. Durham.	WELCH COAL.
	d.	*e.*	*f.*
Fixed Carbon........	61.45	83.27	80.50
Ash.................	5.80	1.52	6.50
Volatile matter......	31.71	8.21	12.10
Sulphur............	1.04	Not given.	0.90
	100.00	100.00	100.00
Coke...............	66 per cent.	84 per cent.	86 per cent.

DRY OR NON-CAKING COALS.

	Mahoning Valley Pa.	Brazil, Indiana.	Straitsville, Ohio.
	g.	*h.*	*i.*
Fixed carbon........	64.30	57.20	55.60
Ash.................	1.95	1.90	6.94
Volatile matter......	32.73	40.15	36.50
Sulphur............	1.02	0.75	0.96
	100.00	100.00	100.00
Coke...............	65 per cent.	58 per cent.	61 per cent.

Analyses as follows: *b. c.* T. T. Morrell. *b. d.* Booth & Garrett. *e.* Richardson. *g. h.* Prof. Cox. *i.* Prof. Wormley. *f.* Truran. *a.* A. S. M'Creath, chemical assistant, Second Geological Survey of Pennsylvania.

The property of caking or not caking in the soft coals does not appear to be clearly made out yet. It does not depend on the amount of volatile matter, for the non-caking coals possess this in the largest volume. Nor, as a general rule, does it appear that the coking property increases with the increase of the hydrogen and oxygen, but rather on the presence of different kinds of bitumen, or to the chemical constitution of the coal as respects the manner in which the gases are combined with the carbon. This combination producing hydro-carbon will account in part for the loss of carbon in coking, but not all.

Ordinary analyses fail to indicate the essential qualities of a good coking coal. They are highly useful, however, in exhibiting the carbon, ash and sulphur, thus clearly indicating the strength and purity of the coal.

The only sure method in the determination of the adaptibility of coal for coking, is to have a quantity of it made into coke, and a study of its physical and chemical properties carefully made.

Other conditions being satisfactory, coal can now be *cleansed from an excess of slate and sulphur by a process of crushing and washing.*

At the Cambria Iron and Steel Works at Johnstown, Bradford's cylinder breaker with the usual jigs are used.

The Kemble Iron and Coal Company, in the Broad Top region, use a modification of M. Bérard's coal washing apparatus with much success.

The Rockhill Iron and Coal Company, in East Broad Top, use Bradford's coal breaker, with the English sluice washer, recommended by I. Lowthian Bell, Esq., and report satisfactory results.

By this washing operation many coals can be made into good coke which otherwise would not prove satisfactory.

With coals adapted to coking the result can never be doubtful, whether the coke is made in open heaps, Beehive ovens or Belgian ovens.

The primitive mode of coking coal, in heaps or mounds, very naturally grew out of the method employed in making charcoal in conical mounds for furnace use.

The plans are essentially the same; but in the case of the coal it has been gradually improved, mainly in respect to uniformity of quality of coke and saving of carbon.

The coke yard is prepared by leveling a piece of ground and surfacing it with coal dust. The coal to be coked is then arranged in heaps or pits, with longitudinal, transverse and vertical flues; sufficient wood being distributed in these to ignite the whole mass.

Beginning on a base of 14 feet wide, coal is spread to a depth of 18 inches, A. On this base the flues are arranged and constructed as shown in the plan—the coal being piled up, as shown in section B. The flues are made of refuse coke and lump coal, and are covered with billets of wood. When the heap is ready for coking, fire is applied at the base of the vertical flues, C, C, igniting the kindling wood at each alternate flue.

As the process advances, the fire extends in every direction, until the whole mass is ablaze. Considerable attention is required in managing this mode of coking, in diffusing the fire evenly through the mass, in preventing the waste of coke by too much air at any place, and in banking up the heaps with fine dust as the operation progresses from base to top.

When the burning of the gaseous matter has ceased, the heap is carefully closed with dust or duff, and nearly smothered out in this way. The final operation is the application of a small quantity of water, down the vertical flues, which is quickly converted into steam, permeating the whole mass. This gives coke with the least percentage of moisture, if carefully applied.

The time necessary for coking a heap, with the Bennington coal, is from 5 to 8 days—depending mainly on the state of the weather.

It will be shown that coke made in this way is beyond any doubt excellent.

The yield of coke, accurately determined at Bennington and Hollidaysburg, is as follows:

BENNINGTON.

Coal used, - - - -	56.87 gross tons.
Coke drawn, - - - -	33.63 " "
Loss, - - - -	23.24 gross tons.

Yield of coke, 59.1 per cent; loss, 40.9 per cent; 1.67 tons of coal to 1 ton of coke.

HOLLIDAYSBURG.

Coal used, - - - -	63.80 gross tons.
Coke drawn, - - - -	38.02 " "
Loss, - - - -	25.78 gross tons.

Yield of coke, 59.00 per cent; loss, 41.00 per cent.

The yield at both places is substantially the same, 59.00 per cent, exhibiting a loss of 24.00 per cent of the carbon contained in the coal.

The *Beehive oven* is evidently well adapted for coking coal, and is a great advance in the production of a uniform quality of coke, volatilizing a maximum quantity of sulphur.

The coal is spread evenly over the floor of these ovens, to an average depth of two feet. The heat of the oven ignites the charge, and, as the coking progresses, the air is more and more excluded by bricking up the door and luting with clay; 48 to 72 hours are usually required to produce coke.

The 3,579 ovens of the Connellsville coke region are all on the beehive plan, receiving an average charge of 100 bushels of coal, dumped through the opening on the crown of the oven, and yielding, according to current tradition, 120 bushels of coke.

The yield in Connellsville region, adopting the above data, is as follows:

100 bushels of coal @ 76 lbs. per bushel, equals	3.39	gross tons.
120 bushels of coke @ 40 lbs. per bushel, equals	2.14	"
Loss - - - -	1.25	"

Yield of coke, 63 *per cent; loss*, 37 *per cent.* One and sixtenth tons of coal to one ton coke.

The coke is silvery, cellular and tenacious, possessing great calorific power and is comparatively free from impurities.

The Kemble Coal and Iron Company use beehive ovens to coke for their furnaces at Riddlesburg, in the Broad Top Coal Region.

The process is substantially the same as at Connellsville, and the coke produced very similar in all respects.

The yield is as follows:

Coal charged into oven, - - -	4.35	gross tons.
Coke taken out, - - - -	2.74	"
Loss equals - - - - -	1.61	"

Yield of coke, 63 per cent; loss, 37 per cent. 1.58 tons of coal to one ton of coke.

The loss of carbon at Connellsville and Broad Top is as follows:

Connellsville, - - - - -	9	per cent.
Broad Top, - - - - -	$22\frac{1}{2}$	"

BELGIAN OVEN.

The accompanying drawings will illustrate the improved Belgian oven, exhibiting its size, arrangement of tracks for supplying coal to ovens, and for the engine that pushes the coke out of the ovens. A number of ovens bearing different names, but operating essentially on the same general principles, and belonging to this type, are now in use, each pressing peculiar claims on public attention.

There appears to be, without any sufficient reason, a wide range given to the discussion of the merits of the several mem-

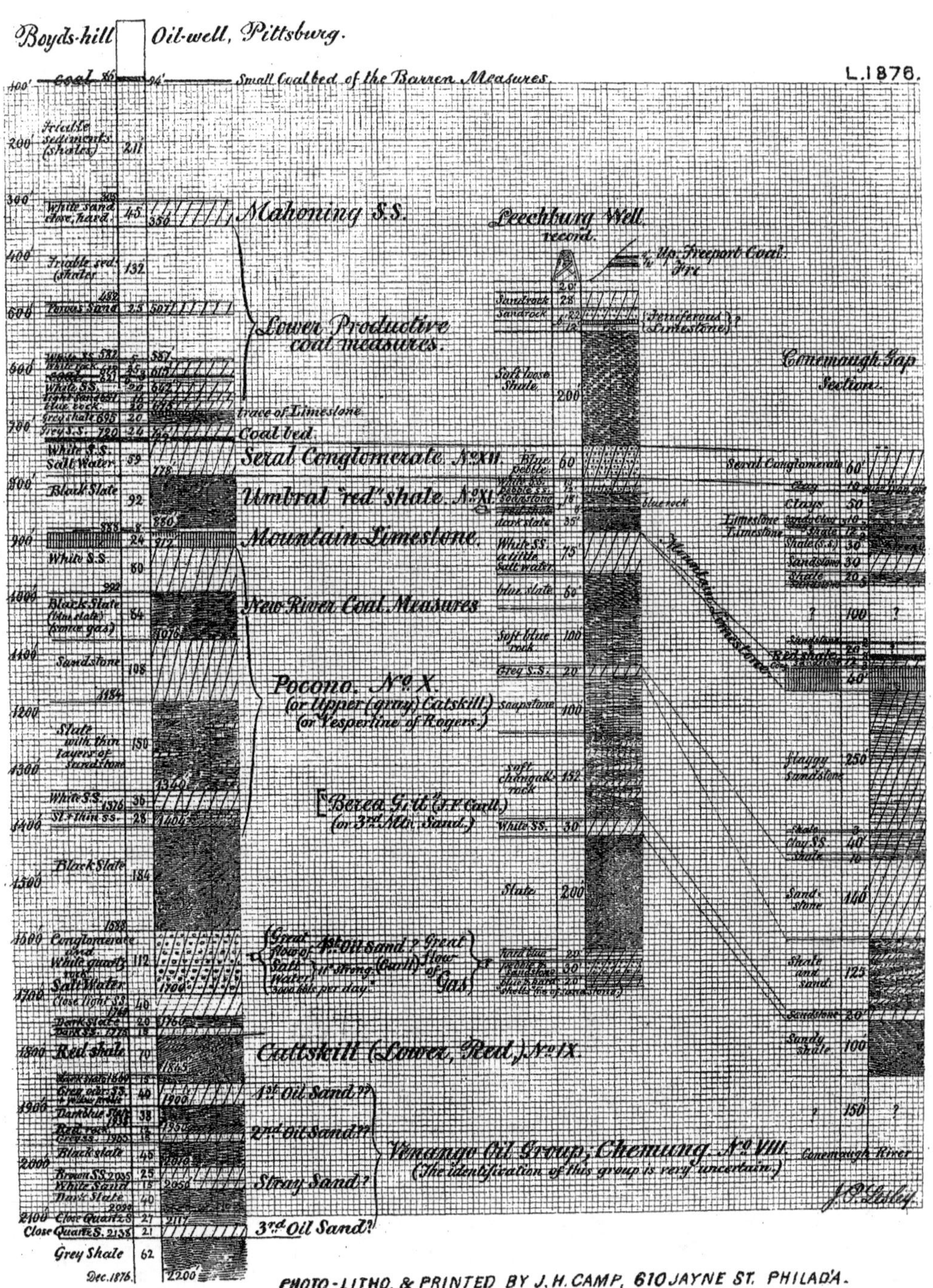

PHOTO-LITHO. & PRINTED BY J.H. CAMP, 610 JAYNE ST. PHILAD'A.

bers of the Belgian oven family. This is certainly "multiplying words without knowledge," for in every case the conclusive evidence consists *in the work done, the economy in doing it, and in the saving of the carbon of the coal.*

The result of coking at Hollidaysburg in Belgian ovens, with Bennington coal, is as follows:

Coal used,	6.86	gross tons.
Coke made,	4.81	"
Loss,	2.05	"

Yield of coke, 70 per cent; loss, 30 per cent. 1.42 tons of coal to one ton coke.

As the coal used contained 68 per cent of carbon and 8 per cent of ash, and the coke produced, 70 per cent of the coal used, the loss is 10 per cent of carbon in the operation.

The make, by the great bank of Belgian ovens, at the Cambria Iron and Steel Works, at Johnstown, under the care of Mr. W. Grist, corroborates this, yielding 70.3 per cent of coke from a rather dry coal holding 73 per cent of fixed carbon and 6 per cent of ash, indicating a loss of 13 per cent of carbon, which is somewhat more than the loss at Hollidaysburg.

The percentage of coke produced, and the loss of carbon by these three typical methods are as follows:

Bennington and Hollidaysburg pits, 59 per cent coke, 24 per cent loss carbon.

Beehive ovens, Connellsville, 63 per cent coke, 9 per cent loss carbon.

Beehive ovens, Broad Top, 63 per cent coke, 22½ per cent loss carbon.

Belgian ovens, Hollidaysburg, 70 per cent coke, 10 per cent loss carbon.

Belgian ovens, Johnstown, 70.3 per cent coke, 13 per cent loss carbon.

It is a remarkable fact that the waste or loss of carbon indicates not only the economy in the three methods of coking, but also the character of the coals as regards their gaseous or dry properties.

In further considering the relative economy of these typical modes of coking, the value of a gross ton of coal will be taken at $1 00 at the ovens.

I. Pits or Mounds.

Hollidaysburg and Bennington, 1.67 tons, @ $1, equals	$1 67
Hollidaysburg and Bennington, labor, wood, &c., -	70
Total, one gross ton of coke, - -	2 37

II. Beehive Ovens.

Connellsville, 1.60 tons, @ $1, - -	$1 60
Labor, charging and drawing, - -	61
Total cost, one gross ton coke, - -	2 21

Broad Top, Kemble Coal and Iron Company.

Coal, 1.58 tons, @ $1, - - -	$1 58
Coking, &c., - - - -	60
Total, - - - -	2 18

III. Belgian Ovens—Cambria Iron Company.

Hollidaysburg, Bennington coal—coal used to one ton coke, 1.42 tons, @ $1, - - -	$1 42
Labor, supplies, &c., - - -	45
Total cost of one ton coke, - - -	1 87
Johnstown, Miller coal, B—coal used to one ton coke, 1.42 tons, @ $1 - - -	$1 42
Labor, supplies, &c., - - -	45
Total, - - - -	1 87

The cost of the coal and labor of coking one gross ton of coke, by the three methods just considered, is as below:

I. Pits or mounds - - -	$2 37
II. Beehive ovens - - -	2 20
III. Belgian ovens - - -	1 87

Exhibiting an increasing cost from the Belgian ovens to the open pits or mounds. But in the first comparison of costs no place has been given to the interest on the investment in preparing the several modes for coking, which is quite an important factor.

Estimated cost of *plant* for the production of 100 tons of coke per day:

I. Pits or Mounds.

Leveling coke yard, fixtures, &c., - -	$1,000 00
Interest on investment, at ten per cent. per year,	100 00
Then, $\frac{\$100}{30,000 \text{ tons}} = \frac{1}{3}$ ct. per ton per year, -	$00\frac{1}{3}$
Cost of coal and labor of coking, - -	2 37
Total cost, - - - -	$2\ 37\frac{1}{3}$

II. Beehive Ovens.

Eighty ovens, (@ $400, - -	$32,000 00
Interest on investment, 10 per cent. per annum,	3,200 00
Annual repairs and renewals, $10 per oven,	800 00
Then $\frac{\$4,000}{30,000 \text{ tons}} = 13\frac{1}{3}$ cents, - -	$13\frac{1}{3}$
Cost of coal and labor of coking, -	2 20
Total cost, - - -	$2\ 33\frac{1}{3}$

III. Belgian Ovens.

Sixty-five ovens, @ $800, - - -	$52,000 00
Annual repairs to each oven, $15, - -	310 00
Engine for pushing coke, - - -	3,000 00
Annual repairs to engine, - - -	50 00
Tracks for engines, - - -	300 00
Interest on investment, $55,3000, @ 10 per cent.,	5,530 00
Then, $\$5,530+\$310+\$50=\frac{\$5,890}{30,000 \text{ tons}}=19\frac{1}{2}$ cents per ton nearly - - - - - -	$19\frac{1}{2}$
Cost of coal and labor of coking, - -	1 87
Total cost, - - - - -	$2\ 06\frac{1}{2}$

The tracks and cars necessary to supply coal to pits and ovens have not been estimated in the foregoing calculation, as it is presumed these several costs would be about equal, adding to each class one-fourth cent per ton for this source of expense.

The ultimate cost then of one gross ton of coke produced by these three methods is as follows:

Mounds or pits, - - - - -	$\$2\ 37\frac{3}{5}$
Beehive ovens, - - - - -	$2\ 33\frac{3}{5}$
Belgian ovens, - - - - -	$2\ 06\frac{3}{4}$

The following table exhibits the physical properties of the cokes made in the State, from the best coking coals, by the three methods of coking most generally in use:

TABLE *exhibiting the physical properties of coke for furnace use, produced from the typical coking coals of Pennsylvania, by three methods now in use.*

LOCALITY WHERE MADE.	Method of coking.	Grammes in one cubic inch.		Pounds in one cubic foot.		Per cent. of coke	Per cent. of cells	Compressive strength per cubic inch in pounds, (¼ ultimate strength,)	Height of furnace charge, which can be supported without crushing	Order of magnitude of cells in coke
		Dry	Wet	Dry	Wet					
Cambria Iron Company:									Feet.	
Bennington	Open pits	13.36	19.74	50.90	75.20	67.68	32.32	281	112	I.
Broad Top:										
Broad Top	Open pits	12.00	19.59	45.72	74.53	61.25	38.75	220	88	I.
Connellsville:										
Seventy-two hour coke	Beehive ovens	12.46	20.25	47.47	77.15	61.53	38.47	284	114	I.
Forty-eight hour coke	Beehive ovens	14.02	20.95	53.41	79.81	62.92	33.08	249	100	I.
Kemble Coal and Iron Company:										
Broad Top	Beehive ovens	11.76	20.18	44.81	76.88	58.27	41.73	240	96	I.
Cambria Iron Company:										
Hollidaysburg—Top of oven	.....	13.19	20.80	50.25	79.25	63.41	36.59	.....	.....	.....
Middle of oven	.....	14.22	20.61	54.18	78.52	69.00	31.00	.....	.....	.....
Bottom of oven	.....	16.92	22.87	64.46	86.13	73.98	26.02	.....	.....	.....
Average	Belgian ovens,	14.77	21.42	56.29	81.30	68.80	31.20	259	104	I.

Cambria Iron Company: Johnstown—24 hour coke.										
Top of oven	....	8.42	17.95	32.08	68.39	46.91	53.09	....	....	.....
Middle of oven	....	12.96	21.00	49.38	80.00	61.71	38.29	....	....	.....
Bottom of oven	....	13.12	21.22	50.00	80.85	61.78	38.22	....	....	.....
Average	Belgian ovens,	11.50	20.06	43.82	76.41	56.80	43.20	245	99	III.
Gap Furnace, near Hollidaysburg:										
Top of oven	....	13.22	20.72	50.37	78.93	63.80	36.20	....	....	.....
Middle of oven	....	13.54	20.67	51.60	78.76	65.50	34.50	....	....	.....
Bottom of oven	....	16.92	24.17	64.46	92.09	70.42	29.58	....	....	.....
Average	Belgian ovens,	14.56	21.85	55.47	83.26	66.57	33.43	248	100	I.
Rockhill Coal & Iron Company;										
Washed coal—Top of pit	....	10.11	17.89	38.52	68.16	56.51	43.49	....	....	.....
Middle of pit	....	11.66	20.22	44.42	77.04	57.66	42.34	....	....	.....
Bottom of pit	....	11.79	19.05	44.92	72.59	61.89	38.11	....	....	.....
Average	Open pits	11.18	19.05	42.59	72.58	58.69	41.31	200	80	II.

This table is designed to illustrate the desirable physical properties of coke exhibiting its capacity to sustain furnace burdens.

The cellular space was obtained by immersing an accurately cut inch cube of coke in a glass of distilled water under the receiver of an air pump, exhausting the air and weighing the cube dry and wet—the difference indicating the cellular space—as the specific gravities of coke and water are very nearly alike.

The best cokes have the cell space to the whole mass, as 33 to 67, or as 1 to 2 nearly. But this proportion can differ widely in cokes, giving equally good results in furnace use; 38 to 62 is obtained from a coke of first class order in strength and purity.

Other conditions being equal, *the size of the coke cells is important*, in giving a first quality of furnace fuel, especially in facilitating its combustion by freely receiving carbonic acid gas, formed lower down in the furnace, thus accelerating its solution and yielding abundant carbonic oxide for the deoxidation of the iron ore.

A very dense coke, with diminutive cells, or rather pores, is always undesirable in furnace operations, as it resists solution with an obstinacy that is truly surprising.

A piece of such coke was handed to me which had passed down and out of a fifty feet furnace, apparently little wasted by its fiery journey. In this connection it may be claimed that anthracite coal is much more dense than coke of any grade, and as the former can be used in the blast furnace, why not the latter?

To this it may be replied, that the operations of these fuels in combustion in a furnace are widely different—the anthracite coal decrepitating, and thus becoming divided into quite small pieces, affording enlarged surface space for solution, whilst, on the other hand, coke is not split into pieces as it approaches the hot zone, and its free combustion is attained only from its large cell structure.

Evidently Mr. I. Lowthian Bell experienced this when he wrote, "My firm has tried these plans," (Belgian ovens,) "but found the useful effect in the furnaces inferior to that obtained from coke made in the ordinary oven," (Beehive.) "In consequence of this, all the more recently erected ovens have been constructed upon the old fashion." *

* I. L. Bell, on iron smelting, page 315.

The table shows that coke made in shallow charges in the beehive ovens is less dense than the coke made in Belgian ovens in deep charges—the bottom section of the charge, in the latter case, showing a very decided increase in density.

When coke of a dense porous structure is produced in large "*chunks*" it is least desirable for furnace use, but its energy and efficiency can be much improved by breaking it in a Blake's crusher or by breaking the larger pieces. This treatment will be more manifest in furnaces under fifty feet in height than in those above this height.

Where coal has a tendency to enter a condition of semi-fusion in coking, agglomerating it usually forms a very decided cellular coke, coked by any of the methods now in use. But, where the coal has a tendency to dryness, and a consequent dense porous structure, it is important that it be coked in thin charges, and rapidly to obtain the best physical condition possible with such coal.

There appear yet to be some defects even in the best methods of coking, or rather a want of adaptability of the methods to the several qualities of coal used.

a. The tendency is noted of some coals to produce a dense, leaden colored coke, with fine pores, increasing in closeness of structure when coked in deep charges in Belgian Ovens, from top to bottom. Such coal should be coked in shallow charges to produce the best possible results. Under such a condition the Beehive Oven would perhaps be the best.

b. The depth of charges, in each of the three methods under consideration, is in many respects objectionable, as it renders the volatilization of the sulphur from the middle and bottom sections more difficult, the amount of which retained is in direct proportion to the depth.

Just here it may be proper to note that in both the Beehive and Belgian ovens the depth of the charge of coal is proportioned to the time determined for coking.

In the Belgian Ovens at Hollidaysburg, using the Bennington coal, the weight and depth of charges have been accurately observed by Mr. W. R. Babcock, Superintendent of Blair Iron and Coal Company, as illustrated in the following sketch:

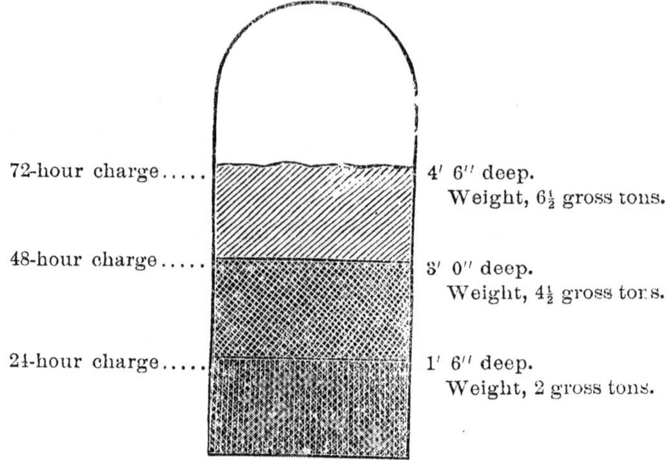

Section of Belgian Oven, showing the depth of charges for 24, 48 and 72-hour coke.

It is manifest that the shallow charges have produced the best and purest coke, but the economy of coking is on the side of the deeper charges.

c. From the bottom bench of the charge being coked under pressure, forming a denser structure, it requires a greater amount of heat in coking just at a place in the oven the most difficult to reach. Mr. J. King M'Lanahan, of Hollidaysburg, who has given these ovens a careful study, suggests that this might be obviated by alternating the charging of the ovens, utilizing the surplus gases disengaged in the early part of the operation for supplying the deficient heat in the floors of the adjoining ovens. This would meet the requirement of thorough coking, but does not remove the objections, in the case of some coals, of a close structure in coke and in obstructing the volatilization of the sulphur.

From the foregoing determinations it follows that two results in coking are *absolute requirements* in order to produce the best possible fuel for furnace use: First, *an open cellular structure, with cells as large as possible by the coal used.* As the tenacity of all the cokes ex-

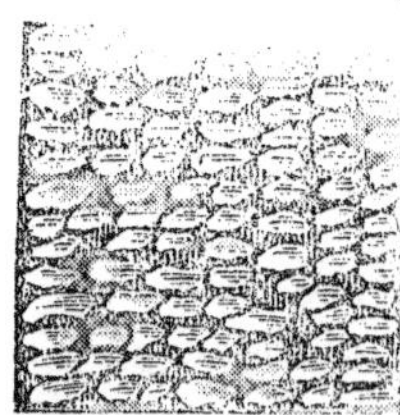

Section of "open" coke, *desirable structure.*

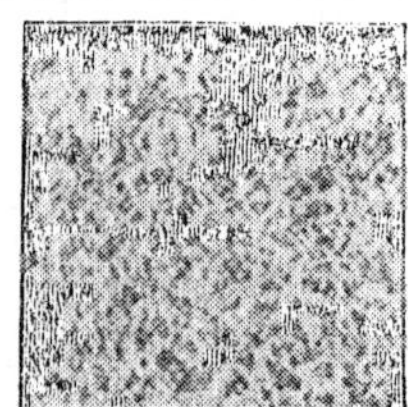

Section of "dense" coke, *undesirable structure.*

amined is greatly above the requirements of the highest furnace now in use, no fears need be entertained in this respect; and, second, *the volatilization of all the sulphur possible in the operation of coking.*

The following table exhibits analyses of the fuels under consideration, indicating also the percentage of sulphur volatilized in coking:

ANALYSES OF TYPICAL FUELS FOR FURNACE USE.

Anthracite Coal, Coke and Dry Bituminous Coal.

NAME OF FUEL AND LOCALITY.	Fixed carbon......	Volatile matter ...	Ash...............	Sulphur............	Phosphorus........	Moisture	Sulphur volatiliz'd in coking—per ct.
Anthracite, best........	89.06	3.45	5.81	0.30	0.024	1.35	......
Anthracite, average....	82.50	5.50	10.50	0.35	0.012	1.15	......
Connellsville coke.....	87.46	....	11.32	0.69	0.029	0.49	......
Connellsville coke.....	87.26	....	11.99	0.746	....	......	40
Bennington............	86.29	....	12.80	0.91	....	......	52
Hollidaysburg.........	87.58	....	11.36	1.06	....	......	34
Broad Top, K. C. & I. Co.	89.28	....	9.66	1.06	....	......	56
Mercer Co. block coal..	68.03	25.49	1.70	1.04	....	3.80	......

Some careful chemical investigation is very much desired to unfold the several conditions in which sulphur is found in coal, and the ratio of each which can be volatilized in the operation of coking.

The greatest volume of the sulphur in coal undoubtedly exists as bi-sulphide of iron, ($Fe\ S_2$). In coking, one equivalent of sulphur is volatilized, leaving the mono-sulphide, ($Fe\ S$) in the coke.

If sulphur is present in the coal united with lime, as sulphide of calcium, it will be volatilized readily; but if it takes the form of the sulphate of lime, (gypsum,) it cannot be driven off in a coke oven.

The results of volatilization by coking given in the foregoing table must be used with caution, because the coking has been performed under various conditions. It indicates, however, that the same quality of coal, coked in mounds at Bennington, parted with fifty-two per cent of its sulphur, but when coked in Belgian ovens, at Hollidaysburg, only thirty-four per cent was driven off.

The work of the beehive ovens shows that the Connellsville coal parts with five per cent of its sulphur, whilst the Broad Top surrenders in coking fifty-six per cent of its sulphur.

These results are submitted more to indicate the wants in future investigations, than to assume any definite work in this department of inquiry.

As the physical structure of coke, and its purity, are the two prime elements which constitute its value as a furnace fuel, it is evident that coke ovens should be planned to satisfy these essential requirements.

It is believed that both these results can be obtained, so far as the qualities of each class of coal will permit, *by shallow charges in the coke oven.*

In view of all the facts collected on the coking of coal for furnace use, and feeling satisfied that perhaps a combination of existing plans could be devised in which the several qualities of coals could be coked with the best results, and, at the same time, with the greatest economy consistent with the production of the best possible quality of coke, I have asked Mr. J. King M'Lanahan to devise such a plan, which is herewith submitted :

This plan unites the good qualities of the Beehive and Belgian Ovens.

1. The charge is made wide and shallow, as in the Beehive, and in the best condition to produce an open cellular coke, also affording the best facilities for the volatilization of the sulphur in the coal.

2. The arrangement of the flues under the oven is such as to utilize the gases, diffuse the heat equally, producing a uniform quality of coke.

3. The shallow charges require only thirty hours for coking.

The coke is to be pushed out *en masse* by an apparatus similar to those used in Belgian Ovens, retaining this element of economy in producing coke.

The method of charging through openings in the crown of the oven is used in this plan as in the other ovens.

It will thus be seen, that with the application of the true

means for producing the best quality of coke, the utmost economy in the operations is preserved.

The oven is 24 feet long, 8 feet wide and $2\frac{1}{2}$ feet deep, receiving a charge of coal 2 feet deep, weighing 9 gross tons and yielding 6.3 gross tons of coke.

A day's work of each class of oven is as follows:

Beehive, - - - - - -	1.25 gross tons.
Belgian, - - - - - -	1.55 "
Composite, - - - - - -	5.04 "

The cost of this improved oven is estimated by Mr. M'Lanahan at $1,000.

Taking this as it is estimated, the cost of producing coke in this oven, including interest on invested capital, is as follows:

1.42 tons of coal, at $1, - - - - - -	$1 42
Labor, supplies, &c, - - - - - - -	40
	1 82

Investment for 100 tons of coke per day:

20 ovens, at $1,000, - - - - - -	$20,000 00
Annual repairs of each oven, $20, - -	400 00
Engine for pushing coke, - - - - -	3,000 00
Annual repairs to engine, - - - -	50 00
Tracks for engine, - - - - - -	600 00
Interest on investment, $23,600, at 10 per cent,	2,360 00

Then, $\$2,360+\$400+\$50=\frac{\$2810}{30000}$ tons$=.09^3$ cents per ton.

Ultimate cost:

Coking, - - - - - - - - - -	$1 82
Interest on above, - - - - - - -	09^3
Total, - - - - - - - -	$1\ 91^3$

Comparing the several methods, the cost per ton of coking is as follows:

Pits or mounds, - - - - - - -	$\$2\ 37\frac{3}{5}$
Beehive ovens, - - - - - - -	$2\ 33\frac{3}{5}$
Belgian ovens, - - - - - - - -	$2\ 06\frac{3}{4}$
Composite ovens, - - - - - -	$1\ 91^3$

A closing consideration in the production of coke claims earnest attention—the means of quenching it in the three methods of its manufacture. The amount of water retained in cokes varies from $\frac{1}{2}$ of 1 per cent to 12 per cent or more, depending on the conditions in which it is quenched.

As has been stated, in the means employed in the pits or mounds, in smothering the coke out with fine dust, only using a very small quantity of water as the last act of the operation, thus giving a very dry coke; with care, certainly a minimum. This is a *very decided advantage in pit coking*, which will be considered hereafter, especially when done near the furnace, giving from the pit a dry fuel.

The coke made in Beehive Ovens is quenched by discharging water into the oven by a hose. The water is quickly converted into steam, which permeates the whole mass of coke, resulting in doing the work with the smallest volume of water and vapor, giving a very dry coke.

The Belgian Oven class is open to serious objection in regard to the manner in which the coke is quenched.

The pushing engine discharges the contents of the oven of red hot coke in a mound 20 feet long, 2 to 3 feet wide and 3 to 4 feet high. A hose is turned on this incandescent mass until it is soaked, pools of water are made on the platform, the vapor escapes, and the coke is charged with moisture from 2 to 12 per cent. It is possible to reduce the average of moisture by a more careful application of the water, but the whole plan of doing this part of the work is essentially clumsy.

As a rule in all methods of quenching coke, the finer the pores or cells of the coke the more moisture it will retain.

This matter is now under consideration. Several suggestions have been submitted for overcoming this wetting of the coke. The most feasible of these is a design in which the charge of coke is to be pushed into an iron receiver, resting on a carriage running in front of the ovens like a transfer table. Water and steam, mixed with carbonic acid gas, to be carefully used in quenching the coke. By this means it is hoped to attain results equally satisfactory with the Beehives or open pits. A single apparatus of this kind is intended to receive all the coke from a large bank of ovens, plying on a rail track in front of them. Wet coke invariably cools the furnace and is in every aspect objectionable.

As a uniformity in the quality of coke as a furnace fuel is an imperative necessity to insure its regular working, so the dryness of the coke is demanded for the same reason. Neither furnacemen or cokers have given this matter the attention its importance demands, for it is an important factor in the harmony and economy of the working of the furnace.

I. The Efficiency and Economy of Coke, as Compared with Anthracite Coal, in the Metallurgy of Iron.

Practically, the true value of furnace fuels, as regards their efficiency and economy, is determined by the quantity of each class required to smelt one ton of pig iron.

In this determination, however, there are many factors, each requiring careful consideration, else the result is practically valueless. The size of the furnace, its blast heat and pressure, the qualities of the iron ores used, with the quantity and character of flux and the resultant quality of pig iron.

That there is a well defined measure of the quantity of coke required to smelt one ton of pig-iron, has been clearly demonstrated by Mr. I. Lowthian Bell, in his valuable work on the Chemical Phenomena of Iron Smelting. On page 388 of this work he sums up the conclusion from an elaborate investigation of the whole matter: "Regarded in this way, I would give it as my own opinion, that taking the ordinary run of Durham coke and Cleveland iron-stone, the iron-master who produces a ton of No. 3 iron, with 21½ cwts., (2,408 ℔s.=1.075 gross tons,) with the blast heated to 500°C. (932°F.) may consider himself as working very closely up to those limits of economy, which are prescribed by the nature of the materials he is operating upon."

Taking this 1.075 gross tons of coke to smelt one ton of pig-iron, using Cleveland iron-stone, giving 41 per cent of irôn, as a standard of comparison, the relative values of other cokes will be made manifest.

The Bennington Furnace, of the Cambria Iron Company, 10′× 40′, blast, 2½ to 3 ℔s.—heat, 600°F.—running on a mixture of Lake Superior and native hematite ores, averaging 56 per cent of metallic iron, producing an excellent quality of Bessemer pig iron—using an annual average of 1.3 *tons of pit coke to* 1 *ton of pig iron.* With an increase of the temperature of the blast to

900° F., and an increase of its pressure, it is probable that the consumption of coke would be reduced to the standard indicated above—(1.075 tons).

The results, however, in a furnace of this moderate size, are very excellent, indicating the energy and efficiency of the coke used.

Pittsburg Furnaces.—Two works have been quite prominent during the past year for their very extraordinary yields of pig iron—the Isabella and Lucy works at Pittsburg. They seem to be competing for the largest yield of a single furnace on this Continent, if not in the world.

The size of the furnaces is as follows:

	Lucy Furnace.	Isabella Furnace.
Height of stack, - -	75 feet.	75 feet.
Width of bosh, - - -	20 feet.	20 feet.
Pressure of blast, - -	4 to 8 lbs.	4 to 8lbs.
Temperature of blast,	750° to 1,000° F.	800° to 1,000° F.
Lake Superior ore, -	62 per cent.	62 per cent.
Pig iron made for week ending Oct. 16, 1875,	$762\frac{1024}{2268}$ tons of Gray forge and No. 1, foundry iron.	Same time, $714\frac{1240}{2268}$ tons, one-third foundry and balance mill iron.

Since writing the above, the Isabella furnace has exceeded all its previous productions, as described in the *Engineer and Mining Journal* of December 4, 1875:

"*The Largest Make of Pig Iron on Record.*

"There is that Pittsburg Isabella Furnace, No. 2, 75×20, that has gone and increased its make of pig iron again, this time to $770\ \frac{660}{2240}$ tons a week (133 tons foundry, 601 tons gray forge, and 36 tons mottled). There seems to be no end to this thing, and it is getting as monotonous as an iron market report. Can't Mr. Crowther give us the 'law of increase,' whether it is in an arithmetrical or geometrical progression, and by putting it in the form of a simple formula in which the product is a function of the time, we could calculate just when Isabella, No. 2, will be making 800, 900 or 1,000 tons a week. This noting in every second number 'the largest make on record,' is getting tiresome."

In these efforts, doubtless the quantity of coke used is quite large—greatly above the standard—how much is not publicly known. The results are evidently attained by forcing the air at high pressure and in large volume with the swift calorific energy of Connellsville coke.

In ordinary work the Lucy furnace is reported to use, "with strictly first class coke, from 3,300 to 3,350 pounds per ton of iron made. This includes an allowance of 5 per cent for waste in handling." This gives 1.47 to 1.49 tons of coke to 1 ton of pig. The coke is made from washed Pittsburg coal.

The Isabella is reported as using, when making foundry iron, 1.16 tons coke, and running on mill iron, 1.07 tons. The coke is partly made from washed Pittsburg coal and partly from the large and excellent coke works of the Pittsburg and Connellsville Gas Coal and Coke Company, of which John F. Dravo, Esq., of Pittsburg, is general manager.

Shoenberger, Blair & Co., in a furnace 13×62 feet, with blast of 3 to 5 pounds, and temperature 800° to 850° F.—ores 57 per cent. Coke from Pittsburg coal, washed, use 65 to 70 bushels, or 1.16 to 1.25 tons to 1 ton of pig metal.

Dunbar furnace—in the Connellsville Coke Region—16½×58 feet; blast, 5½ pounds; temperature, 750° F.; running on native carbonates, stiffened with a mixture of Lake Superior ore, is using 1.58 tons of a roughly made coke to 1 ton of excellent pig iron.

Neshannock Iron Company, New Castle, Pa.—Furnace, 15×60 feet; pressure of blast, 3 to 3½ pounds; temperature, 800° F.; make 300 tons a week from Lake Superior ore. Coke, 1.33 tons for foundry iron and 1.50 tons to 1 ton of Bessemer pig.

Kemble Coal and Iron Co., Broad Top.—Furnace, 16×65 feet; blast pressure, 5½ pounds; heat, 800° F.; ores, 30 to 35 per cent; 1.9 tons of coke to 1 ton of excellent pig iron.

Equating the work of this furnace in reducing these lean ores, with the consequent increase of flux, would give 1.18 tons of coke to 1 ton of pig iron.

Cambria Iron and Steel Co., Johnstown.—Belgian Oven coke. Furnace, 15×70; blast, 4½ pounds; heat, 700° F.; running on native carbonate calcined iron ore, use 1.35 tons of coke to 1 ton pig iron.

It will thus be evident that the quantity of coke to make 1 ton of pig iron ranges from 1.16 to 1.50 tons, with ores and other conditions nearly alike. When these have been exceeded, as in furnaces running on lean ores, the reason is obvious. That with care in furnace work and the use of good coke, there can be no question that the standard of 1.075 tons to 1 ton of pig, from 50 per cent ores, can be readily attained, but, in a State measuring her coal beds by thousands of *square miles*, it is difficult to induce the study or application of economy in the use of this fuel in blast furnaces.

ANTHRACITE COAL.

In No. 26 of the *Engineering and Mining Journal*, of June 27, 1874, a very exhaustive table is given of the work of furnaces running on anthracite coal. This table embraces the years from 1855 to 1873, inclusive. The average of coal given to 1 ton of pig from 1869 to 1873 is $1\frac{2191}{2240}$ tons. The ore averaged 44 per cent. The heat of blast is given at 900° F., which is up to modern practice; pressure of blast not given, but presumably it kept up with the increased temperature.

Mr. Bell, in the notes of his recent visit, noticing a portion of the anthracite furnaces, remarks: "Of course the chief subject for consideration is the question of fuel consumption, and here I am bound to say, as a rule, the Lehigh masters are perhaps a little behind the age. In furnaces 55 feet high, with boshes of 17 to 18 feet, the anthracite used in smelting an ore yielding 50 per cent, with 12 cwt. of limestone, was about 35 cwts. (=1.75 gross tons.) A portion of this waste I conceive to be due to a want of sufficient heat in their blast, which, however, by the pyrometers, always in use, indicated fully 1,000° F. That it really fell short of this, generally speaking, was proved by its inability to melt zinc, which fuses at a couple of hundred degrees below this temperature. The more important cause, however, must be ascribed to the insufficient height of the furnaces, but in this matter no one can feel surprised that the iron smelters, whose fuel is anthracite, should have hesitated before following the example of some English iron-masters.

"The latter have the advantage of using a compact and hard fuel, which comes down in large pieces to the hearth, while anthracite is apt to splinter with the heat and requires, it is said, even in a furnace of moderate height, a pillar of blast equal to from 7 to 9 or 10 pounds to overcome the resistance. One or two manufacturers, however, have been bold enough to venture on the erection of furnaces of 72 feet high, and their experience has proved eminently successful, for the fuel has been thereby reduced to something like 25 cwts. per ton of iron, (=1.25 tons.) I do not say that with a little higher temperature in the blast, and an additional height of furnace, even this is not capable of a little reduction; at the same time, looking at the usual quality of their coal, I am not sure whether this must not be regarded as a very satisfactory result."

Evidently one of the high furnaces referred to in the foregoing notice is at the Glendon Iron Works, Easton, Pa. Mr. Frank Firmstone reports of the furnace as follows:

Size of furnace, 18×72 feet; pressure of blast, 6 to 6½ pounds; ore yields 50 per cent; anthracite 1.29 gross tons. Make per week 289 tons—a very excellent exhibit of anthracite furnace work.

Bethlehem Iron and Steel Works.

Furnace No. 1, 15′×65′, blast, 4½ lbs., anthracite coal, 1.72 tons to 1 ton Bessemer pig.

Furnace No. 2, 15′×45′, blast 4½ lbs., 1.84 tons anthracite coal to 1 ton mill pig iron.

Furnace No. 3, 14′×50′, blast 6 lbs., 2.00 tons of coal to 1 ton Gray foundry pig.

Northampton.—16′×65′, 1.73 tons of anthracite coal to 1 ton Bessemer; blast, 7 lbs.

Harrisburg.—Lochiel furnace, 14′×50′, 2 tons anthracite to 1 ton No. 2 mill pig iron, blast 4 lbs., make 18 tons per day.

By using one-half coke the fuel has been reduced to 1.75 tons to 1 ton pig iron.

The above statements have been verified by several furnaces at Harrisburg.

The testimony of furnace men in relation to the use of coke as a mixture with anthracite coal is harmonious. One-third to one-half of coke not only produces an economy of fuel per ton of pig iron, but also improves the working of the furnaces in every way.

It is very evident that the *low* sizes of anthracite furnaces would be greatly benefited by the use of coke, from its swift combustion and its energy in assisting the slow acting anthracite coal, besides giving a better draft to the blast in retaining its shape without splintering.

If the best results in the economy of fuel is taken from the foregoing statistics of the working of these furnaces running on ores of equal grade, with size, blast and temperature nearly the same, it will be seen that Isabella, in ordinary work, uses 1.07 tons of coke to 1 ton of pig metal, whilst Glendon anthracite furnace uses 1.29 tons of coal to 1 ton of pig iron, exhibiting an excess of fuel in the anthracite coal over the coke of 17 per cent, and indicating from this data, the ratio of consumption of coke to anthracite coal in furnace operations as 1:1.17, or in round numbers, 1½ tons of coke are equal to 1¾ tons of anthracite coal. This, however, does not fully indicate the economy of the coke, for it is evident that quite a saving must be induced in the work of men, and salaries of officers, cost of maintaining machinery,&c., in a furnace yielding, *in ordinary work, double the quantity of pig iron produced in anthracite furnaces.*

These results indicate practically the relative conditions of the work of the best coke and anthracite furnaces at the present time. Comparing all these results, it is manifest that the open cellular structure of the coke facilitates its rapid digestion in the furnace, whilst the anthracite coal is slow in combustion and operation. Whether these relationships of consumption of fuel and energy of work can be equated by subsequent additions or modifications of furnaces, it is a question for the future. It is evident that many of the coke furnaces have attained the standard of economy of fuel prescribed by the chemical conditions of the materials used. Whether an addition to the altitude of the high anthracite furnace stacks would produce increased economy of fuel, has also to be determined.

Probably the physical character of these fuels will, under all conditions of dimensions of furnaces, preserve about their present relationship.

In the smaller furnaces, 50 feet high and under, it appears that coke can be used with decided economy—probably requiring time from furnacemen to learn the method of its most economical application.

BLOCK COAL OF MERCER COUNTY.

The Briar Hill or Block Coal of the north-western corner of the State is used in the furnaces as it comes out of the mines. The Sharon furnaces, 50 feet high, consume about $2\frac{1}{4}$ to $2\frac{1}{2}$ tons of this coal to 1 ton of pig iron, from 66 per cent Lake Superior ores. Pressure of blast, 7 pounds. In most of these furnaces, however, coke is used varying in proportion from $\frac{1}{6}$ to $\frac{1}{4}$, $\frac{1}{2}$ and $\frac{3}{4}$, the increased quantities being used in closed top furnaces. This requirement of a portion of coke appears to be a general law in the use of block coal. Mr. E. C. Garlick, of Brazil, Indiana, writes in regard to the use of the celebrated block coal of his State: "It works as well raw as any bituminous coal, but in furnaces of the size of ours, 62×15 feet, *it is desirable to use a small quantity of coke to keep the furnace open and enable it to take the blast with greater freedom.*" The coke used at this place, a sample of which was kindly forwarded me, is made from the block coal in Beehive Ovens—it is really a *charred coal*, as the structure of the coal is unchanged, the laminæ preserving their plane lines very distinctly.

On the whole it appears to be an excellent furnace fuel. The only practical question which it suggests is, whether it would not be more economical to coke all the coal for furnace use. So far, in practice, the fact has been shown that it requires 2 tons of this quality of coal to do the work of 1 ton of coke. And not only is the draft of a furnace improved by using a portion of coke, but *"it insures regularity in the working of the furnace, and we also derive benefit from its use in the faster driving of the furnace, thus saving in the cost of labor to the ton of iron."* The purity of the block coal and the metal made by it are unexceptionable.

The Hocking Valley coal of Ohio is also used in the furnace raw, under nearly the same conditions as the Indiana block coal, only that in the former case the thickness of the coal is greater

The seam on Sunday creek is fully 13 feet thick, of excellent quality, and can be used in the furnace as it comes from the mine, and from the great thickness of the seam, a great degree of economy induced in its production.

Zanesville furnace, 16′×65′, blast $3\frac{1}{2}$ lbs., temperature of blast 750°F., makes 35 tons per day of No. 1 forge pig iron from a mixture of 1 ton native carbonate calcined ore, 1,120 lbs. Lake Superior specular ore, and 746 lbs. mill cinder, consuming to 1 ton pig, 1.14 tons of Hocking Valley coal and 0.63 tons of coke, which indicate very good results.

In closing it would be instructive to compare the energy of the three classes of fuel, anthracite coal, coke and block coal, in the work of smelting pig iron in a blast furnace, under conditions favorable to each quality. A difficulty arises from the fact of the Block coal being used with varying mixtures of coke, so that an estimate of this class must be somewhat approximate.

Taking the production of Lucy or Isabella furnaces at 550 tons per week, which is a very moderate estimate, the product would be 1 *ton in every twenty-four hours to every* 156 *cubic feet internal capacity.* Bennington furnace, producing Bessemer pig for Cambria Iron Company, gives 1 *ton every twenty-four hours to every* 166 *feet internal capacity.*

These indicate the averages of the work of furnaces running on coke, when applied under conditions to produce true results. The average exhibiting the production *of* 1 *ton of pig iron each* 24 *hours to every* 161 *cubic feet of internal capacity of furnace.*

Taking the anthracite furnaces of the heights of 50, 60 and 70 feet as producing 200, 250 and 300 tons of pig iron per week, respectively, the internal capacity of furnace required to produce 1 ton of pig metal per 24 hours will be as follows: 185, 195 and 256 cubic feet, exhibiting an average of this class of 212 cubic feet.

The determination of the internal space in block coal furnaces to each ton of pig iron produced, per day, is rendered difficult by the coke mixtures. It should be found ranging between the coke and anthracite spaces, perhaps more nearly approaching the latter; say from 180 to 190 cubic feet.

The average relative energies, therefore, of these three furnace fuels, under the present conditions of application, appear to be as follows: Coke, 161; block coal and coke, 185, and anthracite coal, 212 cubic feet.

AMERICAN BEEHIVE OVEN

KEMBLE COAL & IRON CO.

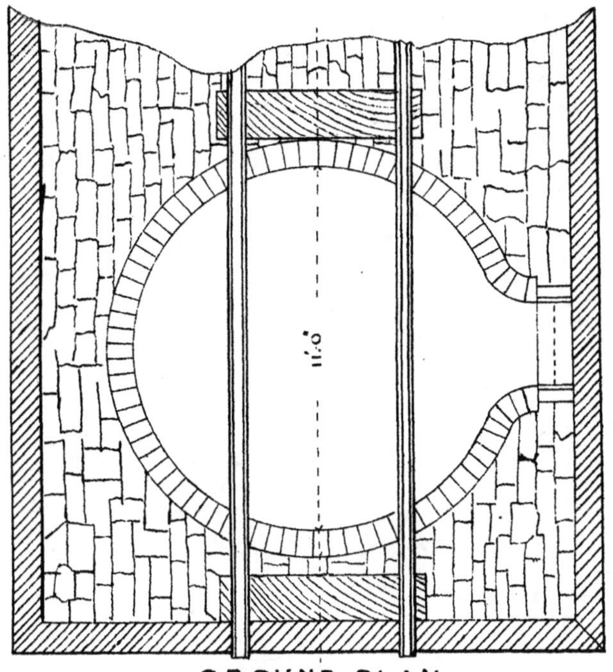

GROUND PLAN

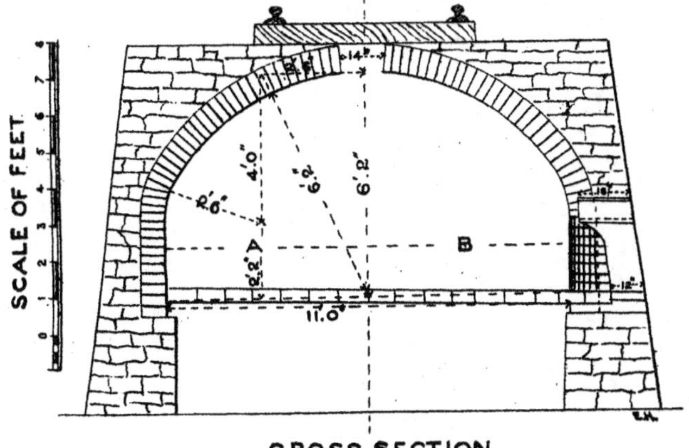

CROSS SECTION.

PHOTO-ZINCOGRAPH, by F. A. WENDEROTH & CO., 1328 Chestnut Street, Philada.

CAMBRIA IRON COMPANY.

BENNINGTON COKE PITS

Jno. Fulton E.M.

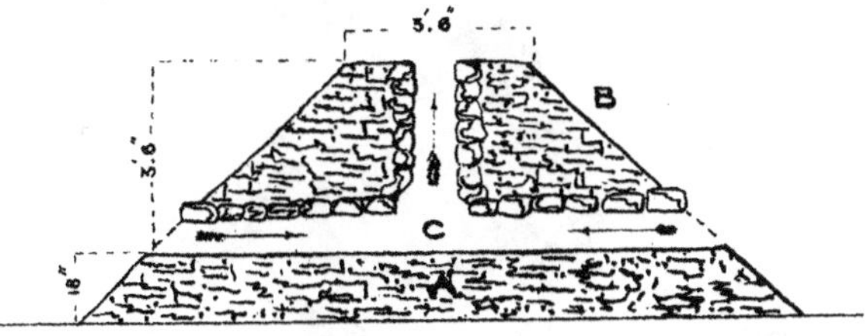

CROSS SECTION.

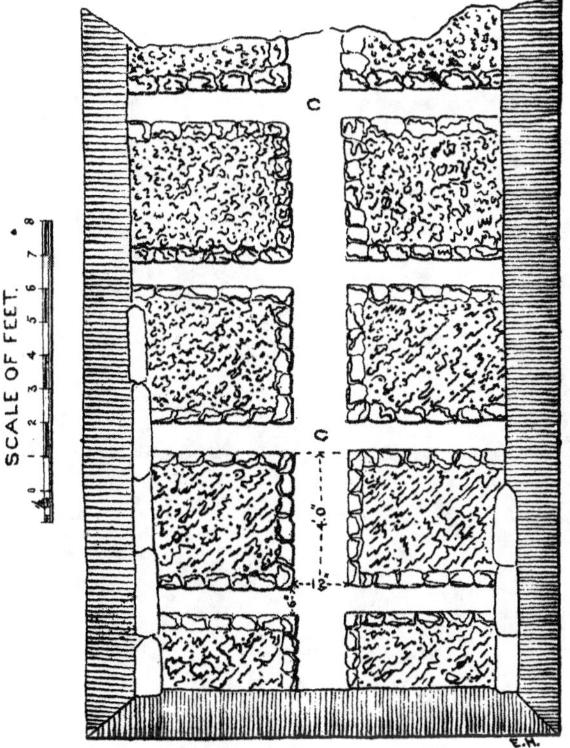

SEE PAGE 122 L.

GROUND PLAN.

PHOTO-ZINCOGRAPH, by F. A. WENDEROTH & CO., 1828 Chestnut Street, Philada.

In the collection of data I have been cordially assisted by Franklin Platt, Esq., Assistant Geologist Second Pennsylvania Geological Survey, and by his associate, C. A. Young, Esq.

Thomas T. Morrell, Esq., Chemist Cambria Iron Co., has laid me under renewed obligations for valuable assistance.

The determinations for the table exhibiting the physical structure of coke were made by my associate, David Peelor, Esq.

Mr. Robert P. Field, my assistant, has been industrious in making and copying drawings for this paper.

APPENDIX B.

Analyses of gas issuing from Oil Wells.

SAML. P. SADTLER, Asst. Prof. Chem., University Pa.

The natural gas issuing from numerous wells in the western part of Pennsylvania, and in the adjacent parts of New York and West Virginia, has been very little studied from a chemical point of view. This neglect is explained when we remember that the finding of a gas well has been considered rather a misfortune than otherwise, oil being the only thing desired. Indeed, until very recently the use of the Fredonia gas in New York for illuminating purposes was about the only case where any attempt was made to utilize this valuable natural product.

Accordingly, there have been almost no analyses whatever made of those gases. In 1866 a French geologist, M. Foucou, visited a number of these gas wells and collected specimens of the gases. These were afterwards analyzed by M. Fouqué, and they are published in *Compt. rendus*, *LXVII, p.* 1045. The localities were Pioneer Run, Venango county, Pa.; Fredonia, New York; Rogers' Gulch, Wirt county, W. Va.; Burning Springs, on Niagara river below the cataract, and Petrolia, Enniskillen district, Canada West. These points are certainly widely enough removed to make the series comprehensive from a geological stand-point. The analyses do not appear to have been complete ones, as M. Fouqué determined the exact amounts of only a few of the constituents. In general the gases were composed of members of the marsh-gas series of hydro-carbons. Thus, the gas from Pioneer run he found to have essentially the composition of propyl-hydride, (C_3 H_8,) with small quantities of carbonic acid and of nitrogen; the Fredonia gas appeared to be a mixture of marsh-gas (CH_4) and ethyl-hydride (C_2 H_6,) with a small quantity of carbonic acid and 1.55 per cent of nitrogen; the Rogers' Gulch gas was CH_4, almost exclusively, with 15.86 per cent of carbonic acid and a small quantity of nitrogen; the Burning Springs gas almost pure CH_4, with a little CO_2; the Petrolia gas a mixture of marsh-gas, (CH_4,) and ethyl-hydride, (C_2H_6,) with a small amount of carbonic acid.

However, in some cases the composition as given above was only apparent, as in the case of the Pioneer Run gas, for on passing the gas through alcohol a part was absorbed, which was afterwards shown to be butyl-hydride, (C_4H_{10},) while the part unabsorbed showed nearly the composition of marsh-gas, (CH_4.) It was evident, therefore, that what appeared to be propyl-hydride, (C_3H_8,) was in reality a mixture of marsh-gas, (CH_4,) and butyl-hydride, (C_4H_{10},).

In 1870 Prof. Henry Wurtz made an analysis of the gas from a well in West Bloomfield, N. Y. The results of this analysis are found in *Silliman's Journal*, (2) *XLIX, p.* 336. He found:

Marsh-gas	82.41
Carbonic acid	10.11
Nitrogen	4.31
Oxygen	0.23
Illuminating hydro-carbons	2.94
	100.00

The specific gravity of the gas was .693.

The methods of analysis were not the usual ones of gas analysis, but some new absorption methods devised by himself, in conjunction with Prof. B. Silliman.

This I believe is the extent of the published information on the subject. Prof. Otto Wuth, of Pittsburg, had made some qualitative examinations of one of the gases to be discussed in this report, and had established the presence of marsh-gas (CH_4) as the main constituent of it.

Through the kindness of Profs. Newberry and Morley, I am also enabled to give the results of an analysis of the famous Neff well, near Gambier, Ohio.

Its composition is as follows:

Oxygen	0.8
Carbonic acid	0.3
Carbonic oxide	0.5
Marsh gas	81.4
Ethyl hydride	12.2
Nitrogen	4.8
	100.00
Specific gravity, (calculated,)	.64
Specific gravity, (observed,)	.65

The gases which I was requested to collect and analyze were, first, the gas of the Harvey well, in Butler county, at that time already used in the mills of Spang, Chalfant & Co., and Graff, Bennett & Co., at Ætna; secondly, the Leechburg well gas, used in the Rogers & Burchfield mill, at Leechburg, and thirdly, the gas bubbling from a spring at Cherry Tree, Indiana county. To this list was afterwards added the gas of the Burns well, in Butler county, which it is now proposed to convey to Pittsburg by a gas pipe-line.

I will therefore describe the collection of these several gases and the qualitative tests made in several cases at the wells.

The first collected was the Burns well gas. The well is located on the Delphy farm, three-quarters of a mile south of St. Joe, in Butler county. It is in the midst of a number of oil wells out of which oil flows from a depth of 1,650 feet. The gas comes from a level 50 feet lower, or from a depth of 1,700 feet. The samples were collected at a pumping-house, one-half a mile south from the well where the gas is used to heat the boilers of the pumping engine of an oil pipe-line. The pressure is here substantially the same as at the well, at the lowest estimate over 100 pounds to the square inch. I fastened my rubber tubing on a quarter-inch pipe connected with the main pipe from the well. The pressure was regulated by a valve. Seven tubes full were obtained and hermetically sealed before the blow-pipe. All necessary precautions were taken to obtain the gas absolutely free from air, a strong current having been allowed to stream through the tubes for five minutes or more.

I also made two series of qualitative tests with different chemical reagents. First, a current of the gas was passed for a considerable length of time through absolute alchohol. Fouqué's results (see above) had rendered probable the presence of other and higher members of the marsh-gas series than (CH_4). Now while marsh-gas itself is nearly insoluble in absolute alchohol, ethyl hydride ($C_2 H_6$) is dissolved to the extent of $1\frac{1}{2}$ volumes, propyl-hydride ($C_3 H_8$) to the extent of six volumes, and butyl-hydride ($C_4 H_{10}$) to the extent of eighteen volumes in one volume of the alchohol. I therefore expected to saturate the alchohol with such of these hydro-carbons as might be in the gas. After ten or fifteen minutes passage of the gas, the bottles were tightly stoppered and sealed shut, to be afterwards examined in my laboratory. Second, a current of gas was passed for a length of time through bromine. This element combines directly with ethylene and other hydro-carbons of the olefine series. I would therefore by the use of bromine be able to ascertain the presence of small quantities of these illuminating hydro-carbons in the gas. The bottles were also stoppered and sealed, to be afterward examined for the presence of the bromides of these hydro-carbons.

The second gas collected was that of the Leechburg well. This well is in reality not in Armstrong county, but across the Kiskiminitas river from Leechburg, and in Westmoreland county. The gas is brought over the river through a large pipe to the rolling mill of Rogers & Burchfield. The gas has been flowing over four and one-half years, and has been used for two years in the mill. It comes from a depth of 1,200 feet, and throws out with it a quantity of salt water. A well was sunk at Apollo, seven miles above, for gas, but none was found. There are also no oil wells nearer than the ones in Butler county, twenty miles distant.

The gas was taken in the mill from a quarter-inch pipe communicating directly with the main supply pipe brought across the river. The pressure was very great, and had to be controlled by a valve. I collected here five tubes full of the gas. The same absorption tests with absolute alcohol and with bromine were made here as those just described under the collection of the Burns' gas. The bottles were sealed and packed away for subsequent examination.

The third gas collected was that from the Harvey well. This gas comes from a depth of 1,250 feet. I did not collect it, however, at the well, but at Spang, Chalfant & Co.'s mill at Ætna, where it is brought through a line of six-inch pipe, eighteen miles long. Its pressure is still very considerable. I took it from a quarter-inch supply pipe, just in the rear of one of the ovens, where its pressure is indicated by a guage. Five tubes full were collected with all needful precautions against contamination by air or other gases. I did not make any absorption tests in this case.

The fourth gas collected was that at Cherry Tree, in Indiana county. This gas escapes in bubbles through what looks like an ordinary spring of water. I was told that a well had been sunk some 500 feet in quest of oil, when the work had been interrupted, and owing to insufficient piping the well filled with water, through which the gas forces its way. The water is not salt. Here I used a large-sized druggists' funnel, which when inverted over the water and dipped slightly under its surface formed an excellent reservoir for the gas. The neck of the funnel was connected tightly by a piece of rubber tubing with the series of tubes prepared for the gas. These were filled and hermetically sealed as before. No absorption tests were made.

Before proceeding definitely to the analysis of the samples thus collected, the qualitative tests made by means of the absorption reagents were attended to. These tests were made with the gas from two of the wells. The natural gas had been passed, as described, through absolute alcohol and through bromine. The first gas thus examined was the Burns' well gas. The alcohol which should have absorbed certain gases was transferred to a small flask, and sufficient additional absolute alcohol added to completely fill the flask. A cork perforated and carrying a delivery tube, was then fitted to it, so that the excess of alcohol filled this tube also. The flask was now heated, and the gas given off was collected in an eudiometer tube over warm water. I obtained thus some 150 cubic centimeters of gas. The operation was pushed until only alcohol vapor was given off, which was absorbed by the water. To the gas in the eudiometer I then added rapidly an equal volume of chlorine, and allowed it to stand exposed to diffused sunlight. Oily drops formed at once, while the volume of gas contracted until it occupied only about one-half of the first volume. This showed the probable formation of ethyl-chloride, (C_2H_5Cl,) which is gaseous at temperatures over 12° C. and of either propyl-chloride (C_3H_7Cl.,) which is liquid at temperatures under 52° C., or of butyl-chloride, (C_4H_9Cl,) which is liquid at temperatures under 77.6° C. On inverting and applying a flame to the gas in the eudiometer, it was found to be inflammable, burning with the greenish flame characteristic of ethyl-chloride. The water upon which the oily drops had collected was put into a small flask, and an attempt was made to separate them by distillation. This was, however unsatisfactory, as there could only have been very small quantities of either propyl-chloride or butyl-chloride. The result of these tests may therefore be summed up as showing the certain pressure in the gas of ethyl-hydride ($C_2 H_6$) and probable presence of either $C_3 H_8$ or $C_4 H_{10}$.

The other qualitative test made upon this gas was with bromine. This was placed in a porcelain dish, and water added. Pure sodic hydrate was then added to neutralize the excess of bromine. The sodium bromide formed dissolved at once in the water. There remained no trace of oily drops such as would be caused by the bromides of the illuminating hydro-carbons. The sodium bromide was afterwards crystalized out perfectly pure. The test was therefore entirely negative in its results.

The other gas examined by these absorption tests was the Leechburg gas. The absorbed gases were driven off from the alcohol in the same way by heat. I obtained here only about 100 cubic centimeters of gas. An equal volume of chlorine was mixed with it, when a contraction of about one-third took place. On inverting the eudiometer tube, the gas proved to be inflammable, and burned with a greenish flame. Oily drops were distinctly seen, forming a thin layer upon the water, but not enough to distil. Ethyl-hydride was therefore the only constituent positively shown to exist in the gas, although either propyl-hydride or butyl-hydride must have been present also, giving rise to the oily drops of chloride.

On examining the bromine used for the other absorption test, there was apparently a slight layer upon the surface of the bromine which might have been ethylene bromide. On neutralizing the excess of bromine, however, no distinct evidence could be had of the presence of the bromide, so that the result was left uncertain.

The quantitative analyses were next undertaken. These were made by the methods of gas analysis devised by Prof. Bunsen. They are rather tedious, and require great care in the manipulation, but are more accurate than any of the other methods since devised.

The analysis of a gas by these methods resolves itself into two distinct parts, viz: the successive absorption of certain constituents by suitable reagents, and the ignition of the inflammable gases mixed with oxygen and air in a closed eudiometer tube, provided with platinum electrodes, between which the spark is passed.

In the following analyses the carbonic acid, carbonic oxide, illuminating hydro-carbons and free oxygen were tested for, and when present removed by suitable absorption reagents, while the hydrogen, marsh-gas and ethyl-hydride were determined by the eudiometer analysis. Any nitrogen present remains over, and is estimated at the conclusion of the analysis.

Burns Well Gas.

Two complete analyses gave the following results:

Carbonic acid	.34	.35
Carbonic oxide	trace.	trace.
Illuminating hydro-carbons	——	——
Hydrogen	6.06	6.15
Marsh-gas (CH_4)	75.75	75.12
Ethyl-hydride (C_2H_6)	17.84	18.39
Propyl-hydride (C_3H_8)	trace.	trace.
Oxygen	——	——
Nitrogen	——	——
	99.99	100.01

The average would therefore be:

Carbonic acid	.34
Carbonic oxide	trace.
Illuminating hydro-carbons	——
Hydrogen	6.10
Marsh-gas	75.44
Ethyl-hydride	18.12
Propyl-hydride	trace.
Oxygen	——
Nitrogen	——
	100.00

Leechburg Gas.

The average composition of this gas, as deduced from two analyses, is as follows:

Carbonic acid	.35
Carbonic oxide	.26

Illuminating hydro-carbons	.56
Hydrogen	4.79
Marsh-gas	89.65
Ethyl-hydride	4.39
Propyl-hydride	trace.
Oxygen	——
Nitrogen	——
	100.00

Harvey Well Gas.

The average composition of this gas is as follows:

Carbonic acid	.66
Carbonic oxide	trace.
Illuminating hydro-carbons	——
Hydrogen	13.50
Marsh-gas	80.11
Ethyl-hydride	5.72
Propyl-hydride	——
Oxygen	——
Nitrogen	——
	99.99

Cherry-Tree Gas.

The average composition of this gas, deduced from two complete analyses, is:

Carbonic acid	2.28
Carbonic oxide	——
Illuminating hydro-carbons	——
Hydrogen	22.50
Marsh-gas	60.27
Ethyl-hydride	6.80
Oxygen	.83
Nitrogen	7.32
	100.00

It will be seen that the first three of the gases just analyzed are very similar in composition, while the gas escaping from the spring at Cherry Tree, differs very considerably from the others. The larger amount of carbonic acid, and the presence of free oxygen and nitrogen are the chief points which distinguish it. It is only natural, however, that a gas escaping from fresh spring water, should contain these gases, as they are the gases usually dissolved in spring waters.

As to the other constituents of these gases, hydrogen, marsh-gas, and ethyl-hydride, are the most important ones. In the case of two of the gases—the Burns gas and the Leechburg gas—qualitative tests directly proved the presence of the marsh-gas and ethyl-hydride. In all the gases the results of the eudiometric analyses were substituted in the same formulas given by Bunsen in his methods of gas-analysis, and it was found that these were the only compounds which would yield the analytical results obtained.

If now we make a comparison of these results with those obtained by Fouqué and by Prof. Wurtz, we find certain points of similarity, with some striking difference. The greatest difference is at once seen to be the presence of free hydrogen in all these gases. Neither Fouqué nor Wurtz found any. However, there is ready proof for the reality of its presence in the gases analyzed.

Fouqué (loc. cit.) deduced theoretically, and proved experimentally, the correctness of the following equation where the gases analyzed in the eudiometer were exclusively members of the marsh-gas series of hydro-carbons like CH_4 and $C_2 H_6$—the carbonic acid formed is equal to twice the contraction produced by the explosion, minus three times the volume of gas taken; or, transposed, twice the contraction equals the carbonic acid plus three times the volume of gas. Now, if hydrogen were present, in the explosion it would give a contraction greater than that of marsh-gas, as the water formed would condense, while no carbonic acid would be formed. The contraction observed would therefore be greater than that required by Fouqué's equation. This was the result obtained every time.

It will be remembered, too, that by the previous absorption tests I removed carbonic oxide and hydro-carbons of the ethylene series, so that there could be no inflammable gases there but hydrogen and the members of the marsh-gas series. The invariable presence of ethyl-hydride, and other higher members of the marsh-gas series alluded to, is in accord with Fouqué's results, and as was stated, was proved also by qualitative tests. Wurtz found none, but it may be that his absorption methods did not allow him to distinguish between them and marsh-gas, of which he finds 82.41 per cent.

The almost complete absence of the illuminating hydro-carbons is also in accord with Fouqué's results. He found absolutely none. Wurtz, on the other hand, found 2.94 per cent of them in the gas analyzed by him. The specific gravity of the gases, as calculated from analyses given above, is as follows:

Burns well gas	.6148
Leechburg gas	.5580
Harvey well gas	.5119
Cherry Tree gas	——

In one case only did I have a sufficient amount of the gas to verify this calculated value by direct experiment. The Burns Well gas was also tested experimentally and a determination of the specific gravity was made. The method used was that given by Bunsen, in which the velocity with which the gas escapes through a minute orifice, as compared with the velocity of air under similar circumstance, is used to give us its specific gravity.

The result of the determination was as follows: Inverse ratio of squares of times of diffusion, 1: .6977, which therefore represents the sp. gr. of the moist gas (as taken from the well). The calculated sp. gr. of the dry gas was .6148.

The calorific value of these gases remains to be discussed. These calculations must, however, be taken with some allowance, as they involve the use of physical constants very difficult of determination and as to the exact value of which there is some doubt. Moreover, the calculations pre-suppose a perfect combustion, which in practice is never reached, although more nearly attained with gaseous fuel than with solid.

Two classes of results will be given—First, the *calorific power* of the gases expressed in what are called calorific heat-units, that is the number of units by weight of water that will be raised 1° C. in temperature by the burning of one unit of the gas; and, secondly, the *calorific intensity*, or the maximum temperature developed in the process of combustion, and to which the products of combustion can be heated in the course of that combustion.

The calculation for the Burns Well gas is as follows:

Composition of the gas (average)—

$$\left.\begin{array}{r} .34\ CO_2 \\ 6.10\ H. \\ 75.44\ CH_4 \\ 18.12\ C_2H_6 \end{array}\right\}\ \text{Equivalent to}\ \left\{\begin{array}{r} .34\ CO_2 \\ 28.58\ H. \\ 71.08\ C. \end{array}\right.$$

28.58 hydrogen in burning require 228.64 oxygen, which, if taken from the air, have 756.9 nitrogen mixed with them. 71.08 carbon in burning require 189.55 oxygen, which in the air are mixed with 627.5 nitrogen.

The products of the combustion are:—

$$260.63+0.34= 260.97\ CO_2$$
$$257.22\ H_2O.$$
$$1384.4\ N.$$

28.58 hydrogen burning generate 28.58×34.462=9849.20 calorific heat-units.

71.08 carbon burning generate 71.08×80.00= 5743.30 calorific heat-units.

15592.50

Deduct latent heat of water, 257.22×537= 1381.20

14211.30

14.211 calorific heat units therefore represent the calorific power of the Burns Well gas.

The calorific intensity of the gas is then—

CO_2 — 260.97×.2169= 56.6
H_2O— 257.22×.4805=123.6
N. —1384.4 ×.2438=337.5

517.7=Specific heat of the products of combustion.

$$\frac{14211}{517.7}=2745^\circ\ C=\text{theoretical temperature attainable.}$$

For the Leechburg gas we have the following calculation:

Composition of gas—

.35 CO_2. .26 CO. .56 $C_n\ H_{2n}$ 4.79 H. 89.65 CH_4. 4.39 $C_2\ H_6$.	Equivalent to,	.35 CO_2. .26 CO. 28.16 H. 71.23 C.

28.16 hydrogen require in burning - 225.28 oxygen.
71.23 carbon require in burning - 189.95 oxygen.
.26 carbonic oxide require in burning, .15 oxygen.

The whole amount of oxygen, if taken from the air, is mixed with 1375.4 nitrogen.

The products of combustion, are

$261.18\times.41\times.35=$ 261.94 CO_2.
253.44 H_2O.
1375.4 N.

28.16 hydrogen burning generate, $28.16\times34.462=$ 9704.40 calorific heat units.

71.23 carbon burning generate, - $71.23\times8080=$ 5755.30

.26 carbonic oxide burning generate, - - - - - - $.26\times2403=$ 0006.25

15465.95

Deduct latent heat of water, $253.44\times537=$ 1361.00

14104.95

14105 calorific heat units therefore represent the calorific power of the Leechburg gas.

The calorific intensity of the gas is then,

CO_2— $161.94\times.2169=$ 56.815
H_2O— $253.44\times.4805=$121.77
N. —1375.4 $\times.2438=$335.22

513.80=Specific heat of the products of combustion.

$$\frac{14105}{513.8}=2746°C=\text{theoretical temperature attainable.}$$

The calculation for the Harvey well gas is as follows:

Composition of the gas—

.66 CO_2 13.50 H 80.11 CH_4 5.72 C_2H_6	Equivalent to,	.66 CO_2 34.674 H 64.656 C

34.674 hydrogen in burning require, 277.39 oxygen, which in the air would be mixed with 918.2 nitrogen.

64.656 carbon in burning require 172.42 oxygen, which in the air would be mixed with 570.8 nitrogen.

The products of the combustion, are

$237.07 \times .66 = 237.73$ CO_2
312.066 H_2O
1489.0 N

34.674 hydrogen burning generate, calorific heat-units. $34.674 \times 34462 = 11949.00$

64.656 carbon burning generate, calorific heat-units. $64.656 \times 8080 = 5223.20$

17273.20

Deduct latent heat of $312.066 \times 537 =$ 1675.80

15597.40

15597 calorific heat units, therefore, represents the calorific power of the Harvey well gas.

The calorific intensity of the gas is then,

CO_2— $237.73 \times .2169 = 51.56$
$H_{2}0$— $312.066 \times .4805 = 149.94$
N—$1489.0 \times .2438 = 363.$

564.5=Specific heat of the products of combustion.

$$\frac{15597.4}{504.5} = 2763^\circ \text{ C.} = \text{Theoretical temperature attainable.}$$

With the Cherry Tree Gas I did not make any calculations as to calorific value, as from the very different circumstances of its occurrence there was no likelihood of its ever being utilized.

If now we wish to compare these gases considered as fuel with other combustibles, we can either take the calorific power or the calorific intensity as the basis of comparison. In the case of hydrogen, or any compound containing hydrogen, the latter is taken as the most reliable basis, inasmuch as the latent heat of the water formed in the combustion has to be deducted from the sum total of calorific heat units, and the specific heat of water is so much greater than that of carbonic acid that the calorific intensity is greatly reduced in this case.

Thus, 100 parts by weight of hydrogen burned in oxygen give 3446200 heat units, or minus the latent heat of the 900 parts of water formed, 2962900 units. The specific heat of 900 parts of water, however, is 432.5, so that the calorific intensity becomes 6850° C.

On the other hand, 100 parts of carbon burned in oxygen give 808000 heat units, with no deduction for latent heat. The specific heat of 366.6 parts of carbonic acid is only 79.5, so that the calorific intensity becomes 10163° C., or greater than that of hydrogen.

Subjoined are given the calorific powers of different combustibles:

Hydrogen	34.462	units.
Marsh-gas	13.063	"
Olefiant gas	11.858	"
Ether	9.027	"
Alcohol	7.184	"
Petroleum	10.000	"
Sulphur	2.221	"
Wood charcoal	8.080	"
Carbonic oxide	2.400	"
Dry wood, (about)	3.654	"

These results are those obtained by Favre and Silbermann and others, by the most careful scientific methods. The following list taken from Kerl and Stohmann's new German edition of Muspratt's Technical Chemistry, gives the theoretical calorific power of different coals &c., and that observed in the best practice.

Combustible.	*Theoretical power.*	*Observed power.*
Illuminating gas	23.975	22.000
Petroleum	11.380	10.200
Anthracite	8.250	8.100
Bituminous coal (mean)	7.700	7.500
Charcoal	7.400	7.000
Coke (pure)	6.800	7.000
Coke (with 15 per cent ash)	——	6.000
Lignite	6.000	5.800
Peat (dry)	4.500	4.800
Peat (with 20 per cent water)	——	3.600
Wood (dry)	4.180	3.600
Wood (with 20 per cent water)	——	2.800

If now we endeavor to classify these combustibles according to their calorific intensity, we get other results entirely. Thus we have:

Combustible.	*Burned in oxygen.*	*Burned in air.*
Carbon	9873° C.	2458° C.
	(Theoretical, 10179°)	(Theoretical, 2703°)
Carbonic oxide	5316°	2121°
	(Theoretical, 7090°)	(Theoretical, 2828°)
Olefiant gas	6308°	2290°
Marsh gas	4766°	1935°
Wood		1575° to 1750°
Peat		1575° to 2000°
Lignite		1800° to 2200°
Bituminous coal, (with 5 per cent water and 5 per cent ash)		2200° to 2350°
Charcoal		2100° to 2450°
Coke, (with 10 per cent water and 5 per cent ash)		2300°
Coke, (with 5 per cent water and 3 per cent ash)		2400°
Coke, (without water and with 3 per cent ash)		2450°

It will be seen from the calculations made with these natural gases that in calorific power they come second only to hydrogen itself, while in calorific intensity they possess a theoretical value higher than almost any known fuel. How much the observed intensity falls short of that ascribed by theory remains to be tested.

APPENDIX C.

Durability of the Natural Gas Supply.

FRANKLIN PLATT.

The chemical composition of Natural Gas has been fully given in Appendix B of this volume, and its efficiency as a fuel in puddling iron, the calorific effect, the method of piping the gas for long distances, and the leakage and loss of pressure thereby sustained, will be discussed in Appendix D. The remaining point, and one of great practical importance, is "What is the probable durability of the natural gas supply?"

The Report of the Second Geological Survey of Pennsylvania on the Oil Regions of the State will contain, with the facts concerning the oil wells, the facts concerning the gas supply; and when all these are gathered and studied, a much more authoritative judgment can be given. But in view of the demand for some immediate opinion on this subject, a judgment necessarily more or less tentative is given below from the material gathered for the purpose of making this report.

The gas is found at different geological horizons, the rich illuminating gas of Fredonia, New York, and the less rich gas of Erie, Penna., underlying by several hundred feet the oil sands which yield the Butler County Gas. These gases differ decidedly in quality, ranging from a five and a half candle power in Butler county to an eight candle power at Erie and a ten candle power at Fredonia, N. Y.

But the chief point is the difference in the quantity of gas yielded by wells down to these different horizons.

The yield of gas from wells on horizons either above or below the oil sands is usually small, while the gas yielded from the oil sands is enormous in amount. So far as past development shows in Pennsylvania, therefore, it is to the oil sand rocks that we must look for large supplies of natural gas.

The gas well of Messrs. Rogers and Burchfield is in Allegheny township, Westmoreland county, on the south bank of the Kiskiminetas river, directly opposite from Leechburg.

The accompanying record was taken from Mr. Beale's book, kept while drilling.*

Leechburg Well.

Conductor	Thickness.		22′
Sand rock	50′	to	72′
Limestone, with gas and water	6′	to	78′
Fire-clay	12′	to	90′
Soft, loose shale	200′	to	290′
Blue pebble } XII ?	60′	to	350′
White sand } XII ?	15′	to	365′
Dark pebble } XII ?	12′	to	377′
Soapstone	18′	to	395′
Blue rock	5′	to	400′
Red rock. XI ?	8′	to	408′
Dark slate	35′	to	443′
White sand, with little salt water	75′	to	518′
Blue slate	60′	to	578′
Soft blue rock	100′	to	678′
Grey sand rock	20′	to	698′
Soapstone	100′	to	798′
Soft, changeable rock, with strong vein of salt water	152′	to	950′
White sand rock	30′	to	980′
Shale	200′	to	1,180′
Blue rock, hard shells (Struck present gas vein.)	20′	to	1,200′
Pebble and sand rock mixed	30′	to	1,230
Blue rock, hard shells	20′	to	1,250′
Depth of well, July 3, 1871			1,250

The sand rock from which this gas comes is probably the first sand. It is noticeable that no coal beds are mentioned as passed through in this well; yet coals are struck in numerous salt wells between Leechburg and the Allegheny river.

The well flowed gas steadily for three years before any effort was made to utilize it. It is said that the flow is about as strong now as when first struck, but there are no well recorded facts about the matter.

At the time of examination, in 1875, the gas was conveyed from the well in a 5⅝-inch pipe into the works of Messrs. Rogers & Burchfield, and was doing work which had required from 1,600 to 2,000 bushels of coal daily.

The gas well at Saxon Station, on the Butler branch of the

*These facts were obtained from Mr. J. F. Carll, Assistant on the Second Geological Survey of Pennsylvania, engaged in the oil regions.

West Pennsylvania railroad, in Winfield township, Butler county, ten miles from Freeport, was put down in the spring of 1874. Very heavy flow of gas. Aneroid barometer elevation 450 feet above Freeport, or about 1,200 feet above tide.

Owner's record from memory, probably not very reliable, except as to gas vein.

Cased at	580
At 270′ (?) black limestone	60′ thick to 330
At 1150′ 1st sand and gas	50′ thick to 1200′
At 1420′ 2d sand and gas	40′ thick to 1460′
At 1700′ 3d sand, shelly and poor	10′ thick to 1710

Ceased drilling at 1,857′. No oil.

Gas from top of first sand when struck, exploded and burnt the derrick.

The gas in the well is from the "first sand."

The "Thorn Creek Well," Two Miles West of Saxonburg, Jefferson Township, Butler County.

Cased at	720′
Black limestone, at	200′
White limestone, at	480′
First sand, show of oil, at	1250′
"Clover-seed pebble," from	1425′ to 1450′
Sand, gas and oil, from	1485′ to 1525′
Slate	25′ to 1550′
Colored pebble	17′ to 1567′
Slate	33′ to 1600′
Sand	35′ to 1635′
Slate	40′ to 1675′
Sand and oil	20′ to 1695′
Slate to bottom	130′ to 1825′

(Dry.)

Mahan Well, Middlesex Township, Butler County.

Cased at	660′
At 200′	Coal seam 4′ thick.
At 290′	Coal seam 2′ thick.
Black limestone	20′ from 295′ to 315′
Coal	8′ from 640′ to 648′
White limestone and sand	90′ from 675′ to 765′
Sand shells and slates	100′ from 1150′ to 1250′
Sand and fresh water	60′ from 1350′ to 1410′
Black loose sand, 10 feet thick, with amber oil and trace of salt water, oil like Smith's Ferry oil, from	1470′ to 1480′
Grey sand	50′ from 1480′ to 1530′
Red rock	10′ from 1545′ to 1555′

Boulder sand	20′ from 1565′ to 1585
"Pebbly corn meal" or "Clover seed,"	37′ from 1623′ to 1660′
Slate..............................	40′ from 1660′ to 1700′
"Pink clover-seed"..................	25′ from 1700′ to 1725
Fine white sand.....................	15′ from 1740′ to 1755′
Producing good gas and about 10 bbls. oil per day.	
Slate..............................	30′ from 1755′ to 1785′
Still drilling, (May 1875). Sample of oil brought to Pleasantville shows a gravity of 40°.	

Record given by one of the owners, Mr. F. A. Conkle, of Butler.

The "Harvey Well" is near Larden's Mill, Clinton township, Butler county.

The following record was furnished by Mr. Smith, an experienced driller and part owner in the well:

Conductor..............................			8′
Slate and fire-clay....................	20′	to	28′
Coal..................................	6′	to	34′
Slates................................	46′	to	80′
Sandstone.............................	50′	to	130′
Slates................................	80′	to	210′
Sandstone.............................	20′	to	230′
Slates................................	50′	to	280′
Black limestone.......................	15′	to	295′
Coal..................................	5′	to	300′
Slate.................................	80′	to	380′
Sandstone.............................	20′	to	400′
Slate.................................	20′	to	420
White limestone, sometimes called "Blue Monday" and "Lightning Rock," on account of its extreme hardness, six weeks being consumed in drilling through it in the well,	100′	to	520′
Blue slate with *gas*..................	40′	to	560′
Slates and shale......................	100′	to	660′
Mountain sand.........................	160′	to	820′
Cased off salt water which came out on top of this rock at 720 feet.			
Slates................................	25′	to	845′
Sandstone.............................	40	to	885′
Sand shells...........................	15′	to	900′
Sandstone.............................	20′	to	920′
Slate, good drilling..................	180′	to	1,100′
Sandstone, with *gas*..................	15′	to	1,115′
Slate.................................	5′	to	1,120′
Gray sand, with a little salt water and gas, increasing all the way through the sand until compelled to stop..........	20′	to	1,140′
Depth of well—1,140′			

This well is is also getting its gas flow from the first sand. The pressure of the gas is enormous. When examined in May, 1875, by Mr. J. F. Carll, the steam gauge attached to one of the pipes indicated a pressure of one hundred and fifty pounds, the gas still having full vent through another two-inch pipe, which they dare not close for fear of lifting the casing out of the well.

In February, 1876, the pressure of the gas at the Harvey Well was one hundred and twenty pounds, a heavy falling off from the figures of May, 1875.

The Burns and the Delamater Gas Wells are about half a mile apart and lie seven miles north-east of Butler, Butler county. The wells are about 1,600 feet deep and are on the "Fourth Sand Rock" of the Butler Region. The Delamater Well produced oil from the "Third Sand." The pressure of the gas was very great (in December, 1875,) and it was reported that at the Burns Well it had been tested up to three hundred pounds to the square inch, and that the pressure was then taken off to prevent the casing from blowing out. The pressure at the Delamater Well was also very great, but has decreased decidedly, though the exact figures and ratio of decrease are not known.

The Fairview Well, one mile west of Petrolia, has yielded enormous quantities of gas. The pressure at first was very great, but not accurately recorded. Of the recorded pressures, it shows first yielding gas at 125 pounds pressure, with a slow and steady decrease. One year later it measured 60 pounds of pressure, and in February, 1876, the pressure was 22 pounds.* The gas is used for lighting Petrolia and other places in the region.

There is no other gas well in the immediate vicinity of this one, and it seems to be yielding less and less gas simply by its own exhaustion of the supply.

The gas struck in several borings for oil made near the mouth of Jacob's creek, an affluent of the Youghiogheny river and forty miles south of Pittsburg, has already been described on pp. 109–111 of the Youghiogheny Valley Report in this volume. It is only needful here to refer to that description, and

*This information was given by Mr. Christy.

to call attention to the fact that the gas was at that time a nuisance, and was likely, if possible, to be underrated as to its quantity and persistency.

This same difficulty is experienced in securing facts concerning the gas flow in the Venango county oil regions, and most of the figures are apt to be estimates from memory, and rarely, if ever, from measured pressure at the time.

The East Sandy Region furnishes an instance of a total cessation to a gas yield. Mr. H. L. Taylor, a well known oil operator, furnishes the facts as observed by him thus:

1. That in this East Sandy region, eight miles south southeast of Oil City, a well yielded large quantities of gas for years, falling off but little in pressure. This was an oil producing well also.

2. Sixty wells were drilled in the vicinity of this first one. Very little oil was obtained, but nearly every well yielded gas. The first well continued to flow gas, but steadily diminished in pressure as the adjoining wells yielded gas, and finally gave out entirely. This decrease was regular, and dependent upon the wells drilled directly around it.

The Milton Well on the Nelson farm, just north of Titusville, Crawford county, yielded gas sufficient to supply Titusville with light and furnish fuel for boilers. This supply has gradually fallen off to a mere small fraction of the original yield. The life of the well was about three years, and no new wells yielding gas were put down near to it to assist in exhausting the gas supply.

A gas well at Freeport, Armstrong county, is now supplying gas to run the boilers of a 40-horse power engine in the planing mill at that place. The well is 1,900 feet deep. The gas was struck at 1,080 feet, and no more gas was found below that point. The well starts about 35 feet below the Lower Freeport Coal Bed. The record has been destroyed by fire and the statement below is from the memory of the owners:

Small coal at	90′
Limestone at about	300′
Shell rock and sandstone from that point down.	
Some pebbles between	1,450′ and 1,500′
White soft sand at	1,500′

The gas shows good illuminating power, but has not been tested for candle power.

Though no accurate measurements have been kept of the pressure at this well, the engineer reports that from the amount of work done by it there has been no falling off in pressure in the two years during which the gas has been used. There is no other well in the vicinity.

In noting these gas wells no attention is paid to those wells where a sudden and generally very violent outflow of gas occurs, lasting perhaps an hour or even for a day, and then ceasing entirely; only those wells are noted which, after their first fierce outburst, continue to yield gas with a regular and normal pressure, and give evidence that they are drawing upon a considerable quantity below.

No gas has ever been utilized in the Venango County Region for iron puddling, and the records of gas pressure and supply have not been kept as they now are in the Butler Region.

Mr. J. F. Carll, assistant on the Second Geological Survey of Pennsylvania for the Oil Region district, who is familiar with the facts in reference to gas flow from the Venango county oil country, is of opinion that the records show the same in the main as the Butler county facts already recorded. These facts from both regions may be summarized thus:

1. That gas wells have a life just as oil wells have.

2. That one well, left alone without other wells around, will continue to yield a regular supply of gas for a long time; but that when numerous wells are put down around it the gas supply is soon entirely exhausted.

3. That when an oil well ceases to yield, a second well in the vicinity may and frequently does find oil; but that when a well ceases to flow gas new wells in the vicinity find no gas.

The records and statistics given above are all for gas wells deriving their gas from the "oil sands." The facts of the gas yields at Erie, Pa., and Fredonia, N. Y., both drawing their gas supply from a lower geological horizon are given below, and their testimony goes far to confirm the conclusions already given in reference to the gas yields from the oil sands.

In and around the city of Erie there are some fifty gas wells.

The first well of which the gas was utilized was put down about one hundred and fifty yards from the Jarecki Manufacturing Company's Work, where the gas was used. It yielded largely at first, but the amount steadily decreased. This well was six hundred feet deep.

A second well, put down by the company on their own ground, yielded largely. It was put down seven years ago; found gas at 200, 250, 400 and 600 feet deep, and is in all 700 feet deep. It at first supplied gas enough to take the place of four tons of coal daily and to light the works. It now only partially lights the works.

These two wells are in the valley of a small creek. When other wells were put down in the same valley to the north of the works, the effect upon the yield of gas from the company's well was immediate and decided.

At Stearn's Works there are two wells, one 700 and one 1,400 feet deep. The supply of gas was originally large, but is now fallen off to a small quantity.

The Erie Gas Company have put down two wells and use the gas in supplying the city.

Gas Well No. 1, is down to a depth of 750 feet. Gas was struck at 300 feet and at 360 feet.

The pressure at first was 50 pounds to the square inch, but this fell off, and the pressure is now extremely irregular, never very great, and sometimes ceasing entirely and then coming back with temporarily much increased pressure.

Mr. Caughey, the President of the Company, who furnished the above facts, states that the natural gas is much heavier than the illuminating gas manufactured by them. He says that the natural gas is an 8 candle gas; their manufactured gas, made from one-half Sharon and one-half Beaver Coal, being a 16 candle gas.

Gas Well No. 2, which was put down close to No. 1, yielded nothing.

In Mr. Evans' well, also, the gas occasionally stops flowing entirely, and then after a few days begins flowing again with as much as double the normal pressure.

Messrs. Oliver and Bacon have two wells. No. 1, down 470 feet, and No. 2, down 600 feet. No. 2 never yielded anything.

In well No. 1 gas was found all the way down, and at 450 feet deep the pressure was very heavy.

The pressure of the well at first is estimated at 60 to 80 pounds. This pressure lasted for six months. The well is five inches in diameter, and the gas originally ran all the power, (100 horse,) taking the place of three tons of coal daily. Now 2,200 pounds of coal daily are used, and the gas does the remainder of the work. The pressure is reported to be now even and regular, and no falling off is noticed.

The Erie Water Works have two gas wells. In No. 1, there was gas at 550 feet, but the amount was small, and the well was abandoned.

No. 2, is 1,200 feet deep, but no gas apparently deeper than 800 feet. The pressure at first was very heavy, but soon settled down to a normal rate, which now keeps very even. The gas yielded takes the place of two tons of coal daily. The well hole is six inches in diameter.

The Swalley well, which is down in the valley of the small run on which the Jarecki wells were put down, is yielding gas, but in the absence of accurate figures, can only be said to have lost three-fourths of its pressure in ten years.

The well at the mouth of this small run, where it empties into Lake Erie, continues to yield gas with a very regular pressure. Messrs. Rawle, Noble & Co., have carried it with pipe from the well to their furnace, one mile to the eastward. The well is 800 feet deep, and shows a pressure of gas of 25 pounds. This pressure is variable, but Mr. Noble thinks, shows no regular falling off.

At the Erie Car Works, (Messrs. Davenport, Fairburn & Co.,) 1½ miles south-west of Erie, there are two gas wells.

Well, No. 1, is down 705 feet, and was put down in December, 1870. Some gas was found near the surface, within the first 60 feet; fresh water at 147 feet; gas at 213 feet; much gas at 580 feet, and again gas in the bottom of the well. The water now pumped is salt; the original pressure was 70 pounds to the square inch, it is now only 17 pounds.

The well is six inches in diameter. The pressure is reported as not now falling off, but on the contrary, that it seems rather greater now than in 1874.

Well, No. 2, is down 700 feet. The pressure of the gas was very heavy at first, but is now about 17 pounds to the square inch.

Mr. F. F. Adams has a gas well one-third of a mile east of the Erie Car Works. The well is down 750 feet. The first gas was struck at about 300 feet deep, and from that on down at various depths to the bottom. The water in the well is slightly salt, and a little heavy oil comes with it.

The pressure at first was heavy, but soon came down to the present moderate flow, which it keeps now apparently with no regular falling off.

The Tracy Gas Well, two miles from Erie, is down 750 feet. Gas found at 400 feet; much gas at 610 feet, and again gas at 675 feet. The pressure kept evenly at about 25 pounds for the first 17 months, when it suddenly fell off to about one-eighth of that pressure, and at that point, it has since remained constant.

At Fredonia, New York, natural gas from an horizon far below that of the oil sands of Pennsylvania, has been utilized for many years.

The gas was first found coming up in the bed of the creek in 1821, and was then used, though in a small way, for lighting some houses in the village.

In 1858 a gas well was put down on the creek, one-half mile north of this old well. Of this depth thirty feet were shafted, and one hundred and twenty feet of a four-inch bore hole. The gas supply from this well has been and is regular in its average amount.

A second well, four hundred and seventy-five feet deep, just along side of this well, failed to add anything to the gas yielded, the amount coming from the two wells being just what had been coming from the first one. The second was therefore abandoned.

A gas well put down at the gas works, one-half mile away, was eight hundred feet deep and yielded nothing.

Mr. Coburn put down a well in the town, at his mill, 1,250 feet deep, which yields a regular supply of gas. The total yield, however, of these wells is only about 6,000 cubic feet daily.

The president of the company reports that Prof. Hadley, of

Buffalo, on testing the gas found: "That of gas from the Buffalo Gas Works a six-foot burner burns six feet of 14-candle power; of Fredonia natural gas, a six-foot burner burns three feet of 16-candle power."

The facts in reference to the natural gas wells, briefly given above, all point to the conclusion that gas wells have their regular life, and that the quantity of gas is a limited amount. If a single well is down and yielding gas, the pressure will remain constant and the supply regular for many years, but as soon as new wells go down in the immediate vicinity the total gas supply is sooner or later exhausted, and all the wells cease yielding gas.

The gas wells at Erie furnish an illustration of this fact. The wells in the city are close together, and materially affect each other's supply, keeping the pressure low and irregular. But the wells on the lake front record much greater regularity of pressure. The whole region north of the wells, under the water of the lake, is untouched by gas wells, and these wells, therefore, along the lake shore draw their even and regular supply from this region.

The necessary result of this would be that natural gas as a fuel for iron puddling and other uses must be confined to the position of an economical adjunct to other fuels. That is, for works in all other respects well situated for successful iron working, with a cheap coal supply immediately available upon a temporary or permanent ceasing of the gas supply, this natural gas can be brought in as a fuel and used with heavy saving of cost. But it is highly improbable that it could ever pay to locate works simply on a gas supply in a position where without the gas the works could not be successfully run. It is therefore as an economical adjunct, and not as a main source of supply that this gas must be regarded.

As to the likelihood of finding gas at any given point, it rests in that respect precisely as does the probability of finding oil at any given point. The geological position of the "oil sands" below the surface can usually be given closely; but whether when that horizon is reached the oil sands will be found as massive sand rock yielding no oil, or as pebble rock, yielding oil and gas, there is as yet no way of determining. Possibly these "belts" of oil-bearing pebble sands follow some regular lines, such lines depending upon the original ocean currents and shore lines, but if so these lines and this law are not yet worked out. Mr. Carll's work for the Second Geological Survey of Pennsylvania may go far towards settling this question.

The "belts" of pebble rock in the Massive Sandstone of XII, the Seral Conglomerate of Rogers, represent a case very similar to that presented by the development of the "oil sands." But so far no study of XII has yet determined any regular laws or lines of pebble deposition.

Take for example where the Fourth Anticlinal Axis west of the Allegheny Mountain crosses the Little Toby creek, in the northern part of Jefferson county. The Massive Conglomerate of XII is here brought high up into the hills, and shows enormous quantities of pebble rock. The axis runs on unbroken to the south-west and crosses the Sandy Lick creek twelve miles away. The same Massive Sand rock of XII is found on the Sandy Lick, but there is not a piece of pebble rock to be seen.

Again the Conglomerate of XII is largely a massive pebble rock on the crest of the Allegheny Mountains, at the Snow Shoe in Centre county; yet at the Tangascootac Basin and at the Susquehanna River to the north-east, the Conglomerate of XII shows no pebbles.

Were these rocks now deep buried and oil rocks, it appears as if the costly and slow process of boring wells would have marked out for us the change in the rocks as we now see it, and that their oil wells would have been on the pebble rock and their dry holes where it had turned to fine-grained massive sandstone.

APPENDIX D.

NATURAL GAS IN IRON WORKING.

JOHN B. PEARSE, A. M., M. E.

Conveyance and Use of Natural Gas.

The greater part of the following observations were made on gas from the well of the Natural Gas Company, (Limited,) the only one at present supplying gas for manufacturing purposes, which is situated on Bull creek, at Ladnorsville, Butler county, about five miles west of Sarversburg, on the Butler Branch railroad. It is an isolated well, situated some miles south of those districts of Butler county, which at present produce oil and in which, within the limits of Parker township the most remarkable gas wells exist. Of these the Fairview, the Delamater and the Burns wells attract the greatest attention from the enormous volume and great force of the gas current issuing from their tubes. The roaring of the gas when struck makes a powerful impression, not lessened by the fierceness of its flame, if accidentally fired, and the great danger and difficulty of extinguishing the conflagration. The well at Fairview emitted gas so powerfully that, when accidentally fired, no flame appeared within 8 or 10 feet of the mouth of its tube, 5⅝ inches in diameter, and it cost five hundred dollars to put out the flame. The contractor accomplished his task by digging a circular ditch round the well as a centre; protecting himself by working on the windward side of the bank raised by the dirt, always thrown inward toward the well, he finally succeeded in controlling the gas, by the cone of earth thus raised over the tube, sufficiently to extinguish the flame.

The Burns and Delamater wells, now the property of Messrs. Kirk and Dilworth, are situated within half a mile of each other, about seven miles north-east of Butler, and some fifteen miles from the well of the Natural Gas Company. In a direct line these two wells are nearly thirty miles from Pittsburg. Both wells are cased with 5⅝ inch pipe, and each is about 1,600 feet deep, being drilled into the so-called "fourth sand." The Burns well never produced oil, while the Delamater well yielded ten barrels per day by pumping so long as it ended in the "third sand," but, on being deepened, gas alone was found. The pressure of the gas was such that the drilling tools, weighing about 1,600 pounds, could be drawn up by hand. It has been difficult to ascertain the pressure at these wells. The casing of the Burns well was fitted with a cap, into which were screwed five two inch pipes. When all were successively closed, the pressure rose to 300 pounds; at that point a vent was opened, because that pressure was estimated to counterbalance the weight of the casing, and any further increase would have blown the latter out of the well.

The following report was made on the Burns well by Mr. Otto Wuth, chemist, of Pittsburg:

PITTSBURG, PA., *October* 18, 1875.

Messrs. Kirk & Dilworth:

At your request I have visited your Burns gas well at the Duffy farm, in order to ascertain the quality of the gas and the amount produced, and now give you the result of my researches. The gas itself is almost altogether hydro-carbon of the composition $C_4 H_6$, mixed with but little oxide of carbon and carbonic acid. Its illuminating power is equal to 7½ candles, coal gas being about 16. Its heating power is about 25 per cent higher than that of good bituminous coal of equal weight. Specific gravity of the gas is 1.56. [0.56, see below.]

The pressure at the well—5⅝ inch tube—being 100 pounds per square inch, by actual experiment, the pressure of the gas when conducted through a 2 inch tube from the well to Freeport, fifteen miles, was reduced from 200 pounds to 125 pounds. It is therefore safe to assume that when starting with a pressure of 100 pounds and conducted through a 5⅝ inch tube to Pittsburg, thirty-five miles, the loss by friction will not be more than one-half, so that the gas has a pressure of fifty pounds per square inch at Pittsburg. The velocity at which the gas at the pressure rushes into the air is in round numbers

1,700 feet per second. This number multiplied by the area of the tube, 17 square feet, gives 289 cubic feet per second, or 17,340 cubic feet per minute, or, in round numbers, 1,000,000 cubic feet per hour.

13.072 cubic feet of air weigh 1 pound.

8.5128½ cubic feet of gas weigh 1 pound.

1,000,000 cubic feet of gas weigh 58.7 tons.

The amount of gas per day will be at the rate 1,408 tons. If you take into consideration that for furnace use the combustion of the gas will be much more complete than that of bituminous coal, and the absolute heating effect is 25 per cent greater, when the combustion is complete in both cases, you can be sure that the above figures are, if anything, too low.

Yours respectfully,

O. WUTH

Mr. Wuth has corrected this letter for me as to the following points: A rough analysis indicated the presence of carbonic acid, (say 0.50 per cent). The specific gravity 1.56 is a typographical error for 0.56, which agrees more nearly with Prof. Sadtler's determinations. The pressure of the gas was found to be 200 pounds per square inch, and on being actually passed 16 miles through a 2-inch pipe to Freeport the pressure was found to be stationary at 125 pounds. The natural inference was therefore drawn that the gas could be conducted to Pittsburg through the larger pipe with substantially the same waste. The estimated quantity of gas results from a calculation based on the fact that air under a pressure of 50 pounds per square inch would escape from the pipe at a velocity of 1,700 feet per second, and supposing gas to act similarly, the result would not be less than 1,000,000 cubic feet per hour.

Prof. Sadtler furnishes me the following additional details of his analyses: The specific gravity of four natural gases was determined experimentally, one of which was out of the Burns well, and had a specific gravity of 0.615. This gas contained 6.10 per cent of free hydrogen, and only 0.34 per cent of carbonic acid gas.

The gases from wells ending in different geological horizons have a wide range as regards their specific gravity and composition. The natural gas obtained at Erie has a specific gravity of 0.805, being the heaviest on record. This gas contains over 2 per cent of carbonic acid gas, and only 0.31 per cent of free hydrogen, the remainder being chiefly marsh gas and other hydro-carbons. On the other hand, a determination of the specific gravity of the natural gas from Sheffield, Warren county, Pa., gives the astonishing result of 0.45, and is the lightest gas yet examined. Though not yet analysed, it must contain a large amount of free hydrogen. We have then a range from 0.45 to 0.80 in specific gravity.

It is thought that natural gas from the wells must be heavier than air for the reason that it will expel air from a pit sunk round the casing of a well and can be seen flowing downward over the sides of oil tanks out of which it has displaced the air. It will also fill a pump log, and can be poured out of the bore like carbonic acid gas. The permanent gases, however, are not heavier than air. When they issue from the well they are charged with the vapor of higher hydro-carbons which, when pure, are liquids or solids. Prof. Sadtler tells me he found, in a qualitative examination, ethyl-hydride, $C_2 H_6$, and propyl-hydride, $C_3 H_8$. These higher hydro-carbons condense or, as the case may be, separate in small quantities from the gas out of a state of mechanical admixture, and the permanent gas remains lighter than air. I found at Erie that it was heavier than coal gas, for no mixture of the two could be obtained at the city gas works, the natural gas sinking to the bottom of the holder.

As a confirmation of this view, it may be stated that during a visit to many of our gas wells, for the purpose of collecting samples, Prof. Sadtler observed that a white solid, of buttery consistency, was deposited by natural gas in the absence of oil. "At Sheffield there is a large gas well where the gas is not accompanied by appreciable quantities of oil. The piping at the mouth of the well is therefore dry and free from any oil. Yet on this dry tubing, for a yard to either side of a joint at which a leakage of gas occurs, a deposit is formed of a white solid, which the oil men call paraffine. I saw the same thing at the Wilcox gas well, in M'Kean county, where I collected a jar of it for examination." The oil men say this deposit is invariably seen in flowing wells, and they therefore regard its presence as a good omen.

The most obvious use of the gas so lavishly going to waste is to light the derrick and raise steam for the pumping engine at the well. Almost everywhere the neighborhood of the wells is lighted at night by a small jet, and on a larger scale the Fairview well supplies four towns with gas, viz: Fairview, Petrolia, Argyle and Karns City. It is burnt in the streets after a generous fashion in large flaring torches, like beacon fires or medieval cressets. A boiler, described as "20-horse power," was connected with the casing of the Fairview well to separate the gas from the water issuing with it. From the boiler a 3½ inch pipe was laid for seven miles to the four towns above mentioned, and connections were furnished in 1873 to 40 pumping and drilling wells, 8 pump stations on pipe lines, 200 gas burners and 40 cooking stoves. The supply of gas exceeded this consumption, the excess escaping at considerable pressure from a safety valve on the boiler. This well still retains a large portion of its force, while the Newton gas well, near Titusville, struck in 1872, has ceased to emit gas much above atmospheric pressure, though during its first year it was estimated to yield 4,000,000 cubic feet per day at a pressure of about 350 pounds per square inch. The enormous pressure forced the gas readily through pipes of small size, not over 3½ inches inches in diameter at Fairview, nor over 2 inches at Titusville.

In the East Sandy district an extraordinary gas well was struck in 1869. After burning for about a year, it was extinguished and the gas was used, instead of steam, in the cylinders of the drilling engines; about 60 wells were thus sunk. The first twelve wells caused little change in the pressure, but when the fortieth was reached, a serious inroad had been made, and when the whole number had been sunk, the pressure, at first estimated at over 90 pounds to the square inch, when fully in use, fell below an available amount. At M'Keesport a well 1,700 feet deep "struck gas" with a pressure roughly estimated at 500 pounds to the square inch. Probably as powerful as any of these are the Delamater well and the Burns well, also in Butler county, not far north of Butler. The combustibility and high calorific value of the gas fromany part of the district at once suggested the value of a fuel so cheap and so readily transportable.

The first application of the gas to Iron-making, which has hitherto constituted its most important use, was made by Messrs. Rogers & Birchfield, in the puddling furnaces of their works at Leechburg, in Armstrong county. Unfortunately, they went soon after into bankruptcy, and the opportunity for a full series of experiments was thus lost. But Mr. J. D. Weeks, of Pittsburg, with the view of ascertaining the qualities of the iron made with gas, took samples of charges boiled with gas and coal, and forwarded them for analysis to Mr. A. S. M'Creath, of the Survey, with the result detailed below at the proper place.

The well used by Messrs. Rogers & Birchfield was one 3 inches in diameter, sunk for oil in 1871 on the left bank of the Kiskiminetas, to a depth of 1,250 feet. No oil being found the abandoned well was bought by Messrs. Rogers & Birchfield, and the gas, which was abundant at a pressure of 70 pounds to the square inch, was conveyed across the creek to their works, by a pipe bridge carrying a 5-inch pipe, with which all their fires were connected. A freshet having carried this pipe away, one 3 inches in diameter was substituted, and proved fully large enough for the purpose. The mill is named the Siberian Mill, and was built in 1872, with 6 single puddling furnaces, 6 heating furnaces, 6 trains of rolls, 2 steam hammers, 1 refinery and 2 "knobbling fires," which are substantially finery forges. The product consisted of tin plate, sheet iron and charcoal terne plate, and the average annual make was about 2,800 tons; all this work, including puddling, heating and raising steam, was done by gas brought through the 3-inch pipe above mentioned.

When the gas was applied no special alterations were made in the furnaces as to dimensions, but the space above the grate, between the fire bridge and the end of the furnace, was converted into a gas chamber, into which the gas was admitted by jets pierced in a half inch pipe led across the end of the grate each way from a half inch T at the centre, on a pipe of the same size, through which the furnace was supplied. The grate was covered with fine broken bricks but not so closely as to exclude air, some of which passed up and mixed with the gas. The fire bridge was built up to the roof, openings being made for the passage of the gas into the body of the furnace by leaving out a brick here and there. Full combustion was effected by a blast of air at about 2 pounds pressure entering through the roof by two 1⅛-inch nozzles in front of the fire bridge and directed toward the center of the hearth. The heat produced by this arrangement is very intense, while the blast of air directed on the metal facilitated the boiling. The operation was more readily regulated than with coal, both the heat and the character of the flame being fully under control, so that the iron could be melted hot, chilled quickly to promote the commencement of boiling, and the heat could be raised to free the balls well from cinder without fear of injury. Extravagant statements were at first made as to the greater yield of iron with less consumption of ore for fettling, 800 pounds of ore fix being said to be required for two turns at a single coal furnace, while 500 pounds were said to last five single gas furnaces an entire week. Ten heats were made in 15 hours by the two turns at one furnace, and with charges of 460 pounds of Lucy pig iron, and 50 to 80 pounds of roll or hammer scale, a yield of 480 to 490 pounds was said to be obtained from each charge. But the 100 pounds of ore fix weekly used would furnish, say 60 pounds of iron, and the 3,575 pounds of scale (55 charges, at 65 pounds each,) would furnish 787 pounds, estimated at 72 per cent going into and 50 per cent on leaving the furnace as tap cinder; the gain was stated at 1,375 pounds (55 charges, at 25 pounds,) that is 528 pounds (1,375—847=528) more metal than could possibly have been procured from the materials. The process, however, needed no such external bolstering, for the use of gas then shortened the charges and certainly worked them hotter, thus making the iron more homogeneous and often softer. The saving in fuel amounted to about 60 tons of coal per day and a cheaper grade of iron could be used. The failure of the owners had thus no connection with the use of natural gas as fuel; on the contrary, the new fuel proved so efficient that arrangements were made to bring the gas of the Ladnorsville well into Sharpsburg and Allegheny. This work has been completed with great success, as will be seen below.

Mr. Weeks recorded the charges of four heats, numbered 1 to 4, as follows:

Number of Heat.	No. 1.	No. 2.	No. 3.	No. 4.
Isabella gray forge pig	312	294	265	241
Old car wheels, &c	160	184	201	230
Total iron	472	478	466	471
Scale from rolls, &c	275	302	260	260
Total *charged*	747	780	726	731
Product in blooms	553	556	540	572
Gain over iron charged	81	78	74	101
Percentage of gain	17	16	15	21

Having obtained these results from the use of gas, Mr. Weeks desired to become acquainted with the chemical properties of the metal used and of the products obtained from gas as well as from coal. He sent Mr. M'Creath samples of the pig iron used, of the scrap used and of the tap cinder and muck bar obtained from two charges, of which one was boiled with gas, which we denominate A, the other with coal, which we denominate B.

Pig Iron and Scrap Used.

	Isabella pig iron.	Scrap iron, &c.
Carbon, graphitic	3.860	2.890
Carbon, combined	0.341	1.135
Silicium	3.008	0.766
Sulphur	0.050	0.098
Phosphorus	0.592	0.353
Manganese	0.511	0.209
Iron, &c	91.638	94.549
	100.000	100.000

The pig was an "open mill iron" in grade, while the scrap consisted of car scrap, wheel scrap and other cast iron scrap mixed together. The same mixture of pig and scrap was used in both charges.

Tap Cinder from Respective Charges

	Charge A.	Charge B.
Silica	24.640	21.040
Protoxide of iron	57.471	62.100
Sesquioxide of iron	5.857	6.143
Alumina	0.942	2.608
Protoxide of manganese	2.072	1.662
Lime	2.363	1.786
Magnesia	0.367	0.230

	Charge A.	Charge B.
Phosphoric acid	3.685	3.609
Sulphur	0.289	0.249
Alkalies and loss	2.314	0.573
	100.000	100.000

Or,

Iron	48.800	52.600
Sulphur	0.289	0.249
Phosphorus	1.609	1.576

Muck-bar made from Respective Charges.

	Charge A.	Charge B.
Carbon, graphite	0.004	0.005
Carbon, combined	.102	.126
Silicium	.289	.212
Sulphur	.011	.008
Phosphorus	.312	.136
Manganese	.051	.072
Iron, &c.	99.231	99.441
	100.000	100.000

The hammer scale used was not sent, but would not have changed the result of the analyses, as it would have had the same influence in both cases. The actual result shows that while the muck-bars are substantially the same as respects other elements, the composition of the gas iron as to phosphorus is greatly inferior to that of the coal iron, as it contains nearly 2½ times more phosphorus than the latter.

The experiments were not conclusive, since the product analysed —muck bar—was one which itself did not admit of mechanical test in the smithery, and being afterwards re-worked into sheet metal, was in a very disadvantageous form for experiment. And further, the irregular composition of scrap iron is such that the chemical results had little value.

These tests indicated a fact novel to those who were using the irons made with gas and coal, for they consider the former superior to the latter, as it is certainly more homogeneous. Considerable doubt was expressed on the subject. The iron made with gas was desirable for many purposes where ordinary iron would not answer, and seemed more ductile and homogeneous than charcoal metal boiled with coal.

It was important, therefore, that the point should be definitely settled, and the following work was undertaken with the view of making a series of exact experiments, and of describing the practical use of the natural gas as a fuel in iron making.

The location of the well of the Natural Gas Company has been specified above. Its early history is narrated by Mr. J. Cumming, U. S. Signal Service observer at Tarentum. "On the night of the 2d of February, 1875, myself, in company with several others, paid a visit to the great gas well, situated about nine miles from Tarentum and fifteen miles south of Butler, at a place called Larden's Mills on the farm of Mr. William Herney. The well was tapped about ten weeks ago, as I learned from one of the proprietors in their search after oil. They had gone down a distance of 1,145 feet, and had just struck the "first sand rock." The well is located in a hollow, about 300 feet wide, between abrupt hills. The gas is conveyed from the well to the distance of about 150 feet by a 6-inch metal pipe, and discharges itself at the end of the pipe with the percussive force of steam."

"Our party came into the vicinity of the well about 9 o'clock at night, having seen the vast light floating in the sky, on many a dark night, on previous occasions, thirteen miles distant; but when we came in its immediate influence, and saw the trees on either hand lit up and thin trunks and branches silvered to their tops by this burning torch, the scene was beyond description. On arriving at the ground we met hundreds of people from all parts of the country, who like ourselves, flock nightly to see this great wonder. The first thing to strike the visitor on arriving is the great mass of fine, white flame, of intense heat and brightness, the hollow noise resembling thunder heard as the outrushing gas plunges into the atmosphere and lights all around by its imposing brilliancy. The sound of its roaring can be distinctly heard at a distance of four miles."

"The flame of this natural torch is about 40 feet long and fifteen feet wide, and keeps at these dimensions night and day with striking regularity. Hence, the light is both regular and constant. The heat emitted by so làrge a body of flame is very great. The trees all around, at proportional distance, are budding, and the grass that has not been trodden down by the throng of visitors is growing finely; and considering this is mid-winter, this circumstance will give some idea of the great heat. I approached within 60 feet of the flame, and supposed it to be at that distance about 140°. The light is grand.

You can see to read with ease a quarter of a mile from this enormous gas jet, and if uninterrupted by trees and the wind of the road, reading could be done at the distance of a mile and a-half."

The well is bored in the bottom of the valley of Bull creek, here an abrupt ravine between hills 150 feet high. It is 7 inches in diameter, tubed with a $5\frac{5}{8}$ inch casing. A coal bed, probably the Upper Freeport bed, crops out 20 feet above the stream. The presence of gas is thus far rather local since a second well 10 inches in diameter sunk about a-half a mile from that of the Natural Gas Company, is nearly 2,000 feet deep, but as yet, has developed nothing. (Vide, note at end of appendix.)

The arrangements at the well are as follows: a boiler 4 feet in diameter and 17 feet long is connected with the 6 inch pipe from the well, and has an exit in the 6-inch pipe of the conduit line, both pipes being fitted to the top of the boiler. In the boiler the greater part of the water is separated from the gas, and is drawn off twice a day; the gas of course has free exit. The ordinary pressure in the boiler is 110 to 119 pounds per square inch, when the gas is in use; the safety valve is loaded to 140 pounds, but is lifted only when the gas is shut off at the mills. So far as is known the pressure has been regular and the supply unchanged since the boiler was put in; the well, however, has never been completely closed so as to obtain the total pressure. The boiler is enclosed in a house, and the premises are fenced in and are in charge of watchmen constantly on duty.

The pipe line was laid with the intention of taking the shortest and most direct line to the works at Sharpsburg and Allegheny, without reference to grade. The line follows a general south-west course, but undergoes frequent bends on account of the formation of the ground and makes many short crooks to avoid obstacles like large trees. Many of its windings are due to the hostility of the farmers, who, fearing conflagrations, refused the right of way, and compelled the location of the line along the township roads. The line leaves the hollow of Bull's creek within a few hundred feet of the well, and crosses four main summits on its way to the head waters of Pine creek. Thence it passes down the valley of Pine creek to Sharpsburg, crossing a fifth and very abrupt ridge 182 feet high above the creek, at the distance of half a mile from the works of Messrs. Spang, Chalfant & Co. The district traversed would be properly termed a rolling country, the ridges, with the exception of the fifth, not being very sharply defined. From Messrs. Spang, Chalfant & Co.'s mill, at Sharpsburg, the line to the works of Messrs. Graff, Bennett & Co., at Allegheny, follows the turnpike on a slightly descending grade along the north or right bank of the Allegheny river.

The pipe used was 6 inches in diameter, of iron ¼-inch thick. It was laid in a ditch 2 to 3 feet deep covered with earth, and at the crossings of streams it was laid exposed on the bottom of the stream. It was put together in convenient sections on the surface and afterwards lowered into the ditch. The lengths were joined by ordinary screw threaded sockets, the pipes being screwed in till their ends butted against each other. Where bends were necessary, the pipe was sometimes heated, but often bent cold.

The Map and Profile of the Pipe Line of the Natural Gas Company (Limited) herewith presented gives full details of the engineering features of the line. Starting at the well, at Ladnorville, the map shows the various needle courses which the pipe line follows to the mills. Every fifth station is marked on the Map in figures. The Profile starting at the same place gives a profile of the line drawn on with the vertical and horizontal scales equal—that is the profile is the natural one. The levels start from a datum point 734 feet above tide, at Bennett's Mills Station, on the Western Pennslvania Railroad. In the Profile every fifth station is numbered in figures, and the stations at which the pressure of gas in the pipe were taken also correspond with the letters used in the table given below. The mill of Messrs. Spang, Chalfant & Co. is taken as the first station, and is marked "O," the rest A, B, C, &c.

The supervision of the line is committed to a Superintendent, in charge of the whole work, and three men who patrol the line, on the lookout for leaks or accidents. When a leak is discovered by the smell or movement of the earth, the repairer closes it by means of sheet rubber pressed against the hole by a clamp ring bolted around the pipe. No malicious obstructions have occurred since the pipe was laid, but during the laying three or four pump logs were surreptitiously inserted and boys threw stones into the pipe at Allegheny, which were blown out at the end, but the pump logs obstructed the pressure for some time very materially. They were finally discovered by the failure to pass through the pipe an India rubber ball introduced at the well. The pipe was then tapped till the obstructions were discovered. They were removed about six months after the opening of the line.

On the completion of the line the gas burned at Sharpsburg 20 minutes after it was let on at the well. With a length of 17 miles the cubic capacity of the pipe is 17,592 feet, so that the supply of gas at Sharpsburg amounted, before the pipe was really open, to more than 53,000 cubic feet per hour. This supply would meet the requirements of Messrs. Spang, Chalfant & Co.'s works, where the connections were equal in area to 75 half-inch pipe, and 10 furnaces are run wholly on gas, viz: 7 puddling, 3 heating; in all there are 45 connections to the gas, including 24 puddling furnaces, 12 heating furnaces and 3 batteries of 3 boilers each. Messrs. Graff, Bennett & Co. run 25 furnaces on gas, only one—a puddling furnace—wholly on gas so far as I am informed. But the pressure at these last works is less by 5 pounds than it is at Sharpsburg, and when used there the pressure fell to 2 pounds above the atmosphere, hence the other works got none. The safety valve at Sharpsburg is set at 15 pounds, and is never lifted when the gas is in use, nor is the one at the well, but when the gas is shut at the mill the pressure would rise to 80 pounds in a quarter of an hour if the safety valve was held down.

In order to increase the supply an attempt was made to suck the gas out, and thereby lessen the supposed friction in the pipe. A Cameron blowing engine was fitted to work as an exhauster, having a 40-inch gas and 18-inch steam cylinder, and 48-inch stroke; at 28 double strokes per minute this was estimated, without allowances, to give 112,000 cubic feet per hour, or probably 80,000 cubic feet after proper deductions. But the attempt was not successful, and after the removal of the obstructions an ample quantity was delivered by the natural pressure. Before the discovery of the obstructions it was thought that a possible cooling of the gas might reduce its volume, and on observing the temperature in winter it was found to be 48° at the well and only 40° at the works, although the pipe crossed streams 20 times and lay above frost line in the ground.

Pressures Observed near Sharpsburg.

DISTANCE TOWARD WELL FROM SHARPSBURG WORKS.		PRESSURE.		Level above Pine creek at Sharpsburg works.
		Before removal of obstructions.	After removal of obstructions....	
	Feet.	Pounds.	Pounds.	Feet.
Spang, Chalfant & Co........................	0	2	....	0
Thence to A..................................	1,938	7	....	+ 182
Thence to B..................................	4,026	11½	....	+ 62
Thence to C..................................	4,531	12¼	....	+ 34
Thence to D..................................	4,812	13	....	+ 43
Thence to E..................................	5,182	13½	....	+ 48
Thence to F..................................	9,736	20¾	....	+ 48
Thence to G..................................	12,316	24	....	+ 84
Thence to well..............................	89,820	119	....	

Distance causing Loss of 1 *pound, estimated from above observations.*

STATION.	Before removal of obstructions.	After removal of obstructions.
	Feet.	Feet.
From Sharpsburg to A..........................	431	
From Sharpsburg to B..........................	447	
From Sharpsburg to C..........................	490	
From Sharpsburg to D..........................	458	
From Sharpsburg to E..........................	471	
From Sharpsburg to F..........................	539	
From Sharpsburg to G..........................	573	
From Sharpsburg to well.......................	771	
From Station G to well........................	816	

Distance causing Loss of 1 *pound, estimated from above observations.*

STATION.	Before removal of obstructions.	After removal of obstructions.
	Feet.	Feet.
Between 0 and A	431	
Between A and B	464	
Between B and C	673	
Between C and D	375	
Between D and E	740	
Between E and F	628	

Datum, being assumed that Graff, Bennet & Co.'s mill is 728 feet above tide.

Station.	Dist.	Course.	Elevation.	Remarks.
0	....	....	710	0 at Spang, Chalfant & Co.'s mill.
0 to 1	280	N. 15½° W	720	Elevation of Station 1.
1 to 2	272	N. 29° W.	730	Elevation of Station 2.
2 to 3	290	N. 27½° W	759	(Etcetera.)
3 to 4	286	N. 3¾° W	825	
4 to 5	320	N. 4° 35′ E....	882	0 to 5 Dove-colored sandstone thin bedded.
5 to 6	280	N. 14½° E.....	889	
6 to 7	210	N. 17° 10′ E...	892	7 gauge cock.
7 to 8	150	N. 15° E......	869	
8 to 9	375	N. 1½° E......	859	
9 to 10	600	N. 11° E......	862	
10 to 11	130	N. 26½° E.....	855	
11 to 12	525	N. 18° 25′ E ..	784	
12 to 13	143	N. 48½° E.....	787	
13 to 14	165	N. 53° E......	772	14 grayish-blue sandstone.
14 to 15	176	N. 41° 10′ E...	758	
15 to 16	180	N. 24° E......	739	16 gauge cock.
16 to 17	149	N. 21° E......	744	17 gauge cock.
17 to 18	281	N. 17° E	753	
18 to 19	420	N. 31½° W	763	19 gauge cock.
19 to 20	125	N. 33 W	753	
20 to 21	202	N. 3½° E......	751	
21 to 22	370	N. 22° E......	750	
22 to 23	270	N. 25° E......	741	
23 to 24	200	N. 17° E......	737	
24 to 25	162	N. 35½° E.....	730	
25 to 26	370	N. 49° E......	728	
26 to 27	1,100	N. 51½° E.....	746	
27 to 28	400	N. 5° E.......	746	
28 to 29	145	N. 1½° E......	754	
29 to 30	400	N. 48° E......	753	30 S. 58° W. 230′ to old coal opening on turnpike.
30 to 31	660	N. 49° 20′ E ..	768	
31 to 32	500	N. 72° E......	764	
32 to 33	1,120	N. 72½° E.....	781	33 at elevation of 15′ above station, bluish-gray shaly SS. 25′ thick; on top light gray massive SS.
33 to 34	440	N. 72½° E.....	786	
34 to 35	400	N. 63¼° E.....	796	
35 to 36	220	N. 32° E......	794	36 gauge cock.
36 to 37	260	N. 32° E......	810	
37 to 38	182	N. 41½° E.....	804	
38 to 39	208	N. 76° E......	810	39 same SS. as at 33.
39 to 40	450	N. 63½° E.....	810	
40 to 41	325	N. 40° 40′ E...	820	
41 to 42	585	N. 9° E.......	825	
42 to 43	132	N. 48° 40′ E...	834	
43 to 44	385	N. 34° E......	834	
44 to 45	355	N. 28° 25′ E...	840	
45 to 46	310	N. 2° W	842	
46 to 47	660	N. 28½° E.....	855	47 Geo. Shaffer.
47 to 48	860	N. 20° 50′ E...	864	
48 to 49	600	N. 15° E......	878	
49 to 50	310	N. 2° 45′ E....	898	
50 to 51	427	N. 11° 20′ E...	924	
51 to 52	290	N. 10¾° W....	935	
52 to 53	275	N. 10¼° E.....	952	
53 to 54	228	N. 8° 50′ E....	947	
54 to 55	200	N. 19° 50′ E...	955	
55 to 56	295	N. 15° E......	941	
56 to 57	150	N. 33½° W	953	
57 to 58	195	N. 3¼° E......	953	

Station.	Dist.	Course.	Elevation.	Remarks.
58 to 59	140	N. 17° E......	958	Elevation of station 59.
59 to 60	690	N. 30¼° E.....	960	
60 to 61	325	N. 30° 25′ E...	948	
61 to 62	340	N. 54° 50′ E...	930	
62 to 63	182	N. 37° E......	917	
63 to 64	590	N. 24° E......	931	
64 to 65	1,000	N. 29¾° E.....	946	
65 to 66	400	N. 47½° E.....	944	
66 to 67	200	N. 66° E......	954	67 Myer's coal mine, 1½′ thick.
67 to 68	175	N. 51° E......	951	68 creek.
68 to 69	340	N. 37° 20 E...	971	
69 to 70	251	N. 30° E......	959	70 creek.
70 to 71	173	N. 26½° E.....	992	
71 to 72	641	N. 30° E......	999	
72 to 73	350	N. 32½° E.....	1,004	73+200′ creek.
73 to 74	620	N. 34° E......	1,013	
74 to 75	760	N. 34½° E.....	1,018	
75 to 76	295	N. 29° E......	1,038	
76 to 77	710	N. 1½° E......	1,039	77 & 78 olive colored shales.
77 to 78	640	N. 31½° E.....	1,144	
78 to 79	230	N. 23½° E.....	1,147	
79 to 80	560	N. 28° E......	1,065	
80 to 81	155	N. 44° 10′ E...	1,080	81+145′ valve in pipe.
81 to 82	440	N. 41½° E.....	1,078	82 road.
82 to 83	420	N. 50½° E.....	1,065	
83 to 84	280	N. 64¼° E.....	1,040	
84 to 85	660	N. 86° E......	1,024	
85 to 86	265	N. 78½° E.....	1,030	
86 to 87	425	N. 52° E......	1,040	
87 to 88	780	N. 49° 50′ E...	1,006	
88 to 89	185	N. 32° 50′ E...	1,002	89 creek.
89 to 90	730	N. 24½° E.....	1,024	
90 to 91	475	N. 39° E......	1,009	91+150′, and 140′ east of line, Blue [Run School House.]
91 to 92	460	N. 34° E......	1,031	
92 to 93	485	N. 39° E......	1,012	93+100′ small run.
93 to 94	430	N. 54° 20′ E...	1,027	
94 to 95	388	N. 59° E......	1,051	
95 to 96	510	N. 49° 50′ E...	1,017	
96 to 97	322	N. 58½° E.....	1,039	
97 to 98	750	N. 31° 40′ E...	998	
98 to 99	432	N. 38° 25′ E...	1,027	
99 to 100	670	N. 32½° E.....	972	
100 to 101	261	N. 4° E.......	972	
101 to 102	170	N. 4° E.......	952	
102 to 103	460	N. 27° E......	919	102 to 103, line has small sharp [turns in woods.]
103 to 104	250	N. 52½° E.....	895	
104 to 105	395	N. 67° E......	839	
105 to 106	565	N. 66° E......	816	106 Deer creek.
106 to 107	612	N. 47½° E.....	841	107 Brown shales.
107 to 108	365	N. 78° E......	875	
108 to 109	195	N. 39° E......	885	
109 to 110	700	N. 8° E.......	939	
110 to 111	670	N. ½° E.......	973	
111 to 112	310	N. 7° E.......	969	
112 to 113	300	N. 6½° E......	964	
113 to 114	385	N. 10½° E.....	942	
114 to 115	300	N. 40¼° E.....	968	
115 to 116	192	N. 22° E......	962	
116 to 117	705	N. 14° 30′ E...	900	
117 to 118	880	N. 23° E......	892	
118 to 119	1,270	N. 26½° E.....	915	
119 to 120	865	N. 37½° E.....	903	
120 to 121	405	N. 58¾° E.....	917	Elevation of station 121.

Station.	Dist.	Course.	Elevation.	Remarks.
121 to 122	805	N. 43° E.	951	Elevation of station, 122.
122 to 123	495	N. 33¾° E.	958	
123 to 124	330	North	947	
124 to 125	225	N. 18½° E.	966	
125 to 126	335	N. 8½° E.	1,021	
126 to 127	840	N. 27° E.	1,117	
127 to 128	520	N. 24° E.	1,089	
128 to 129	600	N. 11° E.	1,104	
129 to 130	1,560	N. 4° E.	1,118	
130 to 131	50	N. 11½° W.	1,115	
131 to 132	770	N. 2° W.	1,036	
132 to 133	135	N. 19° E.	1,015	
133 to 134	280	N. 45½ E.	1,031	
134 to 135	330	N. 46½° E.	1,065	
135 to 136	168	N. 18° E.	1,074	
136 to 137	330	N. 62° E.	1,065	
137 to 138	141	N. 61° E.	1,028	
138 to 139	118	N. 47° E.	1,033	
139 to 140	565	N. 30° E.	997	
140 to 141	390	N. 14° E.	996	
141 to 142	432	N. 19½° E.	966	
142 to 143	290	N. 27° E.	938	
143 to 144	610	N. 20° E.	951	
144 to 145	280	N. 35° E.	977	
143 to 144 (No.2)	625	N. 11° E.	999	
144 to 145 (No.2)	328	N. 28° E.	999	
145 to 146	640	N. 26° E.	1,013	145 Purple shales.
146 to 147	50	N. 25½° E.	1,017	
147 to 148	700	N. 14½° E.	991	
148 to 149	660	N. 10° 40′ E.	939	
149 to 150	440	N. 12° 30′ E.	958	
150 to 151	428	N. 18° E.	997	
151 to 152	310	N. 4° E.	1,010	
152 to 153	122	N. 5½° E.	1,019	
153 to 154	240	N. 12½° E.	1,023	
154 to 155	840	N. 18° E.	1,069	
155 to 156	1,070	N. 18½° E.	954	
156 to 157 (No.1)	175	N. 18° E.	982	157 Valve in pipe line.
157 to 158 (No.1)	200	N. 32¾° E.	986	
158 to 157 (No.2)	241	N. 45° E.	992	
157 to 158 (No.2)	265	N. 17° E.	1,015	
158 to 159	370	N. 1½° W.	1,037	
159 to 160	855	N. 2° W.	1,083	
160 to 161	480	N. ½° W.	1,111	
161 to 162	1,540	N. 2½° E.	1,111	
162 to 163	410	N. 13½° E.	1,121	
163 to 164	390	N. 57° E.	1,129	
164 to 165	385	N. 53° E.	1,137	
165 to 166	545	N. 59¾° E.	1,130	
166 to 167	220	N. 62½° E.	1,107	
167 to 168	300	N. 63° E.	1,015	
168 to 169	380	N. 35½° E.	988	
169 to 170	540	N. 27° E.	926	
170 to 171	345	N. 67° E.	962	
171 to 172	700	N. 68½° E.	1,025	
172 to 173	550	N. 69° E.	1,031	
173 to 174	280	N. 63° E.	977	
174 to 175	260	N. 50½° E.	1,012	
175 to 176	470	N. 40½° E.	1,070	
176 to 177	130	N. 18° E.	1,069	
177 to 178	1,080	N. 32½° E.	898	178 Coal mine.
178 to 179	835	N. 38° E.	830	
179 to 180	1,165	N. 27° E.	826	

Station.	Dist.	Course.	Elevation.	Remarks.
180 to 181	420	N. 16° E.	836	
181 to 182	260	N. 29° E.	846	Elevation of Stat. 182.
182 to 183	320	N. 18° E.	858	Elevation of Station 183.
183 to 184	258	N. 48° E.	898	
184 to 185	145	N. 32° E.	924	
185 to 186	315	N. 28° E.	942	186. 5' below coal bench.
186 to 187	550	N. 30¾° E.	998	
187 to 188	690	N. 33½° E.	1,091	
188 to 189	415	N. 27° E.	1,120	
189 to 190	990	N. 27° E.	1,094	
190 to 191	850	N. 32° 20' E.	1,143	
191 to 192	1,000	N. 37° E.	1,141	
192 to 193	128	N. 40½° E.	1,148	
193 to 194	270	N. 18½ E°.	1,125	
194 to 195	255	N. 17½° E.	1,081	
195 to 196	560	N. 9° E.	991	
196 to 197	95	N. 1° E.	1,009	
197 to 198	640	N. 47° E.	1,094	
198 to 199	258	N. 26° E.	1,100	
199 to 200	940	N. 32° E.	1,098	
200 to 201	340	N. 30½° E.	1,023	[the elevation being 928'†
201 to 202	605	N. 28½° E.	928	202 is at gas well* at Ladnorsville,
0 to 203	313	S. 19½° E.	713	Elevation of Station 203.
203 to 204	530	S. 2° E.	714	
204 to 205	135	S. 1° W.	720	
205 to 206	310	S. 4½° W.	722	
206 to 207	340	S. 5° W.	736	
207 to 208	83	S. 13° W.	733	
208 to 209	320	S. 45½° W.	741	
209 to 210	290	S. 41° W.	726	
210 to 211	452	S. 41½° W.	735	
211 to 212	470	S. 54° W.	752	
212 to 213	470	S. 53½° W.	759	
213 to 214	513	S. 40¾° W.	746	
214 to 215	490	S. 35° W.	751	
215 to 216	251	S. 50½° W.	754	
216 to 217	260	S. 61¼° W.	740	
217 to 218	232	S. 51½° W.	737	218. Belvidere Hotel, Allegheny.
218 to 219	320	S. 43° W.	740	
219 to 220	454	S. 57° 50' W.	740	
220 to 221	510	S. 56° W.	749	
221 to 222	420	S. 53° W.	741	
222 to 223	732	S. 49° W.	740	
223 to 224	575	S. 40½° W.	735	
224 to 225	332	S. 36° W.	750	
225 to 226	310	S. 32½° W.	736	
226 to 227	500	S. 38½° W.	743	
227 to 228	550	S. 49½° W.	739	
228 to 229	760	S. 42½° W.	745	
229 to 230	230	S. 45° W.	733	
230 to 231	30	S. 45° W.	728	At Graff, Bennett & Co.'s mill.

*Survey then returned to the starting point and was completed in the opposite direction, viz., S. E. to Graff, Bennett & Co's Mill.

† Above 202, with its elevation above tide of 928', and 20' higher, *i. e.*, 948' above tide, is an opening on a 3' coal bed, with sandstone roof, slate floor and underlying fire-clay and limestone: probably Upper Freeport Coal.

The mill of Messrs. Spang, Chalfant & Co. is supplied by two 4-inch pipes and a 6-inch pipe, which are laid below the surface, the smaller conducting pipes rising to the furnaces. At the mill of Messrs Graff, Bennett & Co. the line ends in a boiler 40 inches in diameter by 28 feet long. From this boiler a 6-inch pipe, hung to the sides of the building, makes the complete circuit of the mill and is again connected with the boiler. The small supply pipes descend from the main pipe to the furnaces.

At Sharpsburg the pressure is usually two pounds per square inch, and generally the same at Allegheny. A pressure of five pounds was found too great, as it was strong enough to force the flame out of the stack. Mr. Williams stated that with 5 pounds pressure and a 6-inch pipe he could easily run 30 furnaces, and at Sharpsburg it is practically accomplished.

The sketches on page plates 1 and 2, will illustrate the various modes of burning the gas which have been found economical. Figure 1 is the Graff, Bennett & Co. furnace; Figure 2 is the furnace of Messrs Spang, Chalfant & Co., at whose mill two other exclusively gas furnaces are also in use, of which (Figure 3) one is a gas furnace designed by Mr. Robertson, chemist of the Isabella Iron Company.

I tried the effect of the gas in an empty furnace, No. 22 of Messrs. Spang, Chalfant & Co., just after it had done its day's work and had been repaired by bricklayers. It is the Robertson gas furnace, and the one in which were made the trials of gas burning recorded below. The mill was not running; the pressure on the pipe was 13 pounds, and the ½-inch valve opened wide with two full turns. The flame in the furnace, with the valve fully open, was dense, yellow and very smoky, becoming clearer and whiter as the valve was gradually shut, yet not blue till the supply was almost entirely cut off.

Valve open 1¾ turns:	Thick, smoky flame.
" " 1½ "	Flame somewhat smoky.
" " 1¼ "	Flame quite white and clear, filling the furnace and apparently at its full power.
" " ¾ "	Flame quite transparent; ample to work the furnace; would heat a cold furnace up to working point in ¾ hour.

SKETCHES OF NATURAL GAS FURNACES

GRAFF, BENNETT & CO.'S FURNACE.

P Two Pipes about 1 inch diameter about ⅓ entire space from each side.

SPANG, CHALFANT & CO.'S FURNACE.

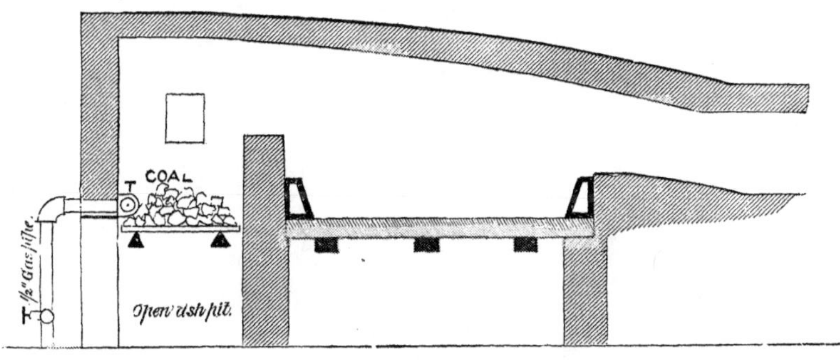

T Pipe extending across entire grate and pierced with numerous holes.

SKETCHES OF NATURAL GAS FURNACES.

ROBERTSON FURNACE

SPANG, CHALFANT & CO.

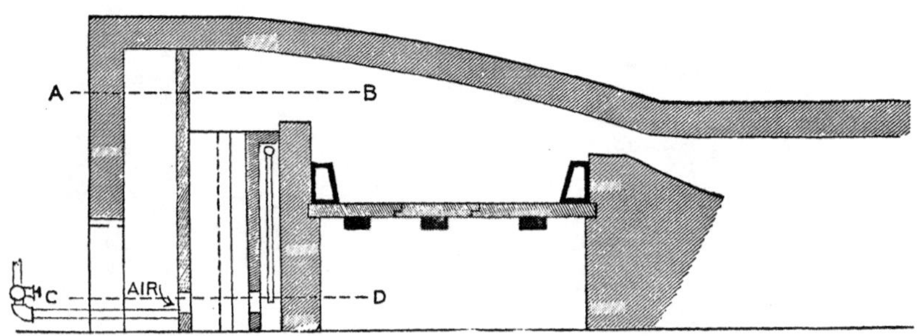

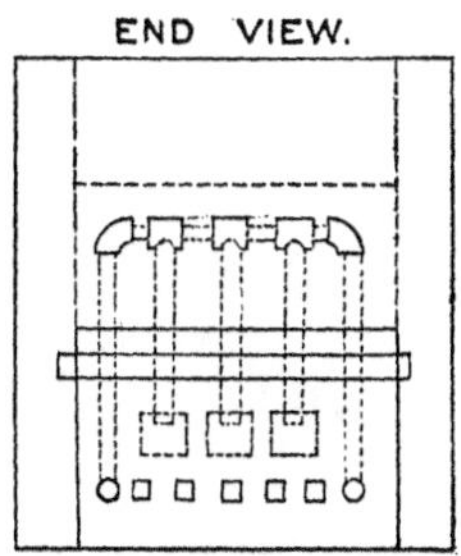

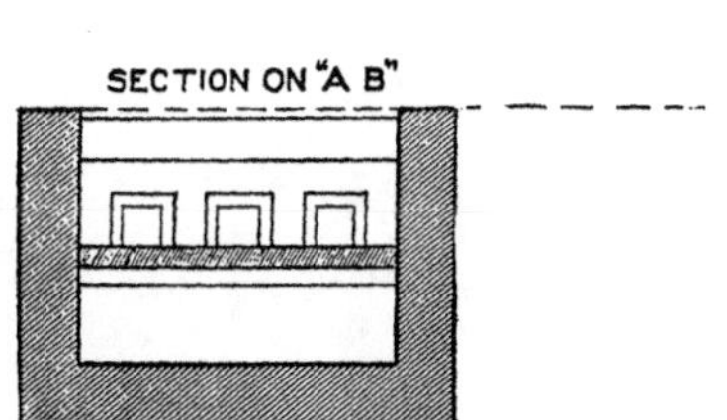

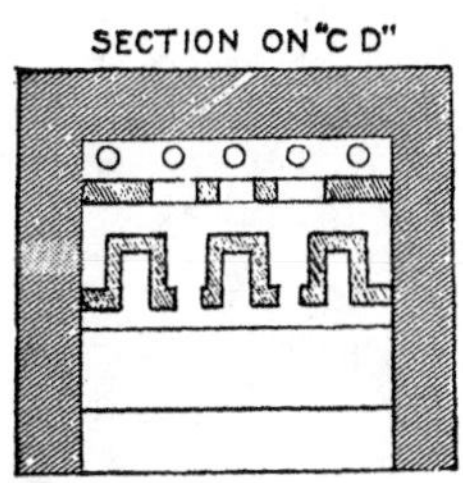

Valve open ½ turns: A good flame, plenty hot enough to melt cinder, and would readily work the furnace when hot.

In order to estimate the heat a 1¼ inch square bar of wrought iron was laid on the bottom of the furnace, which was somewhat heated from the previous experiments, and from the fact that the bricklayers had left the valve open ¾ of a turn. With the valve open one turn the bar was brought to a full yellow in three minutes, and in four minutes in all to a full white welding heat, at which it threw off sparks, and apparently it would soon have been melted if left in.

I am indebted to Robert Young, Esq., the engineer and superintendent of the Allegheny gas works, for the following results of tests made by him at the works of Messrs. Graff, Bennett & Co. on the use of natural gas and the amount of it required.

Mr. Young states that in the first test he made the iron (475 pounds) was charged at 8.5 A. M., and was brought out at 9.53 A. M., the time required being 1 hour and 48 minutes. The meter registered 2,700 cubic feet. The gas gave out, owing to its use elsewhere, and 110 pounds of coal were used in addition. The volatile matter of the coal would equal 550 cubic feet. The second charge was finished in 1 hour 49 minutes from the time of charging; 2,600 cubic feet of gas were measured, and 127 pounds of coal additional were used. The coal would yield in this case about 635 cubic feet of gas. The charge weighed 472 pounds. The third charge was boiled in 1 hour and 42 minutes, with a consumption of 2,700 cubic feet of gas, as registered, and 100 pounds of coal additional; the coal yielded about 500 cubic feet of gas. The charge was 474 pounds. The combustion of the gas appeared to be very complete throughout the tests.

Other trials were afterwards made by different parties with the astounding result that 3,700 cubic feet of Natural Gas would puddle a ton of iron. Mr. Young tested the meter used, and found he could pass five cubic feet of gas through it in 40 seconds without causing it to register at all. How much more might be passed could not be ascertained, as the meter would not register at all.

By Mr. Young's tests, calculating the coal gas as well, it took 14,342 cubic feet of gas per ton of 2,000 pounds. It is not a little remarkable that a ton of iron requires about 35 bushels of Pittsburg coal according to common estimate for boiling, and this would yield about 13,300 cubic feet of gas, allowing nothing for the combustion of the coke. This seems a rather striking coincidence, but probably an accidental one, due to a miscalculation of the coal required. So far as I know I have reason to hold the statement about 30 per cent too high. Yet in view of the common estimate it would be very desirable to boil a charge with street gas, passed through the same meter.

Mr. Young found determined the specific gravity of the gas used at 0.603, and its illuminating power at $9\frac{56}{100}$ candles.

With these explanations the subsequent tests will be intelligible. Their object was to compare the iron boiled by gas with that boiled by coal, as far as possible under similar conditions, and in respect to all their properties. The iron boiled was all Isabella gray forge pig of uniform grade, and borings were taken from *each* piece of *every* pig used in *all* the charges. Exact average samples of all the materials used were taken in a similar manner. The trial charges were boiled as the fourth and fifth charges for that day in their respective furnaces.

A single turn only being on at the time, no other hours could be controlled, and the fifth heat was finished before 12.30 P.M. The furnace, fired with coal only, was No. 21 of Messrs. Spang, Chalfant & Co.'s main mill, and was ordinarily fired with gas, over a small auxiliary coal fire, as shown in Figure 2; but for the purpose of trial the gas was shut off and the T piece of gas pipe taken out of the furnace. The coal used was lump coal of the Upper Freeport vein, and had the following composition:

Water at 225°	0.920
Volatile matter	36.800
Fixed carbon	49.912
Sulphur	1.672
Ash	10.696
	100.000

For the first trial heat in furnace No. 21, being the fourth in the furnace that day, the gas pipe was uncoupled and taken off The furnace was thus brought back to the ordinary condition of a coal furnace, and was then fired during the trial with selected lump coal. The grey forge Isabella iron used had been cast in chills, and was a good No. 3. The total charges were as follows: 70 lbs. best tap cinder; 475 lbs. Isabella iron in broken pigs; 120 lbs. of clean roll scale; 269 lbs. selected lump coal.

TIME CONSUMED.	PERIODS AND REMARKS.
	9h. 3m., A. M., charged best tap 70 lbs. and 475 lbs., Isabella grey forge; charging occupied 2 minutes.
	9h. 24m., iron red, but not yet soft.
	9h. 34m., iron about one-half melted; puddler stirs; 10 lb. scale thrown in.
	9h. 39m., iron about two-thirds melted, helper stirs, pigs covered by cinder bath.
Iron Melted 39*m.*	9h. 42m., nearly all scale in, helper still stirring, and iron chilled by scale, and pasty; coal thrown on fire.
	9h. 45m., bubbles begin to form, helper still stirs; iron risen nearly to stopper hole.
	9h. 48m., iron fallen somewhat, helper still on; fire stirred.
	9h. 50m., rest of scale thrown in; iron rises again.
	9h. 52m., iron rising well; bath still rather liquid; large bubbles formed.
	9h. 53m., cinder runs out of stopper hole.
	9h. 54m., iron fully up to stopper hole; cinder drips steadily; puddler works.
Begins to Boil 55*m.*	9h. 58m., boil begins; fire fixed; puddler still working.

10h. 1m., pasty points on surface of bath; fire stirred; puddler easy and iron falls a little.

10h. 4m., crust over nearly entire surface.

10h. 11m., iron fully over stopper hole; staff put on working plate; ebulition lively with jets.

Iron Granulates, 1*h*. 9*m*. 10h. 12m., iron begins to granulate or "*drop.*"

10h. 13m., Puddler uses "paddle;" fire fixed; doors closed and iron worked.

10h. 15m., a good deal of iron "come to nature;" helper now works.

10h. 16m., iron completely granulated and coheres slightly.

10h. 17m., cinder all absorbed, and bottom dry.

10h. 20 m., damper put down; iron still worked by helper.

Begins to Ball 1*h*. 19*m*. 10h. 22m., iron shows dazzingly white points and begins to boil; coheres well; furnace become hotter; cinder drips out of balls *and puddler balls up.*

10h. 26m., balls well formed; iron sparkles a little.

Balls Ready 1*h*. 24*m*. 10h. 27m., balls ready.

10h. 27½m., *first ball out.*

10h. 29½m., *second ball out.*

Charge Boiled 1*h*. 29*m*. 10h. 32m., *third ball out.*

The iron worked well in squeezer, and roughed down well into 2½ inch muck bars, which weighed when cool, 446 pounds. The percentage of yield was thus 93.9 per cent in the first trial charge.

For the second trial heat the wrong metal was charged at 10h. 35m., but was drawn out completely and the proper iron charged.

TIME CONSUMED.	PERIODS AND REMARKS.
	10h. 44m., heat charged 70 ℔s. tap cinder, and 475 ℔s. Isabella grey forge pigs.
	11h. 4m., iron red and little melted; helper bars up.
	11h. 9m., fire fixed; iron about half melted.
Iron Melted 36*m.*	11h. 20m., all iron melted; damper lowered and helper stirs.
	11h. 21m., scale thrown in.
	11h. 23m., more scale thrown in, and iron made pasty.
	11h. 29m., iron becomes liquid again, and more scale thrown in.
	11h. 36m., both risen a good deal and cinder well mixed; damper raised half up; helper still on, and large bubbles on the bath.
	11h. 37½m., puddler stirs; iron fully up to stopper hole; damper nearly open, and indications of boil.
	11h. 40m., iron fallen somewhat.
Begins to Boil 59*m.*	11h. 43m., iron becomes regularly pasty, and boil begins thoroughly; puddler still on.
	11h. 45m., more cinder thrown in; bath very hot.
	11h. 47m., iron up to stopper hole; cinder doubles out; helper takes his turn.
	11h. 49m., iron fully up; cinder streams out of hole; fire fixed.
	11h. 50m., iron commences to stiffen, and jets come up strongly.
	11h. 54m., metal boiling strongly; fire fixed.
	11h. 57m., bath more pasty, and staff laid on; puddler on; though no cinder runs out over bar.

Iron Granulates 1*h.* 16*m.*	12h., iron begins to "drop" or granulate; puddler still on.
	12h. 1m., paddle used, and metal separated and worked, damper down, nearly shut.
	12h. 2½m., helper on.
Begins to Ball, 1*h.* 20*m.*	12h 4m., iron begins to show in dazzling white points, the cohering masses broken up, helper still on.
	12h. 7m., damper raised, puddler works iron.
	12h. 9m., cinder absorbed in mass, bottom dry and *puddler begins to form balls.*
Balls Ready, 1*h.* 30*m.*	12h. 14m., balls ready, damper down, fire fixed.
	12h. 14½m., *first ball out.*
	12h. 17m., *second ball out.*
Charged Boiled 1*h.* 35*m.*	12h. 19m., *third ball out.*

The balls squeezed well, the metal being good, and rolled well into 2½ inch muck bars, which weighed, when cool, 420 lbs. The yield in per cent of this charge was therefore 88.4 per cent. The quantities charged were 70 lbs. best tap cinder; 475 lbs. Isabella gray forge pigs; 130 lbs. of roll scale and 180 lbs. of selected lump coal.

For the third trial heat, which was boiled solely by Natural Gas in furnace No. 22, built on the plan of Mr. Robertson, the fourth heat in the furnace was chosen as before.

TIME CONSUMED.	PERIODS AND REMARKS.
	9h. 10m., heat charged; 100 lbs. tap cinder and 486 lbs. gray forge Isabella pig.
	9h. 37m., pigs red; the furnace had been run with damper nearly down, the heat being controlled by turning the gas valve.
	9h. 38m., puddler breaks up the pigs.
	9h. 45m., pig half melted; cinder quite liquid; helper works.

Iron Melted 43*m.*	9h. 53m., iron all melted and the bath very liquid; puddler works; a piece of rabble broken off at 9h. 45m. could not be found.
	9h. 55m., bath very hot and liquid; scale thrown in.
	9h. 57m., more scale thrown in and damper lowered.
	10h. 5m., bath stiff and nearly up to hole; the helper stirs.
	10h. 5m., more scale thrown in.
	10h. 8½m., all scale at furnace thrown in.
	10h. 10m., damper closed; metal "hard to raise."
	10h. 12m., 15 lbs. more scale thrown in; large bubbles form.
	10h. 15m., 3 lbs more scale thrown in; a crest barely formed over bath; puddler works.
	10h. 16½m., staff put on door plate; 2 lbs. more scale in; iron well up, but bath still quite liquid.
Begins to Boil, 1*h.* 13*m.*	10h. 23m., begins to boil; damper raised, gas remaining as before; helper works.
	10h. 29m., pasty grains just forming on surface of bath.
	10h. 31m., mass more pasty, granulating well; strong jets out of bath.
	10h. 34m., iron quite pasty and beginning to drop; puddler works and brings it up again by rabbling; Damper up a little more, but gas same as before.
Granulates 1*h.* 28*m.*	10h. 38m., iron all pretty well granulated; jets stronger.
	10h. 42m., iron granulated; quite stiff; getting hotter; paddle used.

	10h. 44m., helper on; iron drops.
	10h. 47m., iron dry, coheres slightly; leaves bottom.
	10h. 49m., puddler on; lumps well broken up.
Begins to Ball, 1*h*. 43*m*.	10h. 53m., bottom dry; lumps cohere well and very solid; iron shows white parts; damper nearly shut.
	10h. 55m., damper closed; more gas on; *puddler begins to make balls;* iron softer and apparently more spongy than the iron in coal heats.
Balls Ready, 1*h*. 47½*m*.	10h. 57½m., balls ready.
	10h. 58m. *first ball out;* damper shut, the flame covering the iron well.
	11h. 0m., *second ball out:* damper up, to ball up a bit sent back from squeezer.
Charge Boiled 1*h*. 52*m*.	11h. 2m., *third ball out;* furnace very hot.

The balls squeezed well and made good muck bars, which weighed, when cold, 475 pounds. The yield in per cent of this charge was therefore 97.74, and the loss only 2.26 per cent. The quantities charged were 100 pounds best tap cinder, 58 pounds Isabella gray forge pig, 145 pounds roll scale.

The fourth trial heat, being the fifth in No. 22 furnace, was charged as soon as the cinder from the third was tapped out.

TIME CONSUMED.	PERIODS AND REMARKS.
	11h. 5m., charged 75 pounds best tap cinder and 484 pounds Isabella gray forge pig iron.
	11h. 7¼m., furnace door shut.
Iron Melted, 40*m*.	11h. 45m., iron all melted, damper down and scale thrown in. Iron quite hot; puddler stirs.
	11h. 52½m., Helper on. Bath stiffer than last and rising better; damper lowered further.

11h. 59m., more scale in; bath up to hole and cinder running out; a light crust on surface, small bubbles.

Begins to Boil 56½m. 12h. 1½m., more scale in, cinder running out of hole; surface pasty, bubbles freely formed.

12h. 6½m., a little more scale thrown in, staff laid on, damper still nearly shut.

12h. 10m., bath risen over staff, very slight granulations show on surface, damper up a little.

12h. 13m., puddler on, bath gone down a little; large bubbles forming.

12h. 18m., iron up again and hotter; bubbles with jets.

12h. 21m., extra scale thrown in (5 pounds) to bring iron down.

12h. 23m., granulations begin to show on surface, bubbles and jets less strong.

12h. 25m., helper on; bath begins to stiffen.

12h. 31m., puddler on; bath quite stiff, "and will go down solid," helper says; paddle used, iron boiling in waves.

12h. 34m., begins to granulate and to cohere slightly. *Drops* hotter than the preceding heat; both, however, being hotter than the coal heats.

Granulates 1h. 31m. 12h. 37m., helper on; iron down, quite granular, cohering well; some cinder on bed.

12h. 39m., puddler on; iron coheres well; bed dry; puddler breaks iron up with slight rabble; more gas on, damper remaining at same height.

12h. 41m., iron hotter, cinder sweats out of lumps; gas shut off again somewhat.

Begins to Ball 1*h*. 38*m*. 12h. 43m., iron shows quite white in specks; gas shut more off; *puddler begins to make balls.*

12h. 44m., damper shut and gas turned on.

Balls Ready, 1*h*. 42*m*. 12h. 47m., balls ready; cinder very liquid on bed.

12h. 48m., first ball out, flame quite smoky.

12h. 51m., second ball out; damper up a little.

Charge Boiled 1*h*. 49*m*. 12h. 54m., third ball out.

The iron squeezes and rolls well. The yield was 462 pounds of cold bars; hence, 95.5 per cent yield and 4.5 loss. There were charged 75 pounds best tap cinder; 484 pounds Isabella gray forge pig; 150 pounds roll scale

Tabulation of Results.

Items for Comparison	COAL AS FUEL.		NAT. GAS AS FUEL.	
	Charge No. 1. Furnace No. 21.	Charge No. 2. Furnace No. 21.	Charge No. 3. Furnace No. 22.	Charge No. 4. Furnace No. 23.
Charged.	*Pounds.*	*Pounds.*	*Pounds.*	*Pounds.*
Isabella Pig-iron	475	475	486	484
Best Tap-cinder	70	70	100	75
Roll scale	120	130	145	150
Coal used	269	180	——	——
Muck-bar got	446	420	475	462
Yields.	*Per Cent.*	*Per Cent.*	*Per Cent.*	*Per Cent.*
Muck-bar	93.90	88.4	97.74	95.50
Loss	6.10	11.6	2.26	4.50
Comparative Periods.	*Minutes.*	*Minutes.*	*Minutes.*	*Minutes.*
Iron melted	39	36	43	40
Beginning to boil	55	59	73	56½
Granulates	69	66	88	91
Begins to ball	79	80	103	98
Balls ready	84	90	107½	102
Charge boiled	89	95	112	109
Total time required.	89	95	112	109

The muck-bars made from these charges, being 2½ inches by ¾ inch in section were speared for piling. The piles consisted of 4 pieces of this size and long enough, say 10 inches, to make a test-bar, ¾ inch square, of sufficient length. The charges were numbered from No. 1, the first charge in the coal furnace, to No. 4, the last charges in the gas furnace. Supposing it possible that there might be a difference in the qualities of the metal made from the middle and that from the ends of the muck-bars, lengths, for piling, were cut from the centres of the respective muck bars. With these piles there was charged in the furnace a special pile of four 4½×¾ inch muck bar puddled on a special order with gas burnt over an auxiliary coal fire. The piles were ready for rolling in 55 minutes from the time of charging, and when rolled, the bars were numbered as follows:

TEST BARS.

No. 1, Rolled from middle of Muck-bars of charge No. 1.
No. 2, Rolled from ends of Muck-bars of charge No. 1.
No. 3, Rolled from middle of Muck-bars of charge No. 2.

No. 4, Rolled from ends of Muck-bars of charge No. 2.

No. 5, Rolled from middle of Muck-bars of charge No. 3.

No. 6, Rolled from ends of Muck-bars of charge No. 3.

No. 7, Rolled from middle of Muck-bars of charge No. 4.

No. 8, Rolled from ends of Muck-bars of charge No. 4.

No. 15, Rolled from iron puddled to a given order for a customer.

No. 16, an inch square bar of iron puddled in regular routine.

Tests for red-shortness were made on bars Nos. 1, 4, 6 and 8, the last three being taken to secure a severe test, if the metal from the ends should prove to be the worst. The ends of the ¾ inch square bars were flattened out, and when the metal in cooling had reached a proper heat, (between a low yellow and a red heat,) a taper drift, ½ inch in diameter at the end and 2 inches long, was driven sharply through to make a ⅞ inch hole in metal about three-sixteenth inch thick. After the hole had been driven through, the end of the bar was bent over sharply on itself. This method afforded two severe tests at temperatures which included those at which red-short irons are always weakest.

TEST FOR RED-SHORTNESS.

No. 1. Punched, drifted out and turned sharply over at centre of hole, without tear or injury to the metal.

No. 4. Treated similarly to No. 1, without developing defect or causing injury.

No. 6. Similarly treated; the metal tore somewhat roughly on the outside of the bar, opposite the centre of hole, when bent over.

No. 8. Similarly treated, and the metal opened out somewhat at side of hole, but to an extent which did not indicate any marked red-shortness.

It appears from these data that in regard to red shortness, the metal puddled with coal is rather the better of the two, though the difference is slight, the quality of all the tests being very high.

In regard to cold-shortness, the sample bars showed far more difference. They were all bent sharply over, across the fibre or direction of the layers of metal, as far as they would go; also, each bar being nicked with a sharp chisel, it was broken, as far as could be, in order to determine the characteristics of the fracture.

TESTS FOR COLD-SHORTNESS.

No. 1. The bar bent close at the unnicked end; but, when nicked at A, it broke with a fracture, 100 per cent fibrous, and of a silky texture of a silvery color.

No. 2. The bar ($\frac{3}{4}''$) happened to be bent round just where it was marked "11," and though it tore at one of the lines on the outside of the bend, yet the bar bent close together. When nicked the bar did not break, but tore partly off, with a fracture about 50 per cent granular, and of a silvery color.

No. 3. The bar ($\frac{3}{4}''$) bent back on itself without injury. When nicked it tore away without fracture, and with a fibrous, silky structure, about 40 per cent granular.

No. 4. The bar ($\frac{3}{4}''$) bent back closely on itself without exposing any defect, and when nicked it tore away with a fracture 40 per cent granular, parting toughly and with a silvery color.

No. 5. The bar ($\frac{3}{4}''$) *broke* when bent through an arc of 150°, and broke at a sound place; when nicked it broke short off, both fractures being about 96 per cent granular.

No. 6. The bar ($\frac{3}{4}''$) when bent *broke* at the 1 of the VI, after bending through an arc of 140°, and with a fracture 100 per cent granular. When nicked the bar broke short off with a fracture almost entirely granular.

No. 7. The bar ($\frac{3}{4}''$) *broke* after bending through an arc of 153°, and with a fracture about 75 per cent granular. When nicked the bar broke short off with a similar (75 per cent) granular fracture.

No. 8. The bar ($\frac{3}{4}''$) *broke* at a sound place after bending 162°, and with a fracture 85 per cent granular.

No. 15. The bar (⅞″) bent back sharply on itself without injury. When nicked it tore away at a depth of ⅛″, the fibres parting with a silver gray wholly fibrous fracture, showing a clear silvery parting all round the torn surface, caused by the bar being bent back on itself.

No. 16. The bar (¾″) bent closely back upon itself without injury. When nicked it tore away without breaking, though hammered flat upon itself, and parted with a fibrous structure, though with some granular portions. Though not broken off, the bar was nearly so after it was hammered together.

The sketches of page plate 3, agreeing with the respective numbers above, show the appearance of the bars after the test was complete. The letter A designates the spot at which the nick was made.

It is evident from the above that the iron boiled in the trial charge with coal is far better, so far as cold shortness is concerned, than that boiled with gas. Yet the tests of bars Nos. 15 and 16 show that iron boiled wholly with gas is equal in quality to the best otherwise made. The reason for this is that the bars, Nos. 5, 6, 7, 8 contain some 40 per cent more phosphorus than the bars Nos. 1, 2, 3, 4; and the phosphorus is present because in the case of the gas the cinder was more liquid, and the mixture of gas and air did not have so strongly reducing an action as the gases of burnt coal. Both these conditions are readily changed, the one by charging less tap cinder, the other by admitting more air, providing, if necessary, a greater heating surface to raise the temperature of the air admitted. For a heating furnace nothing could be better than the furnace using gas alone, as the flame is clear, powerful and reducing in character.

Chemical tests were carefully made from the material used at all stages of the process, *the samples being taken so as to ensure absolute accuracy.* In all samples the drill was made to bury its outside corners completely below the surface before any part of the sample was taken, and all previous borings from that bar were thrown away. The drilled muck bars were rolled into the corresponding finished bars. The analyses were all made in the laboratory of the Survey at Harrisburg by Mr. Andrew S. M'Creath.

ANALYSIS OF COAL USED.

No. 1.

	Per cent.
Water at 225°	0.920
Volatile matter	36.800
Fixed carbon	49.912
Sulphur	1.672
Ash	10.696
	100.000

Coke 62.280 per cent.; color of ash, cream.

ANALYSIS "COLD FIX" USED.

No. 2.

Iron	63.250
Sulphur	0.056
Phosphorus	0.072
Insoluble residue	5.940

ANALYSES OF ROLL SCALE USED.

No. 3. Average sample roll scale used in coal charges.

No. 4. Average sample roll scale used in gas charges.

	No. 3.	No. 3, wet.	No. 4.
Protoxide of iron	61.842	59.597	64.285
Sesquioxide of iron	17.000	16.383	11.428
Sulphur	0.380	0.366	0.311
Phosphorus	0.748	0.720	0.723
Silica	13.990	13.482	18.180
Iron as Fe O	48.100	46.354	50.000
Iron as $Fe_2 O_3$	11.900	11.468	8.000
Total iron	60.000	57.822	58.000
Water	——	3.630	——

ANALYSES OF TAP CINDER.

Nos. 5, 6, 7, 8, 9, 10.

No. 5. Cinder tapped from No. 21 furnace before *first coal charge.*

No. 6. Tap cinder charged with *first coal charge* in No. 21 furnace.

No. 7. Cinder tapped from and after *first coal charge* in No. 21 furnace.

No. 8. Cinder tapped out of furnace No. 22, before *first gas charge.*

No. 9. Tap cinder charged into *first gas charge*, No. 22 furnace.

No. 10. Tap cinder charged into *second gas charge*, No. 22 furnace.

	No. 5.	No. 6.	No. 7.	No. 8.	No. 9.	No. 10.
Protoxide of iron	42.235	72.000	56.571	56.571	56.571	56.571
Sesquioxide of iron	33.785	17.571	10.857	8.786	7.429	7.713
Sulphur	0.151	0.209	0.291	0.401	0.376	0.308
Phosphorus	0.419	0.276	1.088	0.888	0.963	0.968
Silica	17.650	5.970	23.940	26.890	27.130	27.030
Iron as Fe O	32.850	56.000	44.000	44.000	44.000	44.000
Iron as Fe_2 O_3	23.650	12.300	7.600	6.150	5.200	5.400
Total iron	56.500	68.300	51.600	50.150	49.200	49.400

ANALYSES OF ISABELLA GRAY FORGE PIG IRON USED.

Nos. 11, 12, 13 and 14.

No. 11. Pig iron from which the first coal charge was boiled.

No. 12. Pig iron from which the second coal charge was boiled.

No. 13. Pig iron from which the first gas charge was boiled.

No. 14. Pig iron from which the second gas charge was boiled.

	No. 11.	No. 12.	No. 13.	No. 14.
Carbon, graphitic	2.770	2.860	2.880	3.050
Carbon, combined	1.495	1.380	1.425	1.293
Silicium	1.421	1.409	1.566	1.713
Sulphur	0.180	0.198	0.198	0.143
Phosphorus	0.545	0.546	0.548	{ 0.486 0.488
Manganese	0.324	0.289	0.331	0.245
Calcium	0.147	0.141	0.139	0.149
Magnesium	trace.	trace.	trace.	trace.
Iron	93.085	93.050	93.100	92.650
	99 967	99.873	100.187	99.731

Two determinations were made of the phosphorus in No. 14, with the second result 0.486 as recorded above.

ANALYSES OF MUCK-BARS PRODUCED.

Nos. 15, 16, 17, 18, 19, 20, 21, 22 and 23.

No. 15. Muck-bar; being sample from *the ends* of muck-bars of 1st coal charge.

Second Geological Survey of Pennsylvania.

Fractured test bars.

To illustrate Report L. 1875'6 Appendix D. Natural Gas Iron, J.B. Pearse.

Test No. 1. — A — Rolled from middle of muck bars of charge No. 1.

Test No. 2. — A — Rolled from ends of "

Test No. 3. — A — Rolled from middle of No. 2.

Test No. 4. — A — Rolled from ends of "

Test No. 5. — 30° — A — Rolled from middle of No. 3.

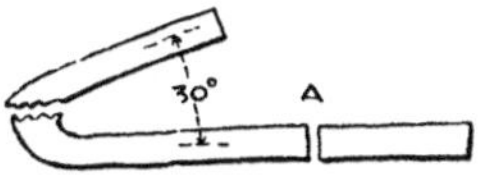

Test No 6. — 90° — A — Rolled from ends of "

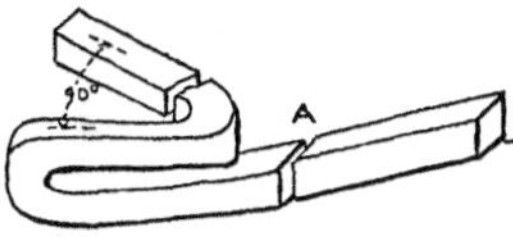

Test No 7. — 27° — A — Rolled from middle of No. 4

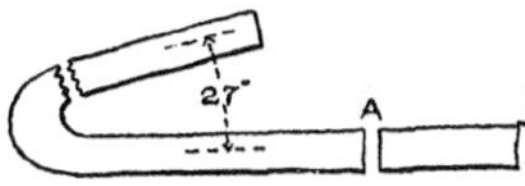

Test No. 8. — 18° — A — Rolled from end of "

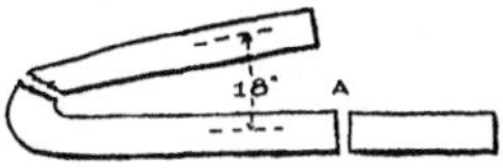

Test No. 15 — A — Rolled from special order.

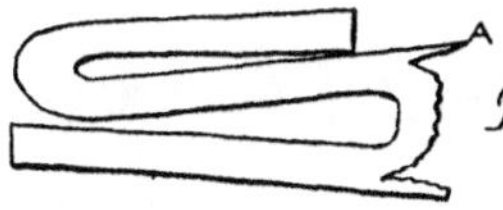

Test No. 16. — A — Rolled from iron puddled in regular manner.

No. 16. Muck-bar; being sample from the centres of the same bars.

No. 17. Muck-bar; being sample from *the ends* of bars of 2d coal charge.

No. 18. Muck-bar; being sample from the centres of bars of the 2d coal charge.

No. 19. *Special sample*; being from *the ends* of a muck-bar of 2d coal charge.

No. 20. *Special sample*; being from the centre of this one bar 2d coal charge.

No. 21. Muck-bar; sample from the centres of bars of 1st gas charge.

No. 22. Muck-bar; sample from the centres of bars of the 2d gas charge.

No. 23. Muck-bar; sample from near the ends of a special muck-bar, from which the trial bar No. 15 was made.

	No. 15. Ends.	No. 16. Centres.	No. 17. Ends.	No. 18. Centres.	No. 19. Ends.	No. 20. Centres.	No. 21. Centres.	No. 22. Centres.	No. 23. Near ends
	Per cent.	Per cent.	Per cent.	Per cent.	Per cent.	Per cent.	Per cent.	Per cent.	Per cent.
Carbon	0.060	0.064	0.054	0.058	0.052	0.055	0.049	0.048	0.055
Silicium	0.246	0.272	0.259	0.235	0.260	0.309	0.269	0.273	0.283
Sulphur	0.055	0.055	0.067	0.065	0.065	{ 0.095 / 0.092 }	0.086	0.087	0.067
Phosphorus	0.198	0.212	{ 0.205 / 0.202 }	{ *0.173 / 0.171 }	{ 0.209 / 0.194 }	{ 0.235 / 0.229 }	{ 0.312 / 0.321 }	{ *0.349 / 0.346 }	0.194
Manganese	0.039	0.036	0.023	0.021	0.030	0.031	0.029	0.029	0.029
Cinder	0.060	0.016	0.076	0.014	0.058	0.098	0.036	0.006	0.050
Iron	99.280	99.250	99.320	99.400	99.260	99.210	99.150	99.100	99.300
Total	99.938	99.905	100.001	99.964	99.919	100.024	99.940	99.889	99.978

The figures marked with an * are duplicate determinations by Mr. David M'Creath.

ERRATA.

Page 211, line 18th, Cinder in No. 25, for "0.114" read "0.014."
In No. 27, for "0.220" read "0.020."

ANALYSES OF TRIAL FINISHED BARS.

Nos. 24, 25, 26, 27 and 28.

No. 24. Rolled from centres of muck-bars of first coal charge, corresponding to muck bar analysis No. 16.

No. 25. Rolled from centres of muck-bars of 2d coal charge, corresponding to muck-bar analysis No 18.

No. 26. Rolled from centres of muck-bar of 1st gas charge, corresponding to muck bar analysis No. 21.

No. 27. Rolled from centres of muck-bars of second gas charge, corresponding to muck-bar analysis No. 22.

No. 28. Rolled in regular routine.

	No. 24. Per cent.	No. 25. Per cent.	No. 26. Per cent.	No. 27. Per cent.	No. 28. Per cent.
Carbon	0.050	0.052	0.054	0.055	0.053
Silicium	0.336	0.329	0.348	0.270	0.260
Sulphur	0.053	0.071	0.083	0.066	0.064
Phosphorus	0.234	{ 0.216 0.224 }	{ 0.342 0.342 }	{ 0.302* 0.300 }	0.186
Cinder	0.040	0.114	0.018	0.220	0.020
Manganese	.029*	.029*	.015*	.029*	.029
Iron	99.290*	99.180*	99.100*	99.250*	99.360
	100.003	99.899	99.959	99.990	99.972

No. 29. Analysis of Carbon deposited by Natural gas in flues of a furnace at places where a slight inward leakage of air produces an incomplete combustion.

Water at 225°	0.023
Volatile matter	0.133
Fixed carbon	92.134
Sulphur	0.102
Ash	7.608
	100.000

The chemical investigation developed so great a uniformity in the composition of the Roll Scale that no difference in the products could be ascribed to the scale charged. The same "cold fix" of the purest Lake Superior ore ground fine, was used in all the charges.

In respect to the tap cinder, charged with the respective coal and gas charges, there is more difference, and rather more indeed than might be expected in a mill working always on one forge mixture. But while there is a good deal of difference between No. 6 and Nos. 9 and 10 in regard to Phosphorus and Silica,

The figures marked with an * are determinations by Mr. David M'Creath.

yet No. 6 is exceptionally low in Silica and Phosphorus for a tap cinder, and No. 7, the cinder from first coal trial heat, agrees very well with the No. 8 cinder out of the gas furnace before first gas trial heat. As the furnaces were charged with similar and regular mixtures the fact that there is more Phosphorus in No. 7 than in No. 8 shows that the coal furnace eliminated more Phosphorus than the gas furnace. The cinder charged with the first coal heat seems much better in regard to Phosphorus than that charged with the gas heats, and this fact, while it seems to indicate greater elimination of Phosphorus in the coal furnace, does not absolutely show that therefore the gas irons should be poorer. For first, the Phosphorus has rather a tendency to remain in the cinder; and second, No. 6 must be a rather irregular sample, as the percentage of Phosphorus in the cinder tapped from the heat in which it was charged, is higher than would be expected from the use of such a cinder as No. 6 with the given charge. Hence, while these analyses are not absolutely conclusive, they show a tendency in the coal furnace to eliminate Phosphorus, which agrees with the subsequent analyses.

In regard to the Pig iron, the uniformity is unusual, especially so in view of the fact that the pigs used came from all parts of the iron pile. If there is any difference in respect to the iron, it is in favor of the gas charges as appears from analysis No. 14. If the Isabella furnace is always run with as great uniformity as seems the case from the analyses, the management is entitled to very great praise.

In regard to the muck-bars, it will be seen that the ends and centres of the respective bars have been analysed—*that is*, samples for analysis were taken from each extreme end of every bar of each heat, just where the iron was most rough and dirty, and also from the centres of every bar of each heat. As the centres are unquestionably the best for comparison, let us take Nos. 16, 18, 21 and 22 as our basis.

As to Phosphorus and Sulphur the muck bars of the gas heats contain much more of both than those of the coal heats; in regard to the other elements both are practically identical, the gas irons containing least carbon. The greatest difference is exhibited in regard to the Phosphorus, the gas trial iron containing nearly twice as much as the coal iron.

In regard to *cinder*, the ends of both kinds of iron are practically the same, one gas iron sample showing least of all. But when we examine the difference between the *ends* and *centres* of the muck bars of the respective charges tested, we find that in the cases of Nos. 15 to 18 the ends show a percentage of cinder four to five times higher than in the centres. Yet in the special bar Nos. 19 and 20 the centre has nearly twice as much as the ends. The final result as to cinder is, therefore, that there is not the difference that might be expected between the centres and ends of the muck bars (the ends of the bar being of course the ends of the puddle balls) and that the preponderance of percentage shows that the centre is slightly freer from cinder than the ends. The latter, however, is shown to have been thoroughly expelled in the squeezer and by the passage through the puddle rolls. In regard to general composition, the ends of the special bar in trials Nos. 19 and 20 are the best; showing less impurity than the iron from the centre; in the other bars the general composition is substantially the same in the ends as in the centres. It cannot be said, therefore, that the ends of the muck bars make a worse finished iron than their centres.

In the analyses of finished bars Nos. 24 to 27 the result is the same as that developed by the analyses of the muck bars. In respect to sulphur the gas irons have more, and of phosphorus much more than the coal irons; and of cinder slightly less when taken together. The differences of composition are, however, less marked than in the muck bars, as the effect of the heating furnace is to eliminate Phosphorus to some extent by sweating it out. The statement by which the finished bars seem to contain more cinder than the centres of the muck bars from which they were made must, in my opinion, be attributed to the almost insuperable difficulty of obtaining an absolutely uniform sample of such a material as puddled iron. The differences are, however, small; and the fact that samples taken entirely independent of each other show similar chemical composition as to questionable points proves that the samples fairly represented the material.

I append the results of mechanical tests made by the Messrs.

Riehle, of Philadelphia. Owing to an unfortunate error, no record was made of the limit of the elasticity nor of the elongation :

Testing Department, Philadelphia Scale and Testing Machine Works, North Ninth street, above Master.

PHILADELPHIA, *February* 6, 1877.

JOHN B. PEARSE, ESQ, *Secretary, Harrisburg, Pa.:*

DEAR SIR :—We have this day tested for you 14 specimens of Wrought Iron subject to tensile strain, with the following result :

Marked.	Size.	Area.	Broke at.	Strain Per Sq. Inch.	Memoranda.
			Pounds.	Pounds.	Pounds.
No. 1......	$\frac{3}{4}'' \times \frac{3}{4}''$ =	0.5625''	29,560=	52,55[illegible]	
No. 2......	$\frac{3}{4}'' \times \frac{3}{4}''$ =	0.5625''	27,280=	48,498	
No. 3......	$\frac{3}{4}'' \times \frac{3}{4}''$ =	0.5625''	30,340=	53,940	[51,791]
No. 4......	$\frac{3}{4}'' \times \frac{3}{4}''$ =	0.5625''	29,350=	52,180	Average Nos. 1 to 4 =
No. 5......	$\frac{3}{4}'' \times \frac{3}{4}''$ =	0.5625''	32,360=	57,529	
No. 6......	0.745×0.745 =	0.555''	30,700=	55,315	
No. 7......	0.745×0.745 =	0.555''	32,770=	59,045	[56,977]
No. 8......	$\frac{3}{4}'' \times \frac{3}{4}''$ =	0.5625''	31,510=	56,020	Average Nos. 5 to 8 =
No. 16......	$\frac{3}{4}'' \times \frac{3}{4}''$ =	0.5625''	30,160=	53,618	
No. 1, M.E.	0.74'' Diam.=	0.4301''	16,930=	39,363	Muck Bar.
No. 2, M.M.	0.74'' Diam.=	0.4301''	20,710=	48,150	Muck Bar.
No. 2, M.E.	0.7'' Diam.=	0.3848''	19,360=	50,310	Muck Bar.
No. 3, M.M.	0.745 Diam.=	0.4316''	22,460=	52,062	Muck Bar.
No. 4, M.M.	0.745 Diam.=	0.4316''	25,130=	58,220	Muck Bar.

Very respectfully,

RIEHLE BROS.

In further explanation of the above report I would add the estimated percentage of fibrous and crystalline iron in the various specimens.

No. 1. 100 per cent fibrous.
No. 2. 97 per cent fibrous.
No. 3. 98 per cent fibrous.
No. 4. 98 per cent fibrous.
No. 5. 90 per cent crystalline.
No. 6. 20 per cent crystalline ; 80 per cent fibrous.
No. 7. 18 per cent crystalline ; 82 per cent fibrous.
No. 8. 10 per cent crystalline ; 90 per cent fibrous.
No. 16. 100 per cent fibrous.
No. 1 M. E. 85 per cent fibrous.

No. 2 M. M. 80 per cent fibrous.
No. 2 M. E. 65 per cent fibrous.
No. 3 M. M. 70 per cent fibrous.
No. 4 M. M. 87 per cent crystalline.

Muck Bars.

No. 1 M. E. is taken from the *end* of a muck bar.
No. 2 M. M. is taken from the *middle* of a muck bar.
No. 2 M. E. is taken from the *end* of a muck bar.
No. 3 M. M. is taken from the *middle* of a muck bar.
No. 4 M. M. is taken from the *middle* of a muck bar.

Finished Bars.

On comparing the results it will be seen that the muck-bars are somewhat irregular, as is right in such an irregular material, but a great uniformity is noted of all the characters of the bars made with coal and an equal uniformity among the bars made with gas, excepting bar No. 5, which is irregular in its almost exclusively crystalline character. Yet it is not irregular in its tensile strength.

For greater certainty, however, an additional analysis, from this special test bar, will be appended.

This variation of characteristics under a chemical composition *practically identical except in regard to Phosphorus*, and the fact that the two trial charges varied by about 0.12 per cent Phosphorus (viz., gas $\left\{\begin{matrix}0.342\\0.300\end{matrix}\right.$ and coal $\left\{\begin{matrix}0.234\\0.224\end{matrix}\right.$) shows that the Phosphorus alone occasioned an average difference of 5,186 pounds to the square inch and *proves that a very small quantity of Phosphorus* materially changes the properties of iron.

It will be noticed that the tests show that all the bars made with gas broke under the smith test. Hence, the greater tensile strength denotes greater hardness and brittleness; and the appearance of the test bars corroborates this view as bar No. 5 broke almost with the original area, and Nos. 5, 6, 7 and 8, with an elongation roughly estimated at 15 per cent, while the coal bars broke with at least 28 per cent elongation. Therefore the bars in question must be graded as *a comparatively inferior iron.* This of course does not *apply generally to iron made with gas*, as shown by charge 6, *but only to the bars in question.* Consumers prefer the gas-iron as being more homogeneous, and more susceptible of polish, and a better iron generally than that made from the same pig iron with coal.

Further, the most important result of the whole work is the conclusion that iron with less than 0.2 per cent Phosphorus and otherwise ordinary composition is *good* and unusually good, and that with 0.3 per cent and more is *comparatively bad.* These trials fix the amount of Phosphorus that can be present in first class high grade irons, and show that iron in this respect resembles steel. With 0.1 per cent of Phosphorus, or less, soft steel is good; with 0.2 per cent it is bad and dangerous, in rails at least.

The fact that iron can be made stronger, when desired, by leaving its phosphorus in it or so regulating its composition as to increase the Phosphorus slightly has been known and practiced; but in the light of the above trials such a course must be regarded as reprehensible.

Also, the suggestion to be drawn from all this is, that if *iron* with 0.3 per cent of Phosphorus and only 0.05 per cent of Carbon can not be made first class what reason have we to expect that steel can be? In the light of these trials the so-called *phosphorus steels* must be regarded as *dangerous materials.*

APPENDIX E.

THE BOYD'S HILL GAS WELL AT PITTSBURG.

J. P. LESLEY.

This well is drilled from a platform at the south end of Boyd's hill, overlooking the Pittsburg Steel Works, on the north bank of the Monongahela river.

The derrick is 70 feet high. The derrick floor is 852.28 feet above ocean level (Pittsburg Union Depot being 745.26); 95 feet (by barometer) above Messrs. Anderson and Woods' office pavement; and 153 feet above low water in the Ohio river. Base of Pittsburg coal bed, 1,050′ (with possible error of 5′) above ocean level. Interval between derrick floor and Pittsburg bed, therefore, 200′±, to be increased by 50′ or 60′ for the southward dip across the Monongahela.

The well is about 2,300 feet deep in January, 1877, having been begun early in 1876.

It was located by Dr. Hunter on a compass line 23° 10′ west of south from the oil producing wells on the Divner and M'-Ginley farms and the large gas wells on the Duffey farm in Butler county, said survey being made by Civil Engineers Edeburn and Cooper, of Pittsburg. "My idea being," adds Dr. Hunter, "that this degree represented the strike of the oil and gas producing rocks of Butler county."

It is needless to remark that this method of locating one oil or gas well from another must necessarily prove ineffectual, because it imagines the plane of the oil to be in the vertical, whereas it spreads horizontally. Land surveyors and civil engineers, not being trained geologists, are naturally disposed to overvalue the powers of their special professional instrument, the compass or transit; and it is not to be wondered at if, in the confusion of men's ideas about oil, and the origin of natural gas, the engineer's compass should have made a stiff fight to keep the field over which it had, so to speak, the right of pre-emption.

Since rock-oil and gas in union with salt water are held by horizontal layers of loose sand and gravel, and since these layers of sand and gravel were of course deposited in and by running water, currents in an ancient and probably rather shallow sea, it is clearly useless to attempt to follow their irregular courses underground by surveying straight transit lines across the present surface of the country. The straighter the compass line is run—in other words, the more skillful the engineer—the less will his line correspond to the real lines of direction of the ancient oil and gas-bearing sand and gravel banks meandering and branching a thousand feet beneath him. He can no more tell by means of his compass through what narrow channels in the narrow and more or less crooked sand-bar the oil is slowly moving, than a boy, by drawing lead pencil lines on the top of a pile of boards, can tell what is the direction of the grain, or the movements of a worm, in the hundredth board down from the top. Even on the impossible supposition that his lines may for once accidentally correspond to the grain ot the hundredth board, they certainly could not correspond also to the grain or worm holes of the hundred and tenth board, representing, say, the Second sand-rock of the oil; and still less to the hundred and twentieth, representing the Stray sand; the hundred and thirtieth, the Third sand, &c.

The Pittsburg Boyd's Hill well is only one more of the multitude of dry wells the locations of which have been chosen on the faith of compass lines. Nor will this faith quite die out of men's minds until *good maps of the underground sand-bars* (or rather of their looser parts which hold gas and oil) shall have been made and widely published. But this can only be accomplished by the united efforts of civil engineers, oil sinkers and geologists; the oil sinkers furnishing reliable well records; the surveying engineers locating and mapping the productive wells on the surface; and the geologists not only making, comparing, grouping and representing in vertical sections the order of the oil sands, but also constructing underground contour-line maps of them, so as to discover and exhibit their slopes or dips. Mr. Carll has set a fair and plain example of the method by which this is done in his Report of Progress I, for 1874, pages 18 and 19, where the reader may find two page plates exhibiting the shape of the upper and under surfaces of the First and Third oil-sands of Venango county. There is no reason why every engineer and surveyor of the oil regions should not do the same for each district or locality with which he is best acquainted; and thus, in an incredibly short time, we should have a series of extensive maps of each and all of the oil-bearing sands over all their extent in western Pennsylvania. Such maps would indubitably show all the central current lines, and the outside irregular limits of each and all of the productive sands. Such is, in fact, the task which the Geological Survey of Pennsylvania has set for itself. But more rapid progress could be made if surveyors, engineers and well-sinkers of the oil regions would co-operate with the survey.

Many hundreds of well records have been collected by Mr. Carll as a preliminary for this work. The first installment of the collection has been printed by the American Philosophical Society in its Proceedings, recently; and extra copies for the use of the survey are in the hands of Mr. Carll for distribution to oil men and engineers, who can obtain them by applying for them with a promise to furnish their own or any reliable materials of the same sort to help forward the study of the oil-rocks. (Address, Pleasantville, Venango county.)

Mr. Carll, in his Second Report of Progress, II, will embody all these well records (and many more) in a classified form, and will give the conclusions to which he has arrived.

The principal obstacle encountered, after that of getting trustworthy records, has been a want of the levels above tide (or above some other known datum level; which amounts to the same thing) of the different well mouths. In the absence of this element a map of the underground cannot be made, however many well records may be on hand, and however accurate may be the measurements down to the Sands.

What is most wanted is this: The levels of 25, 50 or 100 mouths of wells in one locality, say within a radius of two or three miles.

A comparison of the levels of the mouths of two wells at the distance of 20 or 40 miles is of no value whatever, unless the wells lie north-east and south-west from each other; that is, along the strike of the great bituminous coal basins, which all run in that direction, sinking slowly toward the south-west.

For example, what good does it do to compare the levels above tide (of either the top or bottom of) two such wells as the Boyd's Hill well at Pittsburg, and the Fairview well in Butler county 40 miles distant?—seeing that the powerful Brady's Bend anticlinal axis runs between them in a direction diagonal to the line which connects them on the map. (See figure on the opposite page.)

The descent along this anticlinal is so great that the Conglomerate is at A (below Brady's Bend) 100+ feet *above* the Allegheny river bed; it is at B (below Pittsburg) 300+ feet *below* the bed of the Ohio river; and we must add to this the difference between railroad levels at B and A, which will about represent the fall of the river bed, say 830—731=100, feet. The total fall of any one oil-sand rock in a direction south-west along the crest of the anticlinal for 41 miles (from where it crosses the Allegheny to where it crosses the Ohio,) is therefore about 500 feet.

This is why there is no Pittsburg Coal bed in the hills at Brady's Bend. They should be 600 feet higher than they are to take it in.

This is why the depth of a well sunk to strike a certain rock beneath the surface at Pittsburg has no known relation to the depth of a well sunk to strike the same rock at Butler, until the dips of that rock on both sides of the Brady's Bend anticlinal and on both sides of the Brady's Bend synclinal are accurately ascertained.

Explorers for oil and gas, trusting merely to levels or compass lines or any other surface indications, if they intend to *cross that anticlinal from Butler County into Allegheny County*, may just as well abandon their purpose first as last. They have absolutely nothing to go upon—until they have collected all the reliable well records in the two counties—leveled all the mouths of the wells in relation to one another—placed them accurately

A Sketch Map, intended to show how the Brady's Bend Axes, anticlinal and synclinal, cut off all connection, as to levels, between the Butler Co. oil wells and Wells at Pittsburgh.

(Second Geological Survey of Pennsylvania Report of Progress L. App. E.)

Brady's Bend Synclinal.
Brady's Bend Anticlinal.
Fairview gas well.
Butler Co.
A
Centre line of trough of the 6th Basin.
40 miles
The Alleghany River flows down the 5th Basin.
Kittanning
Freeport.
Leechburg gas-well.
Anticlinal axis.
Ohio.
Wood's run
B
Pittsburgh
Boyd's hill gas-well.
Kiskiminitas River.
Monongahela
J.P.L.

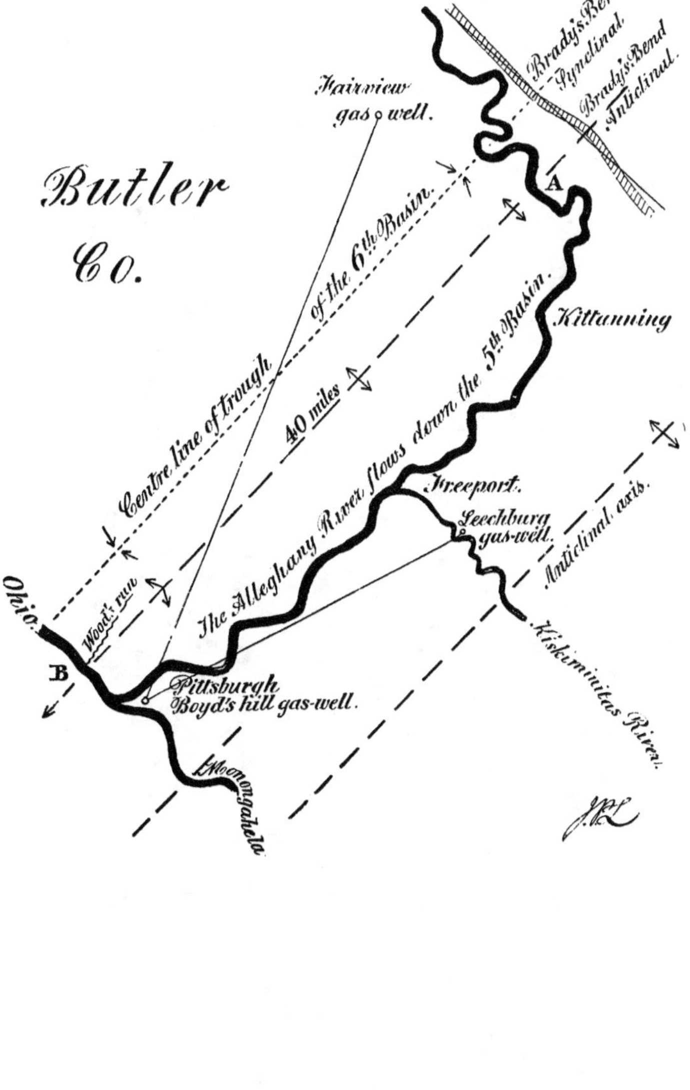

upon a map—and then *calculated the rise and fall* of some recognizable rock in all the wells, first down the south-east slope of the Brady's Bend synclinal, then up the north-west slope of the anticlinal, and finally down its south-east slope.

But, it may now be asked, can we not get all we want to know, *after a deep well* (like the Boyd's Hill well) *has been drilled*, by comparing the rocks it has gone through with the rocks gone through in Butler county?

No. And for two reasons:—

1. The drillings do not tell us *with sufficient plainness* what we go through;

2. Sufficient care is never, and can never be, under ordinary circumstances, taken to get the *entire* record of a deep well; finally—

3. The same rocks do not extend for forty miles without many a local change and sometimes a total disappearance, or substitution by some other kind of rock.

All this will be fully explained in Mr. Carll's forthcoming reports, and it need not here be repeated.

All that is insisted on here is, that the judicious student of this great practical problem of Western Pennsylvania will be slow to theorize,—will refuse to jump across distances of 20 and 40 miles,—will rather study local groups of wells,—will follow on across the synclinals and anticlinals with slow and cautious steps, collecting and mapping one group of wells after another, watching the changes which take place in *all* the rocks of his wells, changes of thickness, hardness, color, porosity, distance between rocks,—until he has the whole changeable series clearly before him, and can *then* safely identify its sand-rocks in wells at great distances from one another.

The Boyd's Hill gas well is one of the most interesting and important bore holes ever drilled. It is also one of the deep wells. It passes through the Barren Measures, the Lower Productive Coal Measures. the Pottsville *Seral* Conglomerate, the Mauch Chunk *Umbral* Red shale, the Pocono *Vespertine* or Mountain sandstones, the Catskill red rocks, and the oil group of Venango and Butler counties, and possibly through even some of the Warren Measures. Its record is tolerably good down to

1,700 feet. Here the great flow of salt-water took place, and the remaining 600 feet are not recorded with all the certainty that is desirable in an investigation of such importance. Circumstances were unfavorable to perfect accuracy, in spite of the earnest efforts of its superintendent to reach that end.

The following record, furnished courteously by Dr. Hunter, gives an excellent general idea of the series of rocks drilled through, and is of immense value in settling some hitherto pending geological questions. But there are some curious defects in it, which, if left unnoticed, would lead to serious misconceptions of our western geology. For example:—

There must be some mistake about the 8-foot bed of coal marked at 86 feet; for at that depth only the well known small 1 or 2 foot coal bed of the Barren Measures crops out both north and south of the derrick, at the foot of the hill in one of the streets of Pittsburg, and in the banks of the river Monongahela.

The Freeport Coal series also, consisting of two coal beds and one limestone, is passed without notice.

The Kittanning Coal bed and ferriferous limestone are also passed unnoticed.

The coal bed marked in the record as lying just on top of the Conglomerate is represented as of most unusual (although not entirely incredible) thickness. (See Coal A, Cambria Report HH.)

No red shale is mentioned under the Conglomerate, but it is quite possible that the Mauch Chunk (*Umbral*) may be destitute of red layers underneath Pittsburg; although it is more likely that the red color of some of the shales passed through at that depth was overlooked for want of knowing the geological significance of the red color.

The 26-foot limestone at the bottom of the *Umbral* (if good measurement) is the most important item in the whole upper half of this record. If the rock here passed through was really limestone, then we have in it a fixed, sure and well known geological horizon from which to measure upwards to and through the Coal Measures, and also downwards through the Pocono and Catskill (or Mountain sand group) towards the oil-sand group. Not only this; we have a means of connecting the underground geology of Pittsburg and its vicinity (which has never happened before) with the Devonian rock sections exposed in the gaps at Blairsville, Latrobe, Mt. Pleasant and Connellsville to the east, and with the underground geology of Butler county to the north-west; for in the wells there the same thick, silicious, *Umbral* (or Mountain) Limestone is indicated.

The Great Sandstone at 1,700 feet represents well enough the lowest conglomeritic layers of the *Vespertine* in the Chestnut ridge gaps above mentioned, and it is indicated at about the same depth below the *Seral.*

Whether this sandstone is the lowest Mountain Sand of the Oil Regions, or the First Oil Sand, is a doubtful point. In the former case it would be the *Berea Grit* of Ohio, according to Mr. Carll.

All below this is in a state of uncertainty. Even the accounts given (for there are three of them) from this part of the well respecting the red rocks in the upper part of the oil group furnish no positive data for working out the exact place in the vertical series where the well stops. It is evident, however, that it has gone down through all the Oil Group, if not a good deal further. And yet it has passed through neither oil nor gas. There is therefore no reason for expecting oil or gas in rocks still lower down. Nevertheless the importance of sinking it a thousand feet further is, in a geological sense, so great that it would justify the Legislature in expending several thousands of dollars in the work. Such an opportuniy will not soon recur. The well is large, well drilled and furnished with a strong 70-foot high derrick and good rig.

While studying the record and section I had an opportunity ot carefully examining an imperfect exhibition of the drillings preserved in eleven jars, about five inches in diameter and eighteen inches high, ranged in order on the mantelpiece in the office of the company. Each jar, however, contains only half a dozen layers of sand &c. &c., obtained in process of drilling from different depths; and although strips of paper are pasted on the outside of each jar, and labels are attached, with figures to indicate depth, some of these strips and labels are missing, and no explanations can now be obtained of the typical character nor of the layers, nor the number of types. The layers in the jars are separated by crumpled sheets of paper; and the interior of the jars could not be examined without much time and labor spent over them. A lens is of little use in looking through the glass, because of oxidation and other changes having taken place against the inner surfaces of the jars; but the general character of each layer can be roughly made out, and the following notes were taken accordingly:

0. Platform of the Boyd's Hill Derrick (250′ below the Pittsburg coal bed.)

86′. Top of coal bed. Here struck fresh water.

94′. Bottom of coal bed. This interval of eight feet represents the 6 feet of *gray slate* (weathering quite black) and 1½ feet of *coal*, to be seen at present in the cutting-down of the streetway, at the foot of the hill, three squares north of the derrick, and (by barometer) 60′ lower in level than the derrick floor; the difference between 60′ and 94′ is made by the *visible dip of the coal bed* towards the derrick.*

305′. Bottom of 211′ of "friable sedimentary strata." In this interval the Lower Barren Measure coal beds ought to have been drilled through.

350′. Bottom of 45′ of [MAHONING] sandstone, "close, white, hard." The layer of these drillings in jar No. 1 consists of cubical fragments (¼″) looking like the grains of the Mahoning Sandstone; mixed with finer sand grains.

482′. Bottom of 132′ "friable sedimentary strata." Here should appear the Freeport Coals (Upper and Lower) and Freeport Limestone. The layer in the jar consisted of gray and rather coarse shale, through which were scattered minute quartz pebbles.

---

* This dip is an important fact in the geology of the vicinity of Pittsburg. It explains why the Monongahela river cuts into the cliffs of its *southern* shore, keeping them very high and steep, with the Pittsburg bed at the top; while Grant's hill and Boyd's hill, on the north bank, in the city, taper down to a lower level.

507′. Bottom of 25′ sandstone, "more porous than the 45′ sandstone above.". "A little show of gas." (Note: This sandstone is not mentioned in the labels on the jar, and may have been meant for the 25′ sandstone, between 587′ and 612′.*) There is another record reading thus: "Dark sand at 350′, which continued about the same to the depth of 580 feet."

580′. Top of 52′ fine sand. "Hard sand following it for 32′.

582′. Top of 5′ sandstone,† "hard, white." (Half inch fragments in jar.)

587′. Top of 25′ hard white rock.—*Salt water.*

612′. Top of coal bed. (Upper or perhaps Lower Kittanning.)

615′. Top of 6′ of blue rock. ("Blue sand rock at 615′, 25 feet thick.")

621′. Top of 20′ of white sand. (The layer in the jar is one of white sand, with many fragments of darker sand and a little shale.)

642′. Top of 15′ of blue rock. (In the jar are many minute pieces looking like fragments of crinoidal discs broken up, but the lens could not be brought to bear on them sufficiently to make their character certain.)

657′. Top of 18′ of slate.

675′. Top of 20′ of dark sand. (In the jar, there is here a layer of entirely fine yellowish sand, iron rusted, with subordinate layers of orange.) In the record it reads thus:—

676′. *A Trace of Limestone.*—"Gray shale and horseback, 20′." (If traces of *genuine* limestone were really got here, it is an important fact, showing either the presence of the Ferriferous Limestone of Clarion county or a still lower layer, such as sometimes occurs in Jefferson county.)

---

* This is rendered more probable by the fact that under it is reported 36′ slate, and then 3′ coal, neither of which appear on the jar, but occur in the record lower down. It is probable, therefore, that the sandstone 482′-507′ ought to be transferred to 582′.

† This is no doubt the same as "fine sand" at 580′.

695′. Top of 25′ of dark sandy shale. (In the jar it is decidedly blackish and coarser than that already mentioned; *truly* a dark shale; no pebbles are noticeable. It is a genuine shale mass, probably churned up by the borers with streaks of coal or coal slates.) But in the record it reads:—

696′. Top of 24′ of gray sand rock.

720′. Top of 9′ coal bed. (This is an unusual thickness for the coal A, overlying the Conglomerate; although there are places, as at Bell's Gap, in Cambria county, where the bed has an equal thickness. No such size is ascribed to it in its numerous outcrops through Indiana, Westmoreland, Fayette, Somerset, Clearfield and Jefferson. It is, however, a variable bed, and may possibly be 9′ thick under Pittsburg. It is represented in the jar by a black layer, streaked with yellow, from the decomposition of pyrites.)

729′. Top of 60′ of sand rock, [Pottsville (*Seral*) Conglomerate, No. XII], white, with *Salt Water*. It is represented in the jars by three layers of drillings: 1. The top layer is of a dove-colored and exceedingly fine, white sand. 2. The middle layer is like it, but with a dash of orange, and brilliant red specks against the glass show oxidation of iron. 3. The bottom layer is of coarse sand, but *without pebbles*, and decidedly red or rather orange, but not at all the color of the hydrated red shales of XI, *Umbral*, or of the hydrated red sands of IX, *Catskill*. Its orange red color accounts for its being marked in the record thus:—

729′. Top of 59′ of "red Mahoning Sandstone," "sandrock resembling the Mahoning Sandstone." (But it is not the Mahoning Sandstone, which, in fact, lies in its proper place, 380′ above it. Nor has it the character of that formation. It is the Millstone Grit, Pottsville (*Seral*) Conglomerate, XII, at the base of the Lower Productive Coal Measures.)

789′. "Black Slate *at* 788′" (Record.) Black slate in jar; very black, but without coal. This represents the coal formation which frequently underlies the Conglomerate.

879′. Bottom of 90′ feet interval; represented on the record section as all black slate, but not so stated in record, nor on the jars. The black slate is said to have occurred *at* the top of the interval. In fact, no such mass of genuine *black slate* is known, even in the Anthracite Coal Measures. No doubt layers of black slate, and even of coal, were encountered in passing this interval. Probably, also, layers of the red shale of XI.

888′. Bottom of 8′ feet of black sand; traces of *coal*.

889′. Bottom of 10′ feet of black sand (in jar); dark greenish black, and not a very coarse sand. Record adds, "followed by a vein of good *Limestone* 24 feet thick, which I take to be the Kittanning Limestone," *i. e.*, the Ferriferous. (But the place for that is 200′ higher up in the well.)

914′. Bottom of 25′ of *Limestone* [Mountain Limestone; *Umbral* Limestone; St. Louis Limestone; W. B. Rogers' Virginia Lewisburg Limestone 600′ thick; the 40′ Limestone of J. J. Stevenson's Report on Fayette and Westmoreland counties, 1877.] The layer of drillings in the jar look like fire clay, and as if mixed with sand grains. No opportunity afforded for testing it with acid. (Fire clays have been repeatedly mistaken for limestones in the Butler county wells. The outcrop in the ravine south of Parker City has been taken for an outcrop of limestone even by experts.) There is very little reason to doubt that the well here goes through the Mountain Limestone, because the proper distances have been passed through. Note the record puts the top of this Limestone at 912′; the jars put it at 914′.

994′. Bottom of 80′ white sandrock. [Pocono Sandstone; *Vespertine* of Rogers; Upper or Grey Catskill, No. X.] The record adds, "corresponding with the 40 and 60 foot sand of Butler county, so called by the drillers." (This is open to the same objection as the identification of the 60′ SS. No. XII above, with the Mahoning.) In the jar, at the top of this 80′ is a brilliant orange layer with specks of crimson all through it. But the mass is of white sand.

1,076′. Bottom of 82′ of black slate "containing gas." (In the record, "Black Sand at 976 [?992] followed by black slate 84′ thick.) In the jar this is a dark blue slate, looking like ground up slate-pencils.

1,076′. Record says, "at this point, 1,076 feet, found what is called the Mountain Sand 108 feet thick, which is known as Seral Conglomerate, (XII,) followed by slate and thin layers of sand rock for 150 feet." (See what is said above at 729′.)

1,186′. Bottom of 110′ of "Mountain Sand, First Seral Conglomerate." (Such is the label on the jar, in which is seen a layer of fine, dove-colored sand, evidently from a massive rock, but no pebbles are to be seen in it larger than a pin's head. This rock is certainly not the Seral Conglomerate No. XII, but one of the mountain sands of Butler county; *which* one is not so evident.)

1,340′. Bottom of 154′ of "slate and shells of sand." (Label on the jar. The layer inside is of dark gray and blue slate, with quartz grains; a confused mass telling nothing.)

1,375′. Bottom of 35′ of "sharp white sandstone." (Label.) The layer in the jar is a dirty dove-colored *coarse* sand, evidently from a hard, massive rock, but without pebbles. The record says: "White sand at 1,340′; here a close white sand, 36 feet." Then slate and thin layers of sand, at 1,376′, 28′ thick, to 1,404′.

1,405′. Bottom of 30′ of "slate and shells of sand." (Label.) The layer in the jar is a pepper and salt mixture of flakes of silicious slate with grains of coarse sand; evidently some layers of hard rock have been passed through.

1,590′. Bottom of 185′ of "black slate." (Label.) The layer in the jar is an homogeneous mass, 8 inches deep, a mixture of quartz grains and slate fragments, all extremely small; darker at the top than at the bottom. But there is no way of finding out how nearly this represents the whole 185′, nor whether it represents better one part of the formation than it does another part of it. The record reads thus:—

1,404'. } 184' { "Black Slate at 1,404'."—when we found a
1,588'. } { black slate 184' thick. From No. XII to this point (1,588') I regard it as Umbral of Prof. Rogers, or No. XI; that is, from the bottom of No. XII, which is 1,184' to 1,588', making 404', the thickness of the Umbral at this point."—(The real *Umbral* has been shown above at 788' to 912', with a thickness of only 134', which agrees well with the thickness of XI in the Chestnut Ridge, allowing for its thinning out westward.)

1,588'. } 112' { "White quartzite at 1,588'. Berea Grit."
1,700'. } { "At 1,588' found a CONGLOMERATE, which continued to 1,700', having a *strong fishy smell*, and producing SALT WATER from the top to the bottom, 11° strong. This I regarded as the Upper Berea Grit No. X, Vespertine."

1,700'. Bottom of 110' of "White First Sand, Conglomerate, traces of oil." (Label.) The layer in the jar is 10 inches deep, composed of beautifully transparent quartz grains, all of them angular, and of about the same size, that of a large pin's head. This drilling differs from all the preceding, as exhibited in the jars. It reminds one of the glass sand from the Oriskany outcrops on the Juniata. It is much tinted with an orange iron wash.

From this remarkable rock issued, and issues still, a flood of strong brine, at the rate of 3,000 to 4,000 barrels per day. Dr. Otto Wuth reported that 348 gallons of it make one barrel (280 lbs.) of salt and 60 pounds of bittern. Bromine, 0.31 per cent.

From this same layer issues, by the well at Leechburg, the stream of gas described in this report.

The plate illustration accompanying this report shows, in parallel vertical columns, 1. the section of measures pierced by the Boyd's Hill well; 2. those recorded at Leechburg; and, 3. a section of the same measures as they appear in the gap of the Conemaugh, above Blairsville, made by Prof. Stevenson;—and there can be no room for doubt that this rock, charged with gas at Leechburg, is charged with salt water at Pittsburg. It is a water-bearing rock also in Virginia.

That there is no gas in it for a long distance around Boyd's Hill seems proved by the absence of any unusual back pressure on the brine, which does not spout from the top of the well, although it runs off freely. But this it ought to do, seeing it has the still higher land of Allegheny county to the north of it. The pressure of brine on the casing at 1,590′ was sufficient to collapse the tube, and this was the only serious misadventure experienced in sinking the well. Considerable delay ensued, and all the subsequent records of drilling are made less valuable by the interference of the stream of salt water. The record of a wet well is never worth as much as that of a dry well.

The *geological* value of this well is therefore good down to the depth of 1,700′, but not so good from that depth to the bottom (2,300′), which is unfortunate, since the interval (1,700′ to 2,300′) must be occupied by the Butler-Venango (and perhaps the Warren) Oil Sand Group.

The *practical* value of the well ceased at this point also. For if the Leechburg gas-flow were to issue at the Boyd's Hill derrick, it would have to come from this 110′ sand. There was, however, a possibility of tapping some other regular oil sand and getting gas from it if the well were sunk to a greater depth. This was done, and the oil sands were all pierced, but neither oil nor gas found.

The records of the next spaces disagree, as may be seen from a comparison of A=the labels on the jars, B=the section and MSS, and C=another MSS report:—

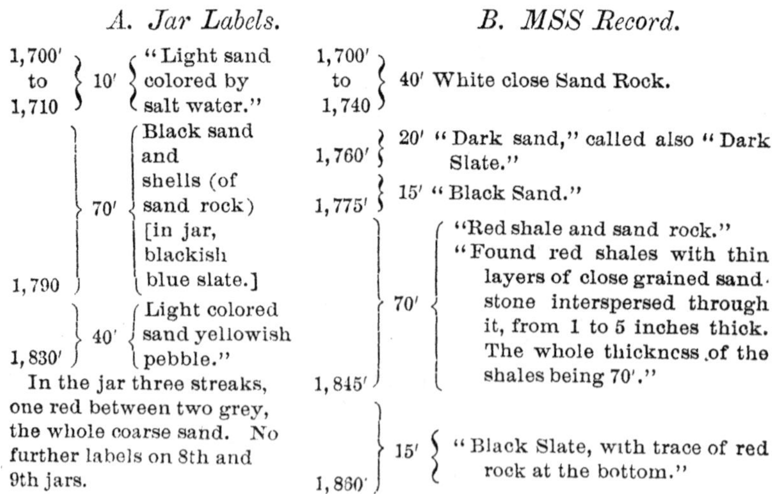

A. Jar Labels.

Depth	Thickness	Label
1,700′ to 1,710	10′	"Light sand colored by salt water."
to 1,790	70′	Black sand and shells (of sand rock) [in jar, blackish blue slate.]
to 1,830′	40′	Light colored sand yellowish pebble."

In the jar three streaks, one red between two grey, the whole coarse sand. No further labels on 8th and 9th jars.

B. MSS Record.

Depth	Thickness	Record
1,700′ to 1,740	40′	White close Sand Rock.
to 1,760′	20′	"Dark sand," called also "Dark Slate."
to 1,775′	15′	"Black Sand."
to 1,845′	70′	"Red shale and sand rock." "Found red shales with thin layers of close grained sandstone interspersed through it, from 1 to 5 inches thick. The whole thickness of the shales being 70′."
to 1,860′	15′	"Black Slate, with trace of red rock at the bottom."

C. Original Copy.	*B. Continued.*
1,845′.	1,845′.
25′ Black Slate, trace of *red*.	15′ Black Slate, trace of *red*.
1,870′.	1,860′.
(not mentioned.)	40′ Grey Slate, colored with iron
	1,900′.
50′ Black Slate, *a*.	38′ Black Slate. *a*.
1,920′.	1,938′.
40′ *Red Rock*, *b*.	12′ *Red Rock*, *b*.
1,960′.	1,950′.
(not mentioned.)	15′ Gray Sand, *c*.
	1,965′.
16′ *Red Rock*.	(not mentioned.)
1,976′.	
34′ Black Slate.	45′ Black Slate.
2,010′.	2,010′.

Going back for a description of some of these layers, we find in the record the following:—

1,938′. Top of 12′ of "red rock." (*b.*) "At this point we found 12′ of red rock, which gave a red color to the water in well. On washing the drillings from this rock they lose most of the red color."

1,950′. Top of 15′ of "gray sand." (*c.*) "Close grained gray sand corresponding to the 'Boulder' found in the Butler county Oil Region."

1,965′ Top 45′ of "black slate."

2,010′ Top of 25′ of "light brown sand; rather close in the grain, corresponding to the stray sand of Butler county."

2,035′. Top of 15′ of white close-grain sand; 3d Sand."

2,050′. Top of 40′ os "dark slate."

2,090′. Top of 27′ of sandstone;"—"slate 27′, and close thin layers of sandstone interspersed through it."

2,117′. Top of 21′ of "close grained quartzite;" "Loose gray sand composed of quartzite. *This sandstone contained a strong smell of oil* This is taken to be the 4th sand of Butler county, found near Great Belt City, on the Sneure and Hame's Farms. On the Sneure Farm, the 4th sand is found at the depth of 1,733′."

(2,117′ On the jar, No. (X,) is the following lable: "Here struck dark corn-meal rock; 21 feet. Strong smell of oil and gas.")

(2,138′ In the jar, is a layer marked, "Mushy Slate, "which looks like a handful of common muddy sea-shore sand; all the fragments are frosted over with what look like angular grains of quartz. Then follows a label: "Grey slate in this 100 feet." Here the jar record ends.)

2,117′. Top of 62′ feet of "grey shale and quartzite."—"At 2,117′ found a gray shale, which still continues at the depth of 2,200′." Here the MSS. and section record ends.

2,200′ Somewhere here I got a handful of fresh drillings from the sand-pump when drawn up December, 1876, and when dried, they had the aspect of ground up Chemung shale.

2,300′. No additional particulars have been reported.

In comparing the above well with that of the Economites at Beaver Falls, now being drilled to a great depth, (and at its proposed depth of 2,000′ it will be in rocks 400′ lower than those in which the Pittsburg well has stopped,) Mr. Carll considers that the 36′ sand at 1,374′ (base) above agrees well with a sand at 675′ (base) at Beaver Falls.

From 700′ down to 1,300′, the B. F. well went through an almost uniform mass of dark grey sandy slates, only broken, in fact, by three streams of *salt water* and one 10′ layer of *red shale.*

Salt water flowed at 820′ (one hundred barrels per day); at 1,060′; and much stronger at 1,280′. Of course there must be some sort of porous rock at these three levels; and they mark the tops of three strata practically tight enough to be water-bearing.

But it is wonderful to see the total disappearance from the Beaver Falls well-record of the 110 foot Boyd's Hill (Pittsburg) brine rock (represented in the Manchester well as 134′ thick!)

The 10′ of red shale at Beaver Falls comes in at 960′. This is about equal to 1,660′ at Pittsburg. But the red shales in the Pittsburg well begin at 1,775′, which is 115′ too low. Yet this (relative) rising of the red shale (going west) agrees exactly (within 5′) with the thinning away of the 110′ sand-rock to 0′.

In an investigation of this nature, new facts being continually collected and collated with those already known, rapid changes of opinion take place and errors are seldom left long undetected.

Thus, on page 162 L, above, it is written: "The sand-rock from which this gas (Leechburg well) comes is probably the third sand," meaning the Third Oil Sand. But the study of the Pittsburg well in connection with that of Leechburg has shown this to be impossible. It is either the First Oil Sand or the Third Mountain Sand, *probably the former.*

On the same page and in the same paragraph it is said that "coals are struck in numerous salt wells between Leechburg and the Allegheny river." This is more precisely stated in Mr. Carll's *Memoranda* of 1875, thus:—

"No coal is noticed in this (Leechburg) well. But in a salt well on the adjoining farm, and in all the salt wells on the Kiskiminetas between this (Leechburg) and the Allegheny river, *a nine* (9) *foot coal bed* is reported *at a depth of about* 90 *feet.* The salt wells are only about 400′ deep, and some of them are still pumping."

There is little risk of committing an error, or of inflicting injustice, by pronouncing such a report a local and popular superstition. We see how easy it is to convert a 1½ foot coal bed, with 6 feet of shales (not even black slates) over it, into an 8 foot coal bed, by reference to the Boyd's Hill record, where, curiously enough, the 8 foot coal is placed just 90 feet down the well. The "8 foot coal bed" at 720′ of the Boyd's Hill well is too low for the "9 foot coal bed" of the salt wells of the Kiskiminetas. The non-record of coal in the Leechburg well is an certain proof of its non-existence, but it raises very strong presumption against a "*nine foot* coal bed."

Mr. Carll's description of the Leechburg well is as follows:—

The Leechburg Gas well was put down in 1871, by Mr. Jos. G. Beale, on the *south* side of the Kiskiminetas, opposite Leechburg, on land of Peter Klingsmith, in Allegheny township, Westmoreland county, 5 miles from the mouth of the river, and Allegheny Valley Railroad Junction.

"It stands on the bed of a small ravine, and about 25 rods up the hollow from the railroad dépôt and the river bank.

"The mouth of the well is 15′ above low water in the river. Casing shuts off fresh water at 350′. A strong vein of salt water flowed in at 825′, which grew weaker after the gas was reached (at 1,200′) and gradually seemed to get exhausted; or, perhaps, it may be held back by the pressure of the gas in the well.

"The gas vein was struck in the top of a pebble rock at 1,200′.

"For nearly three years the well was allowed to pour forth steadily into the air its immense flow of gas, before any attempt was made to utilize it. The flow was thought to be as strong in 1875 as in 1872; but as no tests had been made in the interval, it is quite probably that it had weakened considerably.

"The gas is conveyed from the well in a 5⅝ pipe into what appears to be a common cylindrical steam boiler, furnished with an ordinary safety-valve. Near the bottom is a quarter inch gas pipe, from which the gas constantly forces the water, brought up from the well, in a spray like the steam from a gauge-cock. This pipe gives vent to all the water accumulating in the receiver.

"From the receiver the gas is conveyed in a main across the river and distributed by a network of pipes throughout the works. It is introduced through a ¾ inch pipe into the old furnaces, with very little attention, nothing being required but to cover the grate-bars with ashes and to close up the doors in such a way as to control the draft.

"It required from 1,600 to 2,000 bushels of coal per day to heat the furnaces now fired by the gas from this well. The saving in coal and the greater quantity and better quality of iron produced make a difference to the company of eight hundred dollars per day in favor of the new method. But it should be remembered that this well was bought at only a fraction of its first cost and pays but one hundred dollars a year royalty. Ordinarily the expense and risk of sinking wells, and the customary royalty, would sensibly diminish these figures.

"The advantages claimed for gas are:—1. Furnaces can be built cheaper than for coal. 2. They will last longer. 3. Four heats can be made with gas to three with coal. 4. The product by gas is 30 per cent more than by coal. 5. The iron made is 20 per cent better. 6. The puddler's labor is much lightened. 7. Poor iron is improved by the process.

"The accompanying record was taken from Mr. Beales' book, kept while drilling. (See p. 162 L, above.)

"The data for the contours and section I took with the Aneroid while waiting for the cars.

"The coal seam, which is beautifully exposed in the railroad cutting for a quarter of a mile, appears to be the Freeport bed."

Mr. Carll adds the following notes:—

"*The Apollo Well.*—Messrs. Rogers and Burchfield have other works at Apollo, on the Kiskiminetas river five miles above Leechburg, where they sunk a well for gas last season (1874) to the depth of 1,300 feet. But little (gas) was obtained. Thinking to increase the yield, they inserted a very powerful torpedo, since which it has produced none. They are now sinking another. The present depth (1875) is about 500 feet."

"*The Freeport Well.*—In 1874 Messrs. Rowen and Murphy sunk a well on the east bank of Buffalo creek at Freeport. I could only learn that it was about 1,800 feet deep, and that they struck a gas vein at 1,240 feet, which furnishes enough gas to fire a 40 horse-power boiler."

[As the Upper Freeport Coal bed is at Freeport about 130′ above the Allegheny river, while it is 66′ above the Kiskiminetas river, or 50 feet above the mouth of the gas well at Leechburg, it is evident that 1,240′ in the Freeport well corresponds in about 1,300′ in the Leechburg well; but the Leechburg was struck at 1,230′. The difference (70′) may be diminished by some unknown difference of height of the mouths of the two wells about the river beds. It is in any case not a great variation, considering the irregularity of the sandrock deposits.]

"*The Gas Well, at Saxton Station*, on the Butler and Freeport railroad, in Winfield township, Butler county, is 10* miles from Freeport, and on the supposed prolongation of the 'East Oil Belt' of Middletown." It was struck in the spring of 1874, and had a very heavy flow of gas from a depth of 1,150′ to 1,200, where the First Sand was reported 50′ thick." (See record† given on page 163 L.)

*Distance in a bee-line only 7 miles.

†But this well record was given from memory.

[This well is located on (certainly not a mile west of) the crown of the Brady's Bend anticlinal, which carries the rocks up several hundred feet above their position at Freeport, and accounts for the gas being struck in this well at from 30′ to 80′ less depth than in the Leechburg well, although the mouth of the well must be between 400′ and 500′ higher (above tide) than the mouth of the Leechburg well.]

"*The Thorn Creek Well* stands two miles west of Saxonburg, on the farm of George Welsh, in Jefferson township, Butler county and on the supposed prolongation of the 'West Oil Belt' of Millerstown." (See record,* above, on page 163 L.)

[The gas came in this well from a sand 40′ thick, between 1,485′ and 1,525′. The difference of 335′ greater depth down this well at which the gas flow took place, although its mouth is on high ground, is easily accounted for. As the Saxton gas well was sunk nearly to the ridge of the anticlinal, so this Thorn well was sunk nearly in the trough of the Brady's Bend synclinal. The rocks have a rapid north-west dip down from the top of the anticlinal to the bottom of the synclinal, and the oil and gas go with them.]

"*The Mahan well*, on the Mahan Farm, is in Middlesex township, near the Clinton line, in Butler county." (See record,† above, on page 165 L.)

[The gas in this case is reported to have come from a fine white sand 15′ thick, 1,740′ to 1,755′ down. If the well record were reliable, it would make this gas horizon far below those already described. But as the ocean levels of these wells are not yet all obtained, and very high ground here coincides with the trough of the synclinal, (which moreover goes on deepening more and more towards the south-west,) it remains an open question whether this gas is from the same rock as the gas of the other wells mentioned above.]

"*The Harvey well*, near Larden's Mill, in Clinton township, Butler county, is said to be 360′ above the Allegheny river at Montrose, but the elevation may be questioned. It is probably the most powerful gas well in the country. Mr. Smith, an experienced driller, and part owner in the well, who made the test

*This record, however, was given from memory.

†Not much reliance can be placed the accuracy of this record.

Section and Plan of the Leechburg Gas Well.

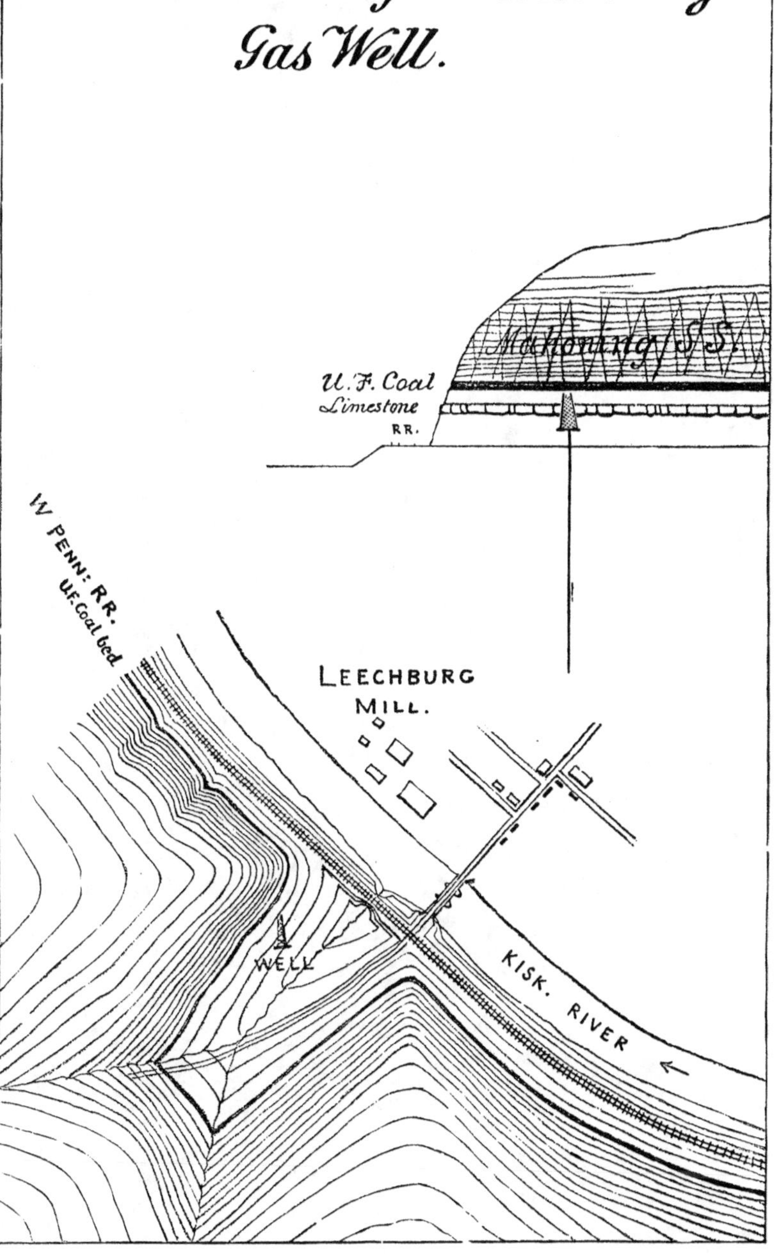

mentioned on page 164 L, above, says he has no doubt the pressure would exceed 400 pounds to the square inch." *

[The gas came from a gray sand 20′ thick at 1,120′ to 1,140′. The well goes down through the coal bed and limestones of the Lower Productive Coal Measures (Freeport and Clarion series, or at least the Clarion series; on coal bed 5′ thick, being reported at 300′. It is therefore impossible that the gas can come from a sand lower in the series than the rock which yields the gas at Leechburg, and the salt water at Pittsburg.]

*Prof. Sadtler's analysis of the gas is given on page 153 L, above.

INDEX

To Report of Progress L, on the Coke Region and the Iron Making Gas Wells.

	Page.
Absence of illuminating hydro-carbons in well gas	154
Addison township	30
Ætna Iron works	148, 149
Allorisma	37
Allegheny city	179, 183, 192
Gas Works	193
Allegheny River Series	12
bluffs	21
Valley railroad	232
Alpsville Station	7, 8, 91
American Phil. Soc. Proc.	219
Ammonites	2
Amount of gas used per ton of iron	192
Analyses of Broad Ford coal,	62, 63
of coals for coke	120
of fire clays	113
of fuels for furnace use	133
of gas (Appendix B)	146
of iron ores under the Pittsburg coal bed	99
of pig, scrap and tap cinder	180
of roll scale	207
of coal used	207
of cold fix	207
of tap cinders	207
of muck-bar	181, 208, 209
of trial finished bars	211
of carbon deposit at gas wells	213
of brine	229
Annularia	37
Anthracite furnaces	147
and coke compared	140
in Wales	87
Anticlinal axes	5, 34
of Brady's Bend	220
Apollo well	149, 235
Appolt's improved oven	65
Area of Coal Measures once larger than now	2, 11
Anderson's railroad map	8
Argyle	177
Armstrong station	7
county	178
Ash analyses	16
Astartella concentrica	35, 37
Athyris subtilita	35, 36
Average relative energies of block coal, coke and anthracite	144
Aviculopecten carbonarius	35
Hertzeri	36
occidentalis	35
Baltimore and Ohio railroad,	38
Bar iron (finished) analysed,	213
Barnet bed for coke in Broad Top	120
Barren red shales	25
Barren Run ore Jacob's cr.	108
Barren Measure coals	222
Barrings' Station level	8
Barton coal bed; (for the correct place of it, see R. P. HHH.)	35
Basin of Connellsville	7
Bayard salt well	114
Bear Wallow ore drifts	28, 31
Beaver Falls well	232
Beck's Run Co.'s works	95
Bed B, mined for coke	120
Bed C, mined in Broad Top	120
Bedford, Huntingdon and Broad Top railroad	3
Beehive oven	63, 83, 123, 136
in Indiana State	143

	Page.
Belgian coke oven	64, 124
section	132
objected to	136
top and bottom coke different in quality	74
Bellerophon carbonarius	37
Montfortianus	37
percarinatus	37
Bennett's Mills station	184
Berard's coal washer for coke,	122
Best coal for coking	62
Bennington station in Blair county	62, 64, 66, 79
coke area	120
iron furnace statistics	137, 144
Berea grit	223, 230
Bethlehem Iron Works	141
Big Bottom ore beds	19, 27, 99, 103
Bigley's mines	91
Big Sewickley creek	4, 11, 12, 90
Birmingham, England	87
Birmingham Bridge Station	8
Birch Cock colliery in Wales,	86
Black limestone of Barren	21
Black Ball Coal Works	89
Black slate XI	226, 228
with gas	227
Blacksmith's Vein	38
Blair Iron and Coal Company,	131
Blairsville	1, 6, 222
coke	73
Block coal	172
area	118
of Ohio	32
versus coke	143
Bloomfield mines in Blair co.,	104
Bloomington (Md)	38
Bliss, Marshall & Co.'s fire brick,	111
Blue lump ore	18, 19, 99, 34, 103
Blue rock in wells	225
Bluff sandstone	17
Boating coke	4
Booth's creek	37, 38, 39
Borings on Jacob's creek	109
Boulder sand of oil men	229
Boyd's Hill well, described in Appendix E	217
Braddock's Station level	8
Gas Coal Company	94
fire brick	111
Bradford's cylinder breaker	122
Brady's Bend anticlinal	220, 236
Brazil block coal in Indiana	143
Briar Hill block coal	143
Brick yards	116
Bridgeport Station	31
level	8, 53, 54
Bridge ore on Jacob's creek	108
Brine, (see Salt)	229
Broad Ford	3, 8, 9, 56, 57, 62
station level	8, 48
coke analyses	78, 105
Broad Top Mountain	6
coal field	22
coal and coke	66, 73, 79
coke area	120
Bromine in brine	229
Bromine works	115
Brook Tunnel Station level	8
Brownville coal bed	38
Brown's Creek	4
Brown's Run	11
Brown's Station level	8
Buckeye mines	143
coke works	54
Buffalo Gas works	171
Bull creek, (Butler county),	173, 183
Burden power of coke	130
Burning Well scenes	173, 183
Burning Spring gas, (Niagara)	146
Brown's gas well, (Butler)	173, 174
Burn's well gas	148, 152, 165
Butler	173
Butler county gas	148, 161
wells	217
Butyl-hydride	147
Caking quality of coking coals	212
Calorific values of well gases,	155
Cambria fire brick works at Braddock's station	111
Cambria Iron Company	120
furnaces	139
coking works	64, 66
Cameron blowing engine	185
Cannel coal	34
Carbon deposit of the gas wells analysed	213
Carbon lost in coking	118
Carbonic acid in well gas,	146, 154, 175
Carr's disintegrator	86

	Page.
Castleman Station level......	8
Catskill Formation (IX, X)..	12, 30
sandstone................	222, 226
Cellular structure of good coke..........................	119, 130
Cement limestone............	15, 113
crusher..................	115
Cessation of gas flow.........	166
Charging the Belgian oven...	132
Charges for gas furnace.......	192
Charlotte furnace............	104
Charred coal..................	143
Cheap coke...................	16
Chemical phenomena of iron smelting..................	137
Chemung oil rocks, (VIII) ..	12, 31
drillings................	232
Cherry Tree well, (Indiana)..	148, 150
gas analyses.............	153
Chestnut Ridge geology, 1, 3, 4, 6, 8, 9, 10, 11, 19, 99.	
ores......................	103
fire brick................	112
Chicago Coke Market........	48
Chonetes granulifera..........	34
Smithii..................	34
Cincinnati as a coke market..	92
Cities lighted by natural gas,	177
City Farm station level......	8
Clarion county.......	225
Clay Pike....	30
Cleaning coal for coking......	122
Cleveland Ironstone in England........................	137
Clinton Township, (Butler)..	164
Coal A................	222, 225, 226, 233
Coal bank ore, Jacob's cr....	106
Coal best for coking..........	69
Coal trade of the Youghiogheny......................	88
Coal for iron gas furnace analysed.......................	207
Coal Beds of the Barren......	21
Coal Measures of the Yough.	1
of the Connellsville Basin, Chapter III........	38
Coals differ in use for coking,	118
Coburn's Creek..............	37
Coke, proportion to iron ore in furnace.............	104
compared with anthracite	137
Coke, region described.... ..	3
area described............	120
yard described............	122
Coking, Chapter V......... ..	61
its object.................	62
for furnace use...........	117
by heaps..................	122
tables.....................	61
trade eastward............	3
Cold-fix analysed.............	207
Cold-short tests...............	205
Compass line location of wells........................	217
Conemaugh river............	12
Condemned Flag ore.........	18
Conflagration at gas wells....	173, 182
Confluence Station...........	9, 30
level.....................	8
Conglomerate, (Seral,) Pottsville,) (see No. XII.)......	4, 23, 31
of the Upper P. C. M.....	34
of No. X. Pocono.........	229
Connection of the Pittsburg and Connellsville coal beds	2
Connellsville..............	1, 8, 48, 220
basin....................	7
station level.............	8
coal bed..................	2
gap.....................	31
coke analysis.............	16
coke trade................	40
coke yield................	61
coal in character..........	62
compared with Bennington coal................	67
coke area.................	120
coal specially adapted to coke....................	83
Gas Coal Company.......	44
sandstone............	17, 18, 19, 35
Conveyance of gas to iron works......................	173
Cook's Mills station level.....	8
Coppeé's improved Belgian oven......................	65
Copper Works station level..	8
Corey & Co.'s works.........	94
Corn-meal rock..............	231
Cornell & Worling's works...	92
Cost of coking..........	65, 77, 126 135
Cost of iron-make at Oliphant's	102

	Page.
Coultersville station level....	8
Cow Rock, see figures........	4
Crinoids (?)..................	225
Crusher for cement	114
Bradford's...............	122
Crushing coal in Wales	87
Cumberland (Md.) station...	8
coal field	34
sandstone................	38
coke.....................	64, 75
coal.....................	66
Cwmllynfell colliery in Wales,	85
Cyathocrinus (?)	36
Datum level.................	8
of pipe survey...........	184
Dawson station level.........	8
Deakey's Bromine works	115
Dicker's creek...............	37
Old Furnace.............	36
Delamater gas well	165, 173, 174
Delphy farm	148
Deltodus	37
Dense coke..................	83
Descent of rocks south-west..	220
Dexter mines.	51
Diamond Fire-Brick works...	112
Gas Coal Co. (Jeff. co.) ..	79, 80
coke described	84
Dip of rocks at base of Ridge,	6
and erosion..............	9
of beds at Pittsburg......	224
Distances to market..........	3
Districts furnishing coke.....	61
Divner farm.................	217
Drakestown Run station level,	8
Drillings in jars.............	223
Duffy farm..................	174, 217
Dunbar......................	12, 14
furnace..........	4, 18, 43, 102, 139
fire-brick................	111
creek.........	4, 17, 20, 22, 23, 26, 29
Duncan's section	55
Brother's mines	105
& Lamb's salt well.......	115
Dunlap's creek..............	4, 11
Durability of the natural gas supply....................	161
Durham coke................	137
East Sandy gas well..........	177
ceased to flow...........	166
Ebbw Vale works, in Wales..	65

	Page.
Economites' well............	232
Economy of coke and anthracite contrasted	137
of Belgian oven..........	126
Edmondia Aspenwalensis....	35
Effects of phosphorus on iron,	215
Efficiency of coke and anthracite compared.............	137
Egypt station level...........	8
Elk Lick Coal (see Errata) ..	35
Elk Rock....................	4, 5
Elk Run.....................	29, 31
Ellerslie station level........	8
Ellrod station................	8
level......................	8
(P. C. R. R.)..........	114, 115, 92
Encrini.....................	21
Engineering and Mining Jour.	74
English sluice washer........	122
Enniskillen gas.............	146
Enterprise works............	46
Erie gas	161, 168
heaviest	176
wells	169
water works wells........	169
Erosion of the Pittsburg Coal bed....................	2, 6
and dip.................	9
Ersocrinus..................	36
Ethyl-hydride	146
chloride	150
Etholene-bromide...........	157
Etna Station................	45
Euomphalus rugosus........	37
Evaporative power of coke...	76
Ewing & Boyd's new furnace,	102
fire-clay	111
Fairview gas well (Butler co.)...................	165, 173, 177
Fall of the rivers westward..	8
anticlinal south-west......	220
Farr's station................	47
Fayette county..............	227
Branch railroad	40
Coal company...........	59
station level.............	44
Fairmount (W. Va.).........	102
Coal company..........	38, 79, 80
coke described	83
Fairhope station level........	8

	Page.
Fairchance iron works	18
coke	40, 68, 98
Fairview gas well	220
Ferguson's station	43
Ferriferous limestone	37
Fibrous bar iron show granulation	214
Figures of gas (iron) furnaces	192
Figures of broken test bars	206
Fire at gas well	173, 182
Final Report of 1858	1, 13
Fire-clays, Chap. VII	98
works decribed, Chap. III.	•
mistaken for limestone	227
Firing for coke	123
First geological Survey	1
First Sand gas	161, 165
Fish remains	31
Flag ore bed	27
Flow through pipe not accurately measurable	192, 193
Fœtid limestone	14
Forge vein ore, Jacob's cr.	106
Forge fire-clay bed, Jacob's cr.,	112
Former sea level	10
Fossil limestone	18
Fossil genera mentioned in this book—	
Allorisma	37
Ammonites	2
Astartella	35
Athyris	35, 37
Aviculopecton	35, 37
Bellerophon	37
Cyathocrinus	36
Encrinus	21, 225
Fish	31
Hemipronites	34, 36
Leptæna	21
Lima	35
Lophophyllum	36
Machrocheilus	35, 37
Macrodon	35
Myalina	37
Nautilus	37
Neuropteris	37
Nucula	35
Nuculina	35, 36
Orthis	35
Orthoceras	21, 37
Fossil genera—*Continued.*	
Phillipsia	37
Pleurotomaria	37
Polyptemopsis	37
Productus	21, 35, 36
Schizodus	37
Solonomya	35
Sphenophyllum	37
Sphenopteris	37
Spirifer	35
Terebratula	21
Yoldia	35, 36
Zeacrinus	36
Fountain Mills station	51
mines	51
Fourth Sand of Butler	231
Frankstown (Westmoreland)	8
Fredonia gas wells in N. Y.	146, 161, 170
Free hydrogen in well gas	154, 176
Freeport	175
coal beds	25, 222
at Pittsburg	224
at Fairmount	69
group ore beds	98
gas well	166, 235
Frick & Co.'s coal, coke	83
ore	105
Friction in pipe for gas	185
Frost station level	42
Fuel gas	158
Furnace clay bed, Jacob's cr.	112
Furnace vein ore, Jacob's cr.	105
Gambier's gas	147
Gap through Chestnut Ridge at Connellsville	3, 31
Garret station level	8
Gas making	71
trade, Chap. IV	88
abundant in Jacob's creek wells	109
above red rocks	110
flow from wells	167, 175, 192, 193
at Leechburg	229
at Erie	168
chiefly from oil sands	161
durability, Ap. C	161
ceased on East Sandy	166
well sections	162
analyses	146, 174
as fuel	158
used in iron working	173, 178

	Page.
Gas (iron) furnaces, how constructed	178
proportion to one ton of iron made	192
well on fire	173, 182, 183
specific gravity	194
pipe line	183
well section, Boyd's Hill. Appendix E	217
Geography of the coke region,	5
Geology of the coal field	4
Geological column at Connellsville	13
George's creek	4, 11, 42
Gist's run	17, 20
Glendon iron works	141
Gorges or gaps of the Yough.,	31
Graff, Bennett & Co's mill	184, 192
Grahamite	34
Granulation. Percentage of in fibrous iron bars	212
Great Limestone U. B. M	14, 33
Great Belt City	231
Greensburg	3
Green Lick N. G. RR	104
Greenwich Point shipping port	90
Gray Catskill Formation, (X.)	30
Grove Station level	8
Growth of coke trade	61
Guffy's station level	7
Gypsum	73
Hame Farm	231
Hammer scale	181
Harrisburg works	141
Harvey well (Butler), 148, 149, 164, 236	
gas analysis	153
Hazelwood station level	8
Hays Station, (P. W. & C. RR.	94
Hays & Bros'. works	94
Hawk-eye Station	46
Heat of furnace	137
in gas furnace	193
of iron bar's furnace	180
Hemipronites crassus	34, 36
Hickman's run	59
History of the coke producduction	61
Hocking Valley coal (O.)	142
Hollidaysburg coke	68
coal	79
Hollidaysburg Belgian oven	125, 131
Honey-comb ore	26
Horizons of iron ore	98
of oil and gas	218
Hydrogen free in well gas	154, 176
Hydro-carbons	164
Illuminating power of well gas	154, 167
of coals	96
Indian Creek station level	8, 9
Inter-Conglomerate coal	32
Irishtown run	29
Iron and Steel Institute, (England)	85
Iron ore of Pittsburg Coal	17, 18
of XII	98
Chapter VII	98
Iron Bridge station	52
Iron-working by gas	173
trials and notes	192 to 201
Iron yield by gas	179
to gas; per cent	192
bars tested	204
Irwin's Station, (P. R. R.)	90
Isabella Furnace	138, 142, 144, 192
Grey forge pig	194
Jacob's creek	4, 6, 7, 9, 11, 25, 26
fire clays	112
ore	98, 105
station, (P. C. R. R.)	108
level	8
gas	165
Jackson, (Fayette county,)	57
mines	58
works	57
Jackson's (R. M. S.) sections,	27
Jameson's Salt works	115
Jar record of drillings	223
Jarecki Manufacturing company's works	168
Jefferson county	225
Township	236
Jefferson county, red hematite ore in coal measures	110
Jimtown mines	59
Johnstown	24, 45
furnace	139
coke works	122
Juniata	229
Karns City	177

Page.

Kemble Iron and Coal Co., Riddlesburg, (B. T.)... 122, 124, 139
Kelly bed coke, Broad Top... 120
Kidney ore bed.............. 27
Kiskimenitas River......... 2, 12, 178
Kittanning.................. 222
  coal bed.................. 225
Kree's & Watt's inclines...... 29
Laboratory coke.............. 73
  at Harrisburg............ 78
Ladnersville, (Butler county) 173
Lake Superior ore........... 104
Lamont Station fire clay..... 117
Landore blast furnaces, coke, 87
Larden's Mill, (Butler)...... 163, 236
Largest iron make of a blast furnace.................... 138
Latrobe..................... 222
Laurel Hill.................. 3, 30
  Run station level......... 8
Laughlin station level........ 8
Layton station level......... 8
  fire brick................ 112
Leechburg well...... 148, 149, 178, 233
  gas horizon............... 229
  gas analysed.............. 152
  gas section............... 162
Lehigh furnaces............. 140
  Valley.................... 49
Lamont station.............. 41
  U. Br. P. & C. R. R....... 102
Leptœna.................... 21
Levels of the region.......... 3
  table of, along P. C. R. R., 8
  of Boyd's Hill well....... 217
  of well mouths........... 219
Lewisbury (Va.) limestone.. 227
Lignite..................... 34
Ligonier.................... 9
  Valley.................. 6, 8, 19, 29
  sandstone............... 20
Lima retifera............... 35
Limestone................... 14
  analyses................. 15
  of Barren Measures....... 20
  of Lower Prod. C. M...... 23
  of XI................ 222, 227, 29
  Ferriferous.............. 225
  at Dunbar................ 103
  over Pittsburg coal bed.. 100
  ore...................... 101

Page.

Lime kilns.................. 113
Limit of elasticity........... 211
Little Toby creek............ 171
  Sewickley creek.......... 4
Lobinger Salt Works......... 17
Locating wells.............. 217
Lochiel furnace............. 141
Locust Point at Baltimore.... 88
Loiseau's artificial fuel....... 85
Long Run Station level...... 8
  P. and C. R. R........... 115
Lophophyllum proliferum.... 36
Loss of carbon in coking..... 67, 118
Lost Land run (Md.)........ 39
Lower Barren Measures.... 17, 35, 224
Lower Coal Measures........ 4
Lower Freeport coal bed.....23, 24, 37
Lower Kittanning coal bed .. 225
Louisville.................. 94
Low furnaces................ 142
Lucy furnace................ 138
  yield.................... 144
Macrocheilus primigenius.... 35, 37
  ventricus............... 35, 37
Macrodon obsoletus.......... 35
Mahan gas well (Butler co.).. 163, 236
Mahoning sandstone....17, 22, 26, 36, 37
  at Pittsburg............. 224, 226
  at ridge................. 6
  described................ 21
Manchester well............. 232
Map of the coke field......... 4
Map of pipe line. 183, 184
Maps of the underground.... 218
Marl of the Barren Measures, 21
Marsh gas.................. 146
  series................... 154
Mauch Chunk Formation (see No. XI)................... 4, 222
Maxwell, Brady & Co.'s fire brick works............... 112
M'Adams & Co.'s lime kilns.. 113
  patent breaker.......... 113
M'Cartney's (J.) quarry...... 30
M'Ginley farm............... 217
M'Kean county............... 38
M'Keesport station level... 3, 7, 8, 93
M'Kinney & Bro.'s Works.... 94
M'Lanahan's oven 134
Meter for measuring gas flow, 192, 193

Page.
Methods of coking........... 63
Appendix A............. 117
Method of collecting gas..... 148
Middle Freeport coal bed.... 37
Middle Run................. 11
Middlesex township, Butler.. 163
Midlothian coke (Virginia)... 75
Miller bed (B) in Blair co.... 62
compared with Connellsville coke.............. 66
with Bennington coke.... 68, 120
Millerstown, Butler county... 236
Milton gas well.............. 166
Milwaukee market........... 48
Mineral Point Station level.. 8
Mixture of ores.............. 104
Mixed coal for coke in Wales, 87
Monongahela river...........1, 21, 215
slackwater navigation.... 3
series of coal measures... 12, 33
Conglomerate 39
Montrose well............... 236
Moore's station (P.& C.R.R.), 90, 91
Morgan station.............. 49
Morgantown.............. 36, 38, 39
sandstone................ 17, 35
Mound coking............... 122
Mountain limestone 30, 222, 227
ores of XI............... 103
Mountain sandstone......... 228
Mount Braddock............. 42, 43
Mount Pleasant 222
Br. P. & C. R. R.... 3, 48, 51, 54, 104
Coke works.............. 56
cement................... 113
Mount Savage coal bed....... 37
fire brick................. 38
Mount's creek............. 4, 7, 22, 25
Muck bar.................... 206
analysed............. 181, 208, 209
tested.................... 203
Mullin's Works............. 54
Myalina..................... 37
Myersdale Station Level..... 8, 9
Names of persons mentioned in this book—
Adams (F. F.) 170
Allen (Charles).......... 8
Appolt & Coppeé 65
Anderson & Wood 217
Armstrong (C. H. & Son), 50, 91, 92

Page.
Names of persons—*Continued.*
Babcock (W. R.)......... 131
Bacon (Oliver &)......... 168
Beale (Hogsette &) 43, 162
Beale (J. S.) 233, 234
Bell (J. Lowthian) .. 75, 121, 122, 131, 137.
Bennett (Graff, & Co.), 59, 60, 148, 184.
Bigley (N. J.)........... 91
Birchfield (Rogers &).... 178
Blair (Schoenberger & Co.) 139
Bliss, Marshall & Co...... 111
Boyle & Hazlett.......... 54, 56
Boyd (Willson, Boyd & Playford) 45
Boyd (Ewing, Boyd & Co.) 42, 102, 111
Brady (Maxwell & Co.).. 112
Brock & Sons............ 85
Brown & Cochran 57, 59, 60
Brown (Paull, Brown & Co) 43
Brown (W. H.).......... 93
Bunsen.................. 154
Birchfield (Rogers &).... 148, 161
Carll, (J. F.,) 31, 162, 165, 167, 172, 218, 219, 233.
Carneige & Co........... 74
Caughey, Mr............ 168
Craven, Major........... 115
Chalfant (Spang & Co.).. 148, 184
Chandler, Prof........... 71
Clark (Speer & Co.)...... 114
Coburn, Mr.............. 170
Cochan (S.) & Co 56, 60
Cochran (J. M.) & Co..... 58, 60
Cochran & Brown........ 57, 59, 60
Cochran & Ewing 53, 56
Cochran & Keister........ 59, 60
Cooper.................. 217
Conkle (F. A.).......... 164
Coppeé (Appolt &)....... 65
Corey & Co.............. 94
Cornell & Werling 92
Cumming (J.) 182
Davenport, Fairburn & Co. 169
Deakey (S. J.).......... 115
Dillinger & Suttle........ 46, 47
Dillinger, Sherrich & Co., 45
Dilworth (Kirk &)....... 173

Page.

Names of persons—*Continued.*

Dravo, (John F.,) ... 44, 77, 94, 139
Duncan Brothers....... 54, 56, 105
Duncan & Lamb......... 115
Edeburn 217
Evans, Mr............... 168
Ewing (Cochran &)...... 53, 56
Ewing, Boyd & Co.... 41, 102, 111
Fairburn (Davenport & Co.) 169
Fawcett (Redmond &)... 94
Firmstone (Frank)....... 141
Fontaine, Prof........... 32
Fouqué.................. 148, 154
Frick & Co., 48, 56, 60, 62, 78, 82, 83, 105.
Frost (F. H.)............ 42
Fulton (Jno.)... 2, 64, 66, 75, 81, 69
Glover (Soisson &)....... 112
Graff, Bennett & Co., 59, 60, 148, 184, 192.
Grist (W.) 125
Hackney, Mr............. 85
Harker (Simpson & Son), 94
Hazlett (Boyle &)........ 54, 56
Heath & White........... 89
Henderson & Co.......... 43
Hurst, Moore & Co 49, 56
Hitchman (Stoner & Co.) 47
Hodge (J. T.)............ 28
Hunter (W. G.).......... 217, 222
Hogsett, Beal & Co....... 43
Hogsett, Watt & Co....... 42
Howell (Frank D.) 109
Hurst, Stoner & Co....... 46
Hutchinson & Co......... 49, 56
Ihmsen, Lake & Co....... 51, 56
Jackson, (Dr. R. M. S.,) 1, 6, 11, 13, 17, 23, 25.
Jameson (J. A.) 115
Johnson (Prof. W. R)... 64, 75, 76
Jones (Howard Grant)... 38, 39
Keifer & Co.............. 50, 56
Keister (Cochran &) 59, 60
Kirk & Dilworth.......... 173
Klingsmith (P.).......... 234
Lake & Co............... 53
Lake (Johnson & Co.) ... 51, 56
Lane (Strickler &) 49, 56
Lamb (Duncan &)....... 115
Laughlin & Co 57, 60
Lesley.................... 215

Page.

Names of persons—*Continued.*

Lomanson & Shaft........ 52, 56
Loisean, Mr............. 85
Markle & Son 90
Markle, (Sherrick & Co.,) 49, 52, 53, 54, 56.
Marshall (Bliss, & Co).... 111
Maxwell, Brady & Co 112
Meek (B. F.)............ 36
M'Adams & Co........... 113
M'Creath, (A. S.,) 70, 78, 79, 80, 84, 99, 100, 101, 104, 105, 108, 111, 112, 162, 172, 178, 207.
M'Kinley, Mr........... 1
M'Kinney & Brother..... 94
M'Lanahan (J. King).... 132, 134
Moore (Thomas).......... 90
Moore (Hurst & Co.)..... 49, 56
Morgan & Co......... 48, 50, 56, 60
Morley, Prof............. 147
Moyer (John)............ 45
Mullin (Wm. D.)........ 54
Murphy 235
Neil (James)............. 92
Neil & Oliver............ 93
Newberry (Dr. J. S.)..... 31, 147
Noble (Rawle & Co.)..... 169
Oliphant, Mr 34
Oliver & Bacon.......... 168
Oliver (Neil &)........... 93
Overholt (J. F.)......... 53, 56
Overholt (A. S. R.) 52, 56
Painter & Co............. 51, 56
Paull, Brown & Co........ 43
Pechin, (E. C.)... 14, 16, 24, 30, 103
Peelor, Mr............... 69
Penny (John)............ 93
Playford (Wilson, Boyd &), 45
Rawle, Noble & Co....... 169
Redmond & Fawcett...... 94
Rice (Sherrick &)........ 46, 47
Rogers (Prof. H. D.), 13, 21, 38, 227
Rogers (Prof. W. B.).... 23, 39, 227
Rogers & Burchfield, 148, 161, 162, 178.
Rosengarten & Sons...... 115
Rowen & Murphy........ 235
Sadtler (Prof.) 175
Sanders.................. 183
Shaft (Tomanson &) 52, 53

Page.

Names of persons—*Continued.*
Sherrick (Markle, & Co.), 49, 53, 54, 56.
Sherrick (Rice & Co.).... 46, 47
Sherwood (A.)........... 31
Shoenberger, Blair & Co.. 139
Silliman, (Prof. B.)...... 147
Simpson, Harker & Son.. 95
Smith (J. R.)........... 113
Smith, Mr............... 164, 236
Soisson & Co............. 111, 112
Soisson & Glover.......... 112
Spang, Chalfant & Co., 148, 184, 192, 194.
Speer, Clark & Co........ 114
Stauffer (Jr., R. & Co.)... 51, 56
Stauffer (J. F. & Co.).... 54, 56
Stearn, Mr............... 168
Stevenson, (Prof. J. J.), 25, 13, 14, 21, 23, 33, 37, 38, 227.
Stone Brothers........... 93
Stoner (Hurst & Co.)..... 46
Stoner (Hitchman & Co.) 47
Strickler & Lane......... 49
Suttle (Dillinger &)...... 46
Taylor (C. W.). 115
Taylor (W. H.) 8
Taylor (H. L.)........... 166
Warden (Samuel) & Co.. 47
Watt, (W. P.) & Co...... 43
Watt (Hogsett & Co.).... 42
Weeks (J. D.)........... 178, 180
Welsh (Geo.) 236
Werling (Cornell &)..... 92
White (Heath &) 89
Williams, Mr............ 36, 192
Wilson (Boyd, Playford), 45
Wormley, Prof........... 72, 96
Wood 217
Wuth (Dr. Otto), 107, 113, 147, 174, 229
Wurtz, (Prof. Henry).... 147, 154
Young, (C. A.).......... 30, 40
Young, (Robt.) C. R..... 192, 193
Natural coke from the Richmond basin (Va.).......... 75
Natural Gas Co. (Limited)... 173
a nuisance to salt borers.. 110
supply discussed......... 161
in iron working, Appendix D.................. 173
well history............. 182

Page.

Nautilus 37
Neal & Oliver's Works....... 93
Neff well gas near Gambier (O.) 147
Nelson farm.................. 166
Neshannock Iron Co.'s F..... 139
Neuropteris 37
New Alexandria............ 1
New Albany 11
New Castle.................. 45, 91
New Orleans................ 94, 95
New Furnace................ 102
New River Coal Measures (XI) 32
Newton gas well 177
Niagara Falls gas........... 146
Nitrogen in well gas.......... 146
Northampton furnace 141
Nucula anodontoides......... 35
parva..................... 35
ventricosa 35, 36
Nuculina bellistriata......... 35
arata..................... 36
No. VIII Formation.......... 12, 31
No. IX Formation............ 12, 31
Nos. IX, X Formations....... 30
No. X Formation............ 12, 229
No. XI Formation............ 12
red shale................. 18
limestones of, ... 29
coal beds in, ... 32
ores in, ... 103
No. XII Formation 23, 31, 37, 38, 39
on the mountain 4
terrace knobs............. 6
coal beds in, ... 32
variable formation........ 171
Oakdale station level........ 8
level (P & C. R. R.)..... 112
Obstacles to oil investigation,. 219
Obstructions put into the gas line pipe.................... 185
Ocean mines.................. 90
Ohio River at Pittsburg...... 4, 220
affluents.................. 3
Conglomerate 31
Ohiopite Falls................ 8
Station level............ 9
Oil wells of St. Jo (Butler co.), 148
Oil well records, Nos. 1, 2, 3, 4, 5, on Jacob's creek.......... 109
Oil sands................... 21, 31, 223
Oil belts..................... 172, 235

	Page.
Oil wells	31
Old Red Sandstone For	31
Old Franklin Iron Furnace	17
Forge	17, 22
Oliphant's new furnace	68
limestones	100
ore section	99
blue lump ore	34
pit coking	70
rick coking	64
wasteful	101
mill iron	180
Ore analyses	24, 28
Ores of Cambria county	24
Ore beds described by Mr. Pechin	26
Ores under XII	103
Ores of Lower Pro. C. M	23
Ore above Mahoning Sand	108
Ore under Pittsburg Coal Bed	105
Orthis carbonaria	35
Orthoceras	21
cribosum	37
Original surface of the earth,	10
Osceola station, Fayette	8
coal works	92
Outcrop of Pittsburg bed	7
Ovens differ in value	119
Ovens in Wales	86
Page's patent kilns	113
Paper Mill at West Newton	90
Parker City	227
Parker Township, Butler	173
Paraffine condensations	176
Pebble rock and gas	234
Petrolia	177
Petrolia gas of Enniskillen	146, 165
Penn Gas Coal Company	90
Penneville station	45
Perryopolis village	17
Persistent coal beds	5
Philadelphia Scale and Testing Machine works	211, 212
Phillipsia Sangamonensis	37
Philson's Mills station level	8
Phosphorus absent from ores	101
in bar iron	181
discussed	213
Physical characters of good coke coal	69
Piedmont Sandstone For	37, 38
Pig iron analyses	180
Pin Vein ore, (XI,)	105
Pine creek, (Butler county,),	183, 184
Pinegrove Station, Somerset,	8
Pinkerton Point, Somerset	8
Pioneer Run gas, Venango	146
Pipe line for gas	173, 183, 184
Pit coking	136
at Bennington	137
Pittsburg	1, 59
level above tide	8, 224
Court House	20
and Connellsville RR.	3, 8, 38, 56, 88
coal bed	2, 33, 217, 220
described	1, 16
undulates	7, 11
at Connellsville	40
thick at Connellsville	85
left in patches	6
P. & C. Gas Coal and C. Co	44, 139
their coke standard	33
Pittsburg Iron furnaces	128
Forge and Iron Company,	94
Pittsburg Limestone	19, 33, 34
Lower limestone	17
Pittsburg Sandstone	20, 34
Steel works	217
Boyd's Hill well	217
Plurotomaria carbonaria	37
Greyvilliensis	37
speciosa	37
(?) *tumida*	37
Pleasantville—Ven. Co	219
Pleasant Unity	11
Pocono Sandstone, (X,)	222
Polyptemopsis peracutus	37
Porous versus dense coke	131
Port Perry Junction level	8
Port Royal Station level	8
Porter, Dennison coke yard	120
Potomac River	39
Pottsville Conglomerate (XII)	4, 226
Pressure in Erie Gas wells	165, 169
of gas in and out of wells,	174, 183
observed in pipe near Sharpsburg	186
at end of pipe	192
diminishes with number of wells sunk	177
Precautions taken in collecting well gas	148

	Page.
Pridevale Iron works	39
Propyl-hydride	146
Productus	21
costatus	35
Nebrascensis	35, 36
Prattenanus	35, 36
semi-reticulatus	35
Production of coke in the region	61
Puddling furnaces heated by gas	185
process	193 to 201
Pushing engine for coke oven,	136
Pyrites in coal	73
Quenching coke	136
Railroads serving the coke trade	3
Rapids of the Youghiogheny,	23
Records of wells defective	219
in jars	223
Red flag ore	99, 103
Red hematite ore in coal measures	110
Red rocks thick in Jacob's creek oil wells	109
Red oil rocks	230, 231
Red shale of B. M.	20, 25
of XI (Mauch Chunk)	222
Red short tests	204
Redmont & Fawcett's works.	94
Redstone creek	4, 11, 13
coal bed	13, 15, 33
Report of Progress, 1876	2, 22
I. Carll's	218
of 1858	11
Results of iron-make with gas	203, 205, 215
Resumé of author	215
Reynoldsville Coal, Jefferson,	79
Richmond (Va.) coke	75
Riddlesburg in Broad Top	124
Rider to Pittsburg Coal	88
Riehle Brothers, tests for strength of gas-iron bars	220
Rising Sun coke works	52, 53
Riverton (Fayette co.) level,	8
Robbinsville level	8
Robertson's gas furnace	192
Rock oil	218
Rocks descend south-west	220
Rockhill Iron and Coal Co	122

	Page
Rocky Mountains	78
Rogers' Gulch gas, Wirt, Va.,	146
Roll-scale analysed	207
Rolling mills	184
Rothrock's Eddy	26
Sadtler's sp. gr. of gas	175
Salisbury	6, 9, 19
Salt Lake City	42, 48
Salt water from wells	115, 221, 225
analysed	229
at Beaver Falls	232
in Conglomerate XII	226
above red rocks in Jacob's creek	110
Salt well (Bayard) (Duncan & Lamb)	144, 120
Sanders' map of pipe line	183
(old) on Jacob's creek	109
Salt works	8
Salt works station level	8, 115
Saltzburg station, P. & C. R. R.,	8, 93
level, Fayette co	8
Sand-bar maps wanted	218
Sand-patch Tunnel level	8
Sand works level	8
Sarversburg (Butler co.)	173
Saxon Station gas well, Butler Br. R. R	162
Saxton Station well	235
Saxonburg, Butler co	163, 236
Sehizodus	37
Scottdale station	50, 104
Scrap-iron analysis	180
Section of C. M. at Duncan's,	55
Jackson's Mine	58
Sections along Dunbar creek,	98
Section of Belgian oven	132
Section of pipe line	183, 184
Sections of gas wells	162
Sedgwick level	6, 8, 69
Seral Conglomerate Formation (see No. XII)	4, 226, 228
ore	103
Sewickley Coal Bed	13, 14, 33
Sewickley creek	4, 11, 14
Shafts on Pittsburg Coal	7
Shales of Barren Measures	21
Shallow versus deep charges in the Belgian oven	132, 134
Shaner's Station, P. & C. R. R.,	91
Sharon furnace	91, 143

Page.
Sharpsburg....... 179, 183, 184, 185, 192
Sheffield well gas (Warren co.) the lightest........... 176
Shipments of coke.......... 85, 95
Shoenberger, Blair & Co.'s furnace.................... 139
Shoo-fly tunnel level......... 8
Siberian rolling mill......... 178
Slack coal coke.............. 69, 74
washing described 74, 91
anthracite, Loiseau's...... 85
Slackwater Navigation of the Monongahela River 3
Small furnaces................ 142
Smith Mills station.......... 88
Sneure Farm................ 231
Snow Shoe Coal Company ... 79
Snyder's level............... 8
Soho level.................. 8
Soison & Co.'s fire brick works 111, 112
Solonomya radiata........... 35
South-west P. R. R. (br. of P. R. R.,)................ 3, 44, 47, 50, 102
Southampton level.......... 8
Spang, Chalfant & Co.'s mill, 192, 194
Specific gravity of well gas... 175, 194
Sphenophyllum............... 37
Sphenopteris................. 37
Spirifer cameratus.
plano-convexus.......... 35
Springgrove Station.......... 40
mines 59
St. Jo, (Butler) Oil well...... 148
St. Louis Limestone.......... 225
St. Louis as a coal market.... 93
Statistics of cost of coking... 126, 127
Stearns works, Erie.......... 168
Sterling mines 57
Stone Bro.'s works........... 93
Stonersville 46, 47
Strata descend south-west.... 220
Strength of cokes 69, 70
Strength of gas iron.......... 203
Strickler coal bank.......... 17
Sub-carboniferous............ 4
Sulphur in coke............. 70, 71
free in coal.............. 72
as gypsum............... 73
division of in coking..... 133
balls..................... 74

Page.
Summit Allegheny Mountain level........................ 8, 9, 30
Summit mines............... 49, 50
"Sunday Coke"............. 77
Survey of pipe line........ 188 to 191
Susquehanna Valley......... 49
Suster's Station.............. 7
Swalley gas well at Erie...... 169
Swansea Coke, (Wales,)..... 87
Table of physical character of cokes made by different methods.................... 182, 128
Tables of results of iron made with gas.................... 203
Tangascootic................. 17
Tap-cinder analysed...... 179, 180, 207
Tarentum 182
Taylor's Salt Works.......... 115
Tender coke................. 70
Terebratula.................. 21
Terrace Knobs............... 62
Tests of coal for coke......... 121, 122
Tests used for gas analysis... 148
Tests for red-shortness........ 204
Theories of well location..... 217
for cold shortness......... 207
bars compared............ 205
by Riehle, Bros........... 213, 214
Thickness of Barren Measures 23
Thickness of Connellsville Coal Bed.................... 85
Third Oil sand............... 233
Thorn Creek gas well, Butler, 163, 236
Tibb's Run.................. 28
Tionesta sandstone........... 38
Titusville 166, 177
Topography of the coke region 5
Tracy gas well at Erie........ 170
Trade in coal at Youghiogheny 88
Transactions Am. Ins't. Min. Eng 14
Transactions American Philosophical Society............ 23
Trials with gas puddling furnace..................... 195 to 201
Tucker's Run 29
Tyrissa Colliery, (Wales,)... 86
Tyrone mines 57

Page.

Umbral Formation, (see No. XI,) 4, 30, 226, 228
Underground maps wanted.. 218
Undulations of Pittsburg coal, 11
Uniformity of coke.......... 137
Uniontown, Fayette county, 3, 11, 15, 18, 19, 40, 98, 103.
Coke.......... 68
Coal bed.......... 15
Br. P. W. & B. R. R...... 3
U. S. Navy Department...... 75
Upper Coal Measures......... 4, 13
Upper Conemaugh in Cambria county.......... 3
Upper Productive Coal Measures scheme in W. Va...... 33
Upper Freeport coal bed, 23, 37, 38, 183.
Ursina.......... 30
Valley of Dunbar creek...... 3
Valley of Mountain creek.... 3
Valley Coke Works.......... 45, 46
Velocity of gas through pipe, 185
Venango county gas.......... 145
oil sands at Pittsburg..... 215
Vespertine Formation (see No. X).......... 30, 223, 227
Virginia salt water.......... 229
Volatile matter in coal....... 96
Volume of gas from wells.... 175, 192
Warren gas.......... 176
oil sands.......... 230
Washer for coke (Bérard's).. 122
Washing coal machinery..... 91
Washing slack coal for coke.. 74
Washington run.......... 22
Waste from use of anthracite, 140
Watts station.......... 43
Waverly Coal Works........ 7, 88
Waynesburg coal bed........ 5, 33
sandstone.......... 33
Wells.......... 31
Well gas analysis.......... 146
Well records, unreliable..... 219
Well record (Bayard's salt).. 114
Well at Boyd's Hill, Pittsburg, 217
at Beaver Falls.......... 232

Page.

Well—Section at Leechburg.. 162
at Lardnor's.......... 182
Well gas not naturally heavy, 175, 176
Welsh coke ovens and yield.. 86
Westmoreland county........ 149
West Bloomfield gas, N. Y... 147
West Newton.......... 7, 11, 89
level.......... 8
cement works.......... 113
paper mill.......... 90
West Overton mines......... 52, 105
Western coals and coke...... 85
Western Penitentiary........ 20
West Pa. R. R.......... 45, 184, 235
West Virginia University.... 36
White Heath Station......... 7
coal.......... 89
White Rock.......... 3
Station level.......... 8, 112
White's mill run.......... 25
Wilcox gas well (M'Kean co.), 176
Winfield T., Butler county... 163, 235
Wirt county, Va., gas........ 146
Wood's run, Allegheny co.... 220
Yellow Flag iron ore......... 99
Yield of coke from Beehive oven.......... 124
from Belgian oven at Johnstown.......... 125
of iron with gas.......... 179
Yniscedwyn anthracite, Wales, 86
Yoldia carbonarius.......... 35, 36
Stevensoni.......... 35
Youghiogheny river.......... 2, 4, 9
mouth at M'Keesport.... 3
Youghiogheny valley........ 3, 12
gorge or gap.......... 31
bluffs.......... 22
rapids.......... 23
gas trade.......... 88
National Coal Company.. 89
Cement Co. Works....... 113
Coal Hollow Coal Co...... 91
Young (C. A.).......... 2, 5
Young's mill run.......... 17
Zanesville (F.).......... 144
Zeacrinus mucrospinus....... 36

ERRATA.

Page 35, Elk Lick bed is the second beneath the Pittsburg.

Page 35, Barton bed, to be called Berlin bed.

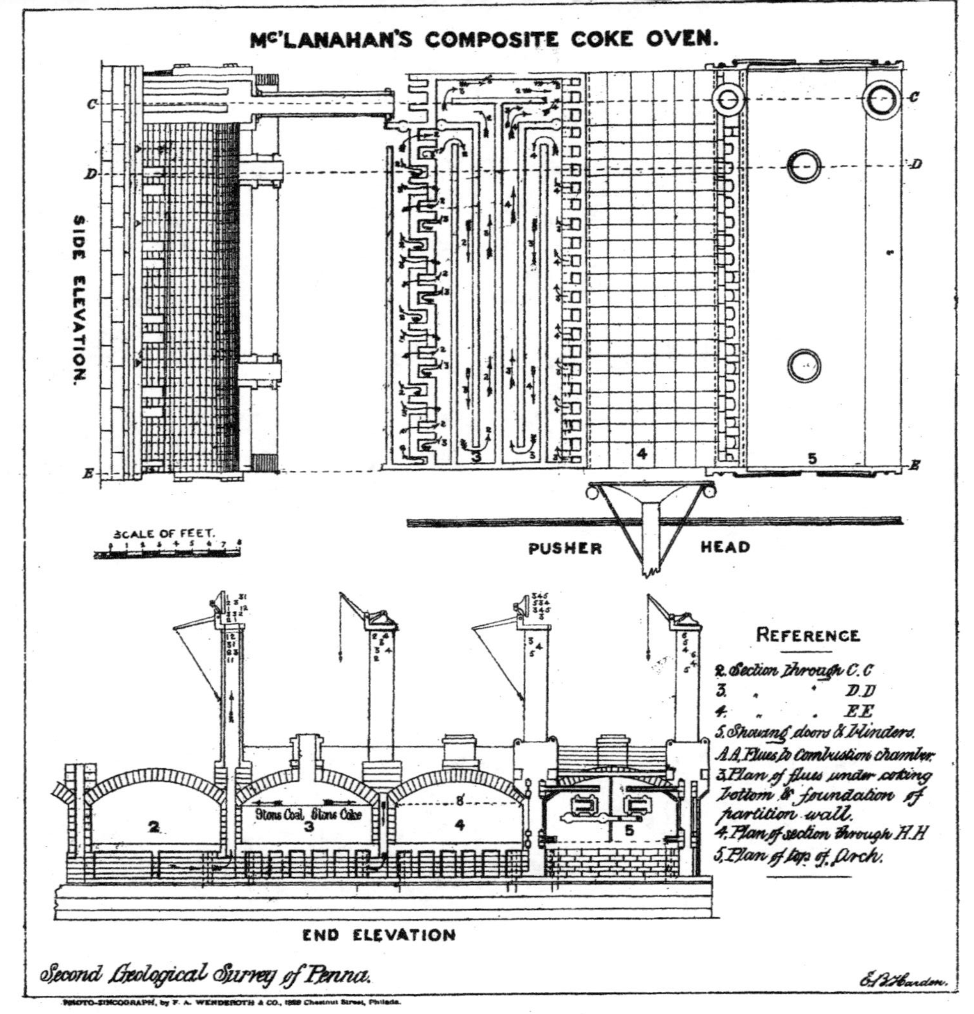

Mc'LANAHAN'S COMPOSITE COKE OVEN.
SIDE ELEVATION.
SCALE OF FEET.
PUSHER HEAD
Stone Coal, Stone Coke
END ELEVATION
REFERENCE
2. Section through C.C
3. " " D.D
4. " " E.E
5. Showing doors & Winders.
A.A. Flues to Combustion chamber.
3. Plan of flues under coking bottom & foundation of partition wall.
4. Plan of section through H.H
5. Plan of top of Arch.
Second Geological Survey of Penna.
PHOTO-ZINCOGRAPH, by F. A. WENDEROTH & CO., 1389 Chestnut Street, Philada.

L.

Second Geological Survey of Pennsylvania.

J. KING McLANAHAN'S IMPROVED COKE OVEN.

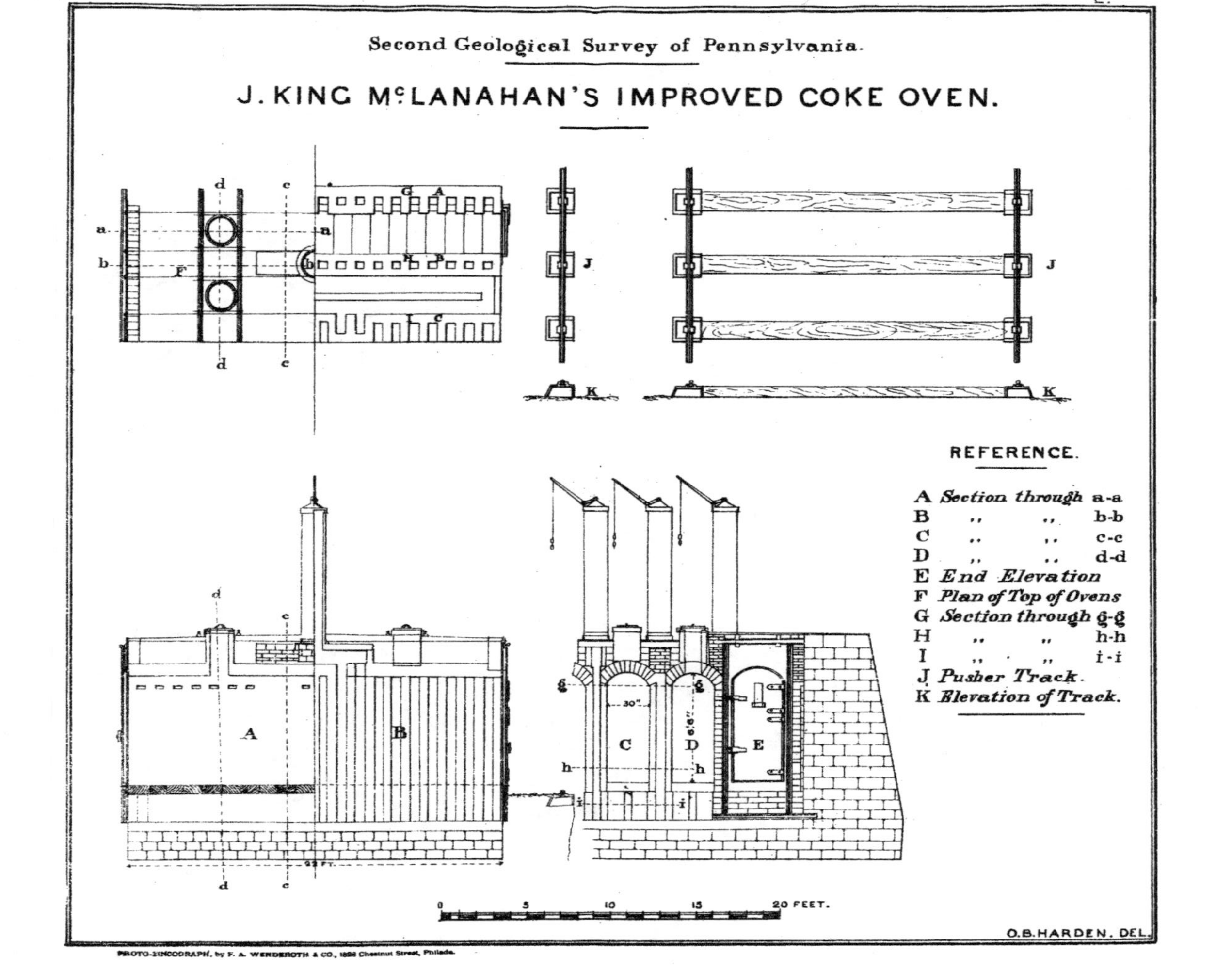

PHOTO-ZINCOGRAPH, by F. A. WENDEROTH & CO., 1828 Chestnut Street, Philada.

The Reports of the Geological Survey of Pennsylvania are, by act of Legislature, sold at cost. The following are now for sale at the Rooms of the Commission, No. 223 Market street, Harrisburg. Mr. F. W. Forman is authorized to conduct the sale of Reports, and letters and orders concerning sales should be addressed as above. Please direct general communications to John B. Pearse, Secretary of Commission.

PRICES OF REPORTS.

REPORTS FOR 1874 AND 1875.	In Paper.		Bound.	
	Report.	Postage	Report.	Postage
A. History of Geological Exploration; Lesley	$0 25	$0 06	$0 50	$0 10
B. Mineralogy of Pennsylvania; Genth,	50	08	75	10
B 2. Mineralogy of Pennsylvania; Genth,	05	02		
C. Report of progress in York and Adams Counties; Frazer	85	10	1 10	12
C C. Report of progress in York, Adams, Cumberland and Franklin Counties; Frazer			1 25	12
D. Lehigh County Iron Ores; Prime	50	04	75	06
H. Bituminous Coal, Clearfield and Jefferson Counties; Platt	1 50	13	1 75	15
HH. Report on Cambria and Somerset District of Bituminous Coal Fields; F. & W. Platt			1 00	12
I. Oil District, Venango County; Carll,	60	05	85	08
J. Special Report on Petroleum; Wrigley	75	06	1 00	08
K. Report on Bituminous Coal Fields of Greene and Washington Counties; Stevenson	65	16	90	18
L. Coke Manufacture; Platt. Methods of Coking; Fulton. Report on use of Natural Gases in Iron Manufacture; Pearse and Platt			1 00	12
M. Analyses, Laboratory at Harrisburg; M'Creath	50	05	75	08

www.ingramcontent.com/pod-product-compliance
Lightning Source LLC
LaVergne TN
LVHW010214110826
845151LV00004B/1078

* 9 7 8 1 4 2 5 5 2 8 0 5 8 *